PLAYS BY WOMEN
VOLUME FOUR

Objections to Sex and Violence *by Caryl Churchill*, Rose's Story *by Grace Dayley*, Blood and Ice *by Liz Lochhead*, Pinball *by Alison Lyssa*.

This is the fourth volume in Methuen's series of anthologies demonstrating the wide range of style and subject matter tackled by women playwrights. Included are *Objections to Sex and Violence*, one of Caryl Churchill's early stage plays, which explores the way political terrorism infiltrates and threatens personal relationships; *Rose's Story* by Grace Dayley, a raw and direct account of the impact of the pregnancy of a young West Indian woman on her friends and family; Liz Lochhead's *Blood and Ice*, about the life and imagination of Mary Shelley, author of *Frankenstein*, and her involvements with Byron and Shelley; and *Pinball* by Australian writer Alison Lyssa, which uses the Biblical myth of Solomon as a way of evoking the emotional and social contradictions of parental custody. Each play has an afterword by the author, and the volume opens with an introduction by the series editor, Michelene Wandor.

PLAYS BY WOMEN

Volume Four

OBJECTIONS TO SEX AND VIOLENCE
by Caryl Churchill

ROSE'S STORY
by Grace Dayley

BLOOD AND ICE
by Liz Lochhead

PINBALL
by Alison Lyssa

Edited and introduced by **Michelene Wandor**

A Methuen Theatrefile
Methuen · London and New York

A METHUEN PAPERBACK

This volume first published in Great Britain as a Methuen Paperback original in 1985 by Methuen London Ltd, 11 New Fetter Lane, London EC4P 4EE, and in the United States of America by Methuen Inc, 733 Third Avenue, New York, NY10017.

Set in IBM 10 point Press Roman by 𝍪 Tek-Art, Croydon, Surrey.
Reproduced, printed and bound in Great Britain by
Hazell Watson & Viney Limited,
Member of the BPCC Group,
Aylesbury, Bucks

British Library Cataloguing in Publication Data

Plays by Women. — (A Methuen theatrefile)
    Vol. 4
    1. English drama — 20th century   2. English drama — Women authors
    I. Wandor, Michelene
    822'.914'0809287   PR1272
    ISBN 0-413-56740-0

CAUTION
All rights whatsoever in these plays are strictly reserved. Applications for performance, including professional, amateur, motion pictures, recitation, lecturing, public reading, broadcasting, television, and the rights of translation into foreign languages, should be addressed to:-

Objections to Sex and Violence: Margaret Ramsay Ltd, 14a Goodwin's Court,
    St Martin's Lane, London WC2N 4LL.
Rose's Story: c/o Methuen London Ltd, 11 New Fetter Lane, London EC4P 4EE.
Blood and Ice: John Johnson Ltd, Clerkenwell House, 45-47 Clerkenwell Green,
    London EC1R 0HT.
Pinball: c/o Methuen London Ltd, 11 New Fetter Lane, London EC4P 4EE.

CONTENTS

ACKNOWLEDGEMENTS

This book, as well as being the fourth volume in the series, is also by way of a salute to all the women working in Australian theatre for the improvement of the position of women – particularly the Association of Women Theatre Workers in Adelaide, the energetic group running The Syndicate in Sydney, and everyone working to increase the number of women writers on the other side of the world.

INTRODUCTION

The four plays in this fourth anthology of *Plays by Women* could all be called 'early' plays — but 'early' in different senses. They range from a lesser-known play by Caryl Churchill, who is already well established as a playwright, to a first play by a young black student, Grace Dayley. Between these are two other 'early' plays — for Liz Lochhead a first piece written for the stage, although she is no newcomer to writing, since before embarking on this play she was already a fine and accomplished poet, well-known on the poetry-reading circuit for her entertaining presentations. The other play is by an Australian playwright, Alison Lyssa, for whom this play was a first full stage production. In earlier volumes there have been plays from other English-speaking cultures — in Volume Two, *Letters Home,* by the American Rose Leiman Goldemberg, and in Volume Three, *Blood Relations* by Sharon Pollock, from Canada.

I met Alison Lyssa in Australia in August 1984. I had been invited by the Association of Women Theatre Workers, a group in Adelaide who, among other things, were running workshops to increase the number of women writing plays in South Australia. I spent a demanding and rewarding fortnight there, and then went on to Sydney and made contact with other women working in theatre. Many of the debates about theatre over there contained echoes of issues which have been hashed over in England since the late 1960s: 'establishment' versus 'community' theatre; what are the many, and best ways of improving the position of women in the theatre industry. There are also cultural questions which are quite specific to Australia — a continent in the Southern hemisphere, where the dominant culture is spelled out through the English language, which has a tortuous and complex relationship to the other major 'English' cultures of Britain and America, and a relatively short history of white culture, a very ancient indigenous Aboriginal culture — and a rich range of various European and Asian communities. I had only a short amount of time in which to absorb and try and make sense of such a complex culture, but I felt that there were enough recognisable points of contact between feminist concerns and style in theatre in this country and Alison Lyssa's play to make it well worth including.

Objections to Sex and Violence was Caryl Churchill's third play to be produced at the Royal Court, the London theatre which introduced her as a professional playwright to the stage — she had already been writing for some years for radio. The play also stands at a transitional moment in her work, since it was produced just before she began working in a more collaborative way with theatre companies — in 1976 she wrote *Light Shining in Buckinghamshire* with Joint Stock and *Vinegar Tom* with Monstrous Regiment. In her Afterword to the latter play (*Plays by Women, Volume One*) Caryl Churchill wrote: 'Though I still wanted to write alone sometimes, my attitude to myself, my work and others had been permanently changed by the two shows I had written since, for Joint Stock and Monstrous Regiment.' Although some of her subsequently successful plays (*Cloud Nine* and *Fen*) were also written in collaboration with Joint Stock, she has continued to write plays 'alone' as well: *Top Girls* and *Softcops*, for example. However, although she developed different ways of writing, and took up new ideas and techniques, it is interesting to trace, in *Objections*, some of the preoccupations and stylistic interests which have maintained continuity in her later plays. Her interest in the ways people are subversive is a recurrent theme in other plays: *Vinegar Tom* and *Cloud Nine* demonstrate subversive sexual choices; it is often a life-choice by characters who cannot find happiness in conventional ways, and by striking out and making new choices, find they are taking up a subversive relationship to society. In *Objections* the 'subversion' appears in two forms: in the secret fantasies of the postcard character Arthur, and in the alternative lifestyle and possible espousal of political violence of Jule. Alternative lifestyles are demonstrated in the second act of *Cloud Nine,* and the satirical use of character 'types' is something drawn on in a number of other plays. There is also another interesting parallel between the fraught, emotional interdependence of the two sisters Annie and Jule in *Objections,* and the very powerful scene between the two sisters which closes *Top Girls;* in both plays the sisters struggle to find some resolution to the differences between them, but in very different styles. In *Objections* the relationship is spelled out in a relatively conventional realist style; in *Top Girls* the dialogue is taut, overlapping, as if the form itself reflects and conveys the impossibility of arriving at resolution. Doubtless there are many more equally interesting comparisons and contrasts to be made — I'll leave those to the reader for now. Perhaps there is a far less rigid distinction to be made between the 'collaborative' and 'individual' plays than a description of different working methods suggests.

Rose's Story was written while the author was still a student, and its boldness and occasional rawness of style is typical of a new (and therefore culturally 'young') area of work. In recent years increasing attention has been drawn to the difficulties which black and ethnic minority performers have in British theatre; groups such as the Black Theatre Co-operative in London have done energetic work in presenting British/West Indian experience and performance — with a very successful series on Channel Four television. But, in line with many radical beginnings in theatre, the 'black' or 'ethnic' theatre work has so far been dominated by men. Very few black women have written for theatre, and Grace Dayley's play is therefore very welcome for a number of reasons. *Rose's Story* is raw, survival experience; the responses of family, friends and community to a young woman's desire for independence and her need to cope with an unexpected pregnancy. It makes no concessions to sentimentality, and is slice-of-life writing in a direct and vivid way, weaving between patois and 'English' English, in a way which demonstrates a cultural mix in which different value systems have to survive. It is jagged and immediate, and hopefully is only the first of many plays from its author.

Blood and Ice has its roots in a very different cultural time and ambience. The story of Mary Shelley, her Romantic poet accompanists, Byron and Shelley, it draws on Liz Lochhead's skills as a poet. The language here combines lyricism, literary formality, reverie and artifice, shifting in style to fit the shifts between time and place in the play, and between the 'reality' of Mary's life as lover and mother, and the obsessions of her imagination which emerged in her famous novel *Frankenstein.* Countless films, plays, novels have taken the theme of *Frankenstein* and re-told it in their own way; *Blood and Ice* is refreshing in its attempts to make some connections between Mary Shelley's own experiences as a woman with her imaginative life. In theme, then, the play engages directly with the fictional, 'illusory' nature of theatre, by taking place, as Liz Lochhead explains in her Afterword, in the consciousness of Mary herself. In this way Mary Shelley is rehabilitated, not as the wife of the poet Shelley, nor as the daughter of the feminist Mary Wollstonecraft, but as mother and poet in her own right. A rare thing.

Finally, Alison Lyssa's play also draws on literary and mythological sources, to transform what might have been a straightforward polemic on behalf of lesbian mothers into something much more, and thus, perhaps, much more effective. The surface metaphor is obvious: the figure of Solomon takes us to the wellspring of Western mythology, and also embodies (in his many agitprop-theatre changes) various reactionary attitudes to women. However, there are two other sub-cultural myths which permeate *Pinball:* the hi-tech, modern world of a child who has already formulated an (offstage) set of tastes and securities, and the subverted motif of Cordelia and her sisters, *pace* Shakespeare's *King Lear.* Alison Lyssa's style, at its strongest, is delicate, ironic and demanding. She is a daring and challenging writer whose sense of stagecraft ensures that each scene, however verbally rich, is also rooted in event and action.

A final, polemical and campaigning note on women playwrights. In 1984 an *ad hoc* group of women directors and administrators produced a survey into the status of women directors and writers in British theatre in 1982-1983. The report (Conference of Women Theatre Directors and Administrators) was not exhaustive, but even so, it revealed as statistics what many people already knew to be the stark reality. Taking figures overall, for the large subsidised theatres, repertory theatres, fringe and community theatres, only about 7% of all plays produced are by women writers. Of these, nearly half are accounted for by Agatha Christie plays. Obviously there is nothing wrong with producing plays by Agatha Christie. But there is a great deal wrong with such a vital medium which represents women writers (and to some degree, by implication, also the 'image' or function of women in plays themselves) in such a scandalous minority way. One of the most interesting findings in the report is completely in line with similar, but far more thorough and exhaustive surveys into the place of women playwrights in Australia and Canada:

'The survey demonstrates clearly that the more money and more prestige a theatre has, the less women will be employed as directors and administrators; the less likelihood that a play written by a women will be commissioned or produced, excepting Agatha Christie; and the less women there will be on the Boards. It is therefore demonstrated that women . . . contribute very little to the production of the cultural matter . . . This is in painful contrast to their majority in higher education Arts courses, in audiences, and in their supporting role in offices.'

There are important professional and aesthetic implications which follow from this:

'The greatest concentration of women occurs in the Alternative and Community categories of theatres. These are the least subsidised and least well-equipped, and offer the smallest stages, the smallest audiences, the least predictable and controllable venues, the smallest budgets, the least likelihood of classical work; in other words, the most difficult circumstances in which to produce art.'

This means that women are not only badly under-represented, but that where we are represented, it is in relative poverty, with a precarious professional hold. This makes much of theatre in which women take an active part an uphill struggle, where it is not only content or subject matter which has to prove its validity, but where aesthetic satisfaction, technical choice and professional sophistication have to be fought for twice as hard. The occasional exception to this — the company or theatre which makes real efforts to commission women writers — does not affect the overall picture in any significant way. What is needed is something more structured, something more structural: a policy which takes very concrete steps to ensure that the position of women playwrights changes.

The policy needed is one which would come under the heading of 'positive discrimination' — or, as it is called in America, 'affirmative action'. Given the theatre's dependence on subsidy, at both national and regional level, it should be very easy (if the will is there) to implement a policy which would ensure that the number of women playwrights increases. The way to do it is to make the granting of subsidy to theatres which do new work conditional on those theatres applying a graduated quota system, the aim of which, over a period of years — three? five? seven? another magic number? — would be to increase the number of women writers until half the plays produced are by women. Such a structural condition on the granting of subsidy would at least provide a framework within which change is not left to the whims and occasional liberal goodwill of those who control the theatre.

There are two objections which are likely to be raised to such a suggestion: 1) There aren't enough women writers to go round, and 2) There aren't enough good women writers/good plays by women. The answer to the first is that there's nothing like the genuine creation of opportunity to produce people eager to do the work. The answer to the second is in two parts: a) There aren't enough good plays by men, and b) the only way in which playwrights learn their craft is by working in the theatre, being produced, and improving on the shop floor, as it were.

If such a policy towards women writers can be tied in with policies of affirmative action towards women in other areas of theatre work, then we may begin to see a real change in representation: not only of women in the theatre work force, but of their points of view, and of their imaginations.

Michelene Wandor

OBJECTIONS TO SEX AND VIOLENCE

Objections to Sex and Violence was first performed at the Royal Court Theatre, London on 2 January 1975 with the following cast:

ANNIE, *mid to late twenties*	Anna Calder-Marshall
JULE, *a little younger than Annie*	Rosemary McHale
ARTHUR, *in his fifties*	Ivor Roberts
MADGE, *in her fifties*	Rose Hill
PHIL, *mid-thirties*	Stephen Moore
ERIC, *younger, early twenties*	Paul Seed
MISS FORBES, *about sixty*	Sylvia Coleridge
TERRY, *about thirty*	Michael Harrigan

Directed by John Tydeman

Place: a sandy beach with rocks behind it.
Time: a June day.
Act One: Low tide.
Act Two: High tide.

ACT ONE

Low tide. Sunny morning.
    JULE *and* ANNIE. JULE *is in a
bathing suit. She has just been swimming
and is wet and slightly cold.* ANNIE *is in
a coat. She has just arrived.*

ANNIE: I never thought I'd find you so
    easily. I came on the beach more for
    the breath of air. Because seeing the
    size of the town I said at once how
    silly of me to come. It seemed a pity
    to waste the sunshine and not start
    with a look at the sea. Then I thought
    I'd get down to it and ask at every
    single bed and breakfast and then at
    least I would have done my best.

JULE: What did you come for?

ANNIE: You sent me a postcard.

JULE: I didn't say come. I was keeping in
    touch.

ANNIE: I read about the trouble in the
    paper, but when I took a train up
    you'd vanished. You weren't just out
    because I waited all day. The police
    said they hadn't kept you.

JULE: It's not my fault you waited all
    day. I can't always be where you
    might drop in.

ANNIE: So when I knew from the
    postmark you were here, I came here,
    that's all.

JULE: Without the others the house felt
    wide open. There were still two of us.
    But even in bed I felt a detective
    sergeant might walk in. They had the
    mattress off that afternoon. They
    went through every shelf and every
    drawer. You don't know you've got so
    many things. And even here I think
    they're still keeping an eye — I think
    I'm paranoid to think that but you
    can't be sure. They're sly buggers and
    they try to be thorough. There's
    probably one of them watching you
    now.

ANNIE: I only came to make sure you
were all right.

JULE: They won't hurt you. You haven't
    done anything.

ANNIE: Nor have you, really, Jule, have
    you? It was more the other people in
    the house the paper said were
    remanded in custody. They wouldn't
    have let you out on bail.

JULE: No, it can't be serious, can it, if
    I'm swimming.

ANNIE: But what have you done, Jule?

JULE: You saw in the paper what the
    charge was.

ANNIE: You can't think 'possession of
    cannabis' would have me running all
    over the country. It's the way the
    paper made all those arrests come in
    the same story as something much
    worse. Everybody smokes. But I'm
    sure the other's nothing to do with
    you. Newspapers usually get it wrong.
    I expect you can set my mind at rest.
    (ANNIE *waits but* JULE *doesn't say
    anything.* JULE *gets her towel and
    puts it round her shoulders.*) Your
    own sister's hardly going to tell. Do
    you feel you have to be loyal to
    somebody?

JULE: It was very good of you to come,
    Annie. I'm really grateful. You came
    all this way.

ANNIE: It makes an excuse for a day by
    the sea. I like an outing. I never get to
    see you in the normal way. It takes a
    catastrophe to get me moving.

    ARTHUR *comes in with two
    deckchairs and a beachbag. He starts
    to put up the deckchairs, trying
    different places to be out of the wind,
    and constantly glancing at* JULE.

JULE: All well your end? Still with that
    bloke that had the accident?

ANNIE: He's out there by the edge of the
    sea.

JULE: What's he doing?

ANNIE: He thought I'd better come over

first and see it was all right.

JULE: Is he frightened?

ANNIE: He's very considerate, that's all it is. Shall I call him?

JULE: You're happy enough with him, are you?

ANNIE: There are things. If I had time to tell you some time. But yes I am.

JULE: You're not sorry about the divorce anyway?

ANNIE: Oh no, that was the best thing I ever − I think if I'm having a bad day, at least I'm not still married to that.

JULE: He doesn't come round and worry you? He's not someone to let it go, from when I knew him.

ANNIE: Not any more, no. There were a few bad times. I had the police one night, he cut my eye. I still haven't got over with Phil just being with someone that isn't going to hit me. He's not going to come unless I call him.

JULE: Better call him, then.

ANNIE: And you, are you with someone?

JULE: Off and on. Things shift about a bit.

ANNIE: How exactly?

JULE: Anyway, I'm not staying in a bed and breakfast so you would have had to knock on a lot of doors. I'm in a tent up on the cliff with someone.

ANNIE: You came down here together, then?

JULE: What if I met him down here on the beach?

ANNIE: Just this last few days?

JULE: I can't know him very well, can I? No, I don't.

ANNIE: Don't start getting at me, Jule, because I'm not like that anymore. It's up to you.

JULE: Call him over. Give him a wave.

ANNIE: Phil! Phil! Jule, I want you to

know. I don't blame you. In a way I think I admire − of course, I don't know what it is you've done. But knowing you, I'm sure it's something I wouldn't blame − I'm sure I could understand anything you told me, Jule. I do so little myself.

JULE: Are you working?

ANNIE: Jobs always fail me, don't they?

JULE: You manage to type.

ANNIE: Oh yes, I stuck it out well this time. I was secretary to a top executive. But you know how it is. I go to pieces. They bust me down to the typing pool for a rest, they were quite concerned. That's when I should have left. But I like to feel committed. I don't know how to keep my distance. I bring my work home in my head as if it was interesting. As if I was competing like the men. You'd love the men, Jule, you'd laugh so much. You can tell the grade of a man by his car. The company provide them with different sizes so there's no mistaking who's important. Regardless of the number of passengers they have in real life. My boss had worked up to a silver grey model with overdrive. The seats are so soft it's quite hard for a girl to get out. But just lately I switched to doing cleaning. It rests your head anyway.

ARTHUR *is doing less and less with the deckchairs. Some time ago he folded one up to move it and now stands holding it, watching* JULE.

JULE: You'd be better if there was something you cared about.

ANNIE: It's not as if you'd ever stayed with a job.

JULE: But I always think you'd make a nurse or a teacher. Something where you could wear yourself out.

ANNIE: I do that whatever I do.

JULE: But over nothing.

ANNIE: Oh it's too late, Jule, to start

training for any of those vocations. The boring detail's too much once your mind's mature. Things keep striking me as irrelevant. I could never settle for discipline nowadays.

JULE: Matrons.

ANNIE: There you are. Headmistresses.

JULE: Executives.

ANNIE: The money's got to be earned. I'm not involved. For some time now I've only cleaned his house.

JULE: The same one, with the grey car?

ANNIE: I drifted into it one afternoon. He knew the company was driving me mad and his wife was just then wanting a char. It was kindly meant. There was no way I could have known.

JULE: I'm not saying teaching's worthwhile. I was thinking more what you might enjoy.

ANNIE: I don't expect to enjoy work, Jule. I rely on Phil to put me out of my misery.

JULE: Where is Phil? Collecting shells, I think. Or it might be bottletops. Yes, I do remember him as very polite.

ANNIE: But, Jule, it's one thing to be fed up. Would you kill people?

JULE: Phil!

ANNIE; Jule, if you take some part in explosions. I don't know what you've done. But the passersby who just happen — and children.

JULE: Come on, let's walk up the beach and meet him. I'm getting cold, let's walk.

ANNIE: But Jule.

JULE: Children are killed in most wars.

ANNIE: Jule.

JULE: I'm not saying I've killed anyone.

They go out.

ARTHUR *takes a step or two after them, dragging the deckchair, then remembers it and stops. He leaves it*

and sits in the other deckchair. From inside his jacket he takes a worn pornographic magazine, from the beach bag the Daily Express. *He hides the magazine inside the paper and reads it.*

MADGE *comes in.*

MADGE: Where did you slip off to, Arthur? I might be dead.

ARTHUR *folds up the paper, leaving the magazine in it.*

ARTHUR: I was trying to get a spot out of the wind.

MADGE: I'm two minute spending a penny and you take advantage to set off by yourself, leaving me to handle a most sinister character.

ARTHUR: What did he do, dear?

MADGE: He didn't dare to do anything because he could tell at a glance I would call the police. But he looked at me unmistakably. And followed.

ARTHUR: Where is he now? Do you want me to deal with him?

MADGE: I shook him off by pretending to go into a café. I watched him pass, through the lace curtains. It's lucky that class of degenerate person is always stupid. Because where were you all this time? Enjoying yourself by yourself on the beach.

ARTHUR *sets up the other deckchair.*

ARTHUR: I was getting a deckchair set up for you, dear.

MADGE: It's the wrong side of the rocks.

MADGE *sits in it.*

ARTHUR: The breeze is blowing straight in off the sea. You won't get shelter either side.

MADGE: This side's very chilly.

ARTHUR *sits in the other deckchair.*

ARTHUR: It was you wanted to take the holiday early. You don't like people.

MADGE: I do indeed like people. I love people.

ARTHUR: You don't love them on the same beach.

MADGE: I'm of service to people fifty weeks a year. Everybody needs a break, Arthur. It's less of a strain to take holidays off peak. And far more public spirited.

ARTHUR *unfolds the* Express *as if to read it again. We can see, though* MADGE *can't, the magazine inside.*

ARTHUR: It doesn't seem a proper holiday unless it's in August. It's not too bad this morning, mind you, there are a few swimmers.

MADGE: While I was being pursued along the front you were off gawping at young girls in no better than their underwear.

ARTHUR: Bathing suits aren't underwear. If a girl came down on the beach in her underwear —

MADGE: While I was in danger of attack. He would have stopped at nothing in an alley. Luckily there's a good crowd on the front.

ARTHUR *folds up the magazine and puts it back in his jacket.*

ARTHUR: Why don't we have a cup of tea?

MADGE: No, I'd rather wait till I'm really cold.

ARTHUR: If you will come to the seaside in June, you have to take the weather as you find it.

MADGE *gets out knitting, a sweater for* ARTHUR, *from the beach bag, and knits.*

MADGE: We could go to the Lake District. Or a coach tour of Scotland would make a change. But oh no. It has to be a beach with bathing beauties or it's not a proper holiday.

ARTHUR: Sitting in a coach all day wouldn't take me out of the furniture department the way I can trust the sea to do.

MADGE: And don't I work hard too? A local government office is no joke.

ARTHUR: Perhaps we should take our holidays apart, dear.

MADGE: We'll have none of that, thank you, Arthur.

ARTHUR: I'm going to have a cup of tea now, whether you are or not.

ARTHUR *gets a thermos flask from the beach bag.*

MADGE *gets a cardigan from the beach bag and puts it on.* ARTHUR *pours himself some tea.*

Madge, did you choose an early holiday on purpose so there wouldn't be so many people swimming?

MADGE: June often has glorious weather. Flaming June.

ARTHUR: If you think that badly of me I want you to say so.

MADGE: I just long to get away from it all. It's not much to ask.

ARTHUR: I want you to have a nice holiday, Madge, I really do.

MADGE: Come on, let's have a cup of tea. I'm just a bit shaken by my experience.

ARTHUR *pours a cup of tea for* MADGE.

ARTHUR: Some girls do go too far. Remember that one last year with the red —

MADGE: I don't want to hear anything like that. We're away from television for two weeks and I hope we've left sex and violence behind. The world is a very beautiful place if you know how to see it. I come on holiday to get my eye in by gazing at nature, which I can't do surrounded by people on towels.

ARTHUR: It is distracting when they're very close.

MADGE: Holidays should be kept for the few who really work. There's no service in shops. You even take your own shoes off the shelf. I said no thank you, I'll go where a fitting expert will bring me shoes in boxes. Because I've always had trouble with my feet, haven't I, Arthur?

ARTHUR: All our married life.

From time to time ARTHUR *glances along the beach.*

MADGE: Feet are like teeth. It's important to be in the hands of a good dentist who knows your history and doesn't cause unnecessary pain. Think of your dentures. I believe we owe it to our bodies to put them into some authority's care. I don't believe in self-service. What are you looking at, Arthur?

ARTHUR: Just gazing at nature. The little children making a sandcastle.

While MADGE *talks,* ARTHUR *stands up and takes a few steps.*

MADGE: Children are said to be a blessing but some people could restrain themselves without threatening the survival of the species. Hydra simply grow little hydra like arms and they drop off, which isn't such a messy arrangement, and they can't enjoy it. But the child must be identical with the parent, which would stand in the way of progress, when I think of my mother. Arthur, where are you going?

ARTHUR: I wondered if it wasn't so breezy . . .

MADGE: Where?

ARTHUR: Further along, by those rocks.

MADGE: There are people there already.

ARTHUR: There's plenty of room.

MADGE: In bathing suits.

ARTHUR: That's what gave me the idea it might be warmer.

MADGE: Young people don't seem to feel the cold.

ARTHUR: I thought I'd just take a turn along the sand.

MADGE: Come here and let me measure your jersey.

ARTHUR: Don't make it too small this time, Madge. If you look at me you'll see I'm quite a medium-sized man.

MADGE: Take your jacket off.

ARTHUR *takes his jacket off and the magazine falls to the ground. He puts a foot on it.* MADGE *is busy with the knitting and doesn't notice.*

I do believe in progress because it must be possible to make people perfect. I've always been a believer, Arthur. I used to believe in fairies as a child. We had to clap to save Tinker Bell. Yes, yes, yes, I used to say, leaning out of my bedroom window in the dark. Bunions, cavities, we struggle as best we can. Another two inches. We have to help each other forward and that's why I resent the disappearance of service. If the wind can be trusted to have dropped I might take my cardigan off again. I'll take my shoes off and have a rest. (*She bends down to take off her shoes. She sees the magazine and picks it up.*)

ARTHUR: I struggle too. I struggle against the flesh. I have particularly strong passions, that's all it is. Saint Augustine had the same problem.

MADGE (*reading*): 'He bit her nipple till she screamed with agony then plunged his foot long red hot weapon —' What shall we do with this?

ARTHUR: I can take it back to the shop and get half the money —

MADGE: We will burn it.

ARTHUR: We're very different, Madge. I've always said that. You long to merge in something mystical. But I can't always manage to dislike what I know is disgusting. I'm always very sorry afterwards. (*He tries*

*ineffectually to light the magazine
with a match.)*

MADGE: You won't do it like that. Let
me. (*She tears the magazine into
pieces and heaps them on the sand.*)
Match. (*She tries several times to light
the paper.*)

ARTHUR: It's too breezy.

MADGE: We'll dig a hole and bury it.

ARTHUR *and* MADGE *dig a hole with
their hands and bury the magazine in
the sand.* MADGE *pats it firmly down.*

I always hope we'll get closer on
holidays. There's nothing in the nature
of the sea to bring women to mind. It
always makes me think of the lifeboat
service.

ARTHUR: I hate women really, you
know that. Young women today want
to be whipped.

MADGE: They'd take it the wrong way,
Arthur.

ARTHUR: You and I, Madge, do mean
the same thing by right and wrong. It's
just that I have a weakness for what's
wrong. But most people give those
words a different meaning.

MADGE: Your weakness, Arthur, is the
result of weak government.

ARTHUR: People want to be told what to
do.

MADGE: They long for a strong man.

ARTHUR: Then if I saw a young girl not
properly dressed I should know I
could ask a policeman to take action.

MADGE: They don't take care of us as
they should. Even law and order is self
service. Have a go, indeed. What we
want is an ideal of service and force.
The armed services are at the same
time the armed forces. Young men did
national service as a national force.
The police force is also a service. The
civil service is a civil force. Public
services should force the public. Then
we could have a well-deserved holiday.

ARTHUR: Self service could mean
yourself using force. Hence the daily
violence in the papers.

The sun goes in.

MADGE: I think I'll need my cardigan
again.

ARTHUR: I do think we might try over
there. Those people haven't put on
cardigans. They're still in the sun.

MADGE: If you can promise me some
peace, Arthur.

ARTHUR *looks down the beach the
way* JULE *and* ANNIE *went out.*

ARTHUR: I've seen that young lady
before.

MADGE: What do you mean? She's not
the person who was on the cliff last
night?

ARTHUR: Lying on the grass with her
young man in full view of the public
footpath and we saw —

MADGE: I was there, Arthur, it doesn't
need to be put into words. Is it the
one?

ARTHUR: I got a good look — I think it
is.

MADGE: It's not enough having penalties
for litter.

ARTHUR: Shall I give her a piece of my
mind?

MADGE: We can't be responsible for
what we see. The television authority
is just as bad. The cliffs would have
been so beautiful in the evening light.

ANNIE, JULE *and* PHIL *come in.*
PHIL *has a camera.*

PHIL: I hope we're not intruding on you
at a time . . . Annie said not. She
insisted we come. If there's anything
we can do.

ARTHUR *goes up to them.*

ARTHUR: Excuse me. Good morning.

PHIL: Good morning. Lovely day.

ARTHUR: Have you got the time?

PHIL: Just gone a quarter to twelve.

ARTHUR: Thank you. (*Pause. Then to* JULE): I believe I saw you yesterday evening.

JULE: Me? You might have done.

Pause.

ANNIE: It's turning a bit cold.

ARTHUR (*to* JULE): Yes, you can't be too warm in that condition.

JULE: No, I'm frozen. I must go and get dressed.

ARTHUR: That's a good idea.

Pause.

PHIL: Here on holiday, are you?

ARTHUR: Yes, my wife and myself. We go for walks sometimes on the cliffs.

PHIL: It seems very pleasant here for walking.

ARTHUR: It can be.

Pause.

PHIL: I hope it keeps fine for you.

ARTHUR: Thank you very much. That's clear, I hope. A quarter to twelve. Good morning. (*He goes back to* MADGE *and helps with folding the deckchairs.*)

PHIL: You're very welcome to come and stay with us. I don't know what your plans are at all. There's a couch in the sitting-room that makes up into a bed. You may remember. If that would be any use.

JULE: No, it's kind of you.

PHIL: You've been in touch with a solicitor, I expect.

JULE: I don't need anything.

PHIL: Because I'm sure it's important to get the legal side right.

JULE: We'll do our own defence, thank you.

PHIL: Because it's rather an expert field.

JULE: We know what we're doing.

PHIL: It's quite embarrassing to make the offer but just so you know we are on hand. If and when, if and when, or not.

JULE: It's not that I'm rude. I just don't want anything.

MADGE: How did she take that?

ARTHUR: She said she was going to go and get dressed.

MADGE: And now she'll see us pointedly move away. Small victories all add up. Now where will we be snug?

MADGE *and* ARTHUR *go out with their things, except the thermos flask, which is left behind on the sand.*

ANNIE: Oh Jule, I wish you would come to us. I hate to think of you here all alone, and the police. If you were living with us — we couldn't stop them but it might look more reliable. They wouldn't have any excuse to get suspicious. I can't believe this holiday maker in a tent's going to look after you. You did the right thing to leave the house. You don't look so connected to the crime as you would do sitting waiting at the scene of it. But if you came to us I'd feel much safer.

The sun comes out.

JULE: You don't know what you're talking about, Annie.

ANNIE: Why don't you tell me what I'm talking about? Why, if it's just a small drugs charge, does it come in a newspaper story that starts with explosions? I know the police pick up a lot of people but why was one of them you? Is it the other people in the house and you didn't know what they were up to? It may even just be them that got you into the drugs charge. You just happen to live in the same house.

PHIL: I expect the police planted it themselves. That's the impression I get in these sort of cases. Once they make up their minds for a conviction.

JULE: Police finger prints were everywhere.

PHIL: Were they, Jule? You must be sure to bring that out in your defence.

JULE: They must have been by the time they'd finished searching, mustn't they? (*She spreads her towel out on the beach and lies down on it.*)

PHIL: Why is it you and one other were let out on bail while the other two were remanded in custody?

ANNIE: The others might have previous convictions. They might even be connected with the explosions. Because the newspaper story did say 'following explosions police raided houses'. They're friends of hers, she's just involved by association. Even the police can tell the difference. That's why I wish you'd come home with us, Jule, to somewhere normal and have a rest. It must be a strain, you're far too white. Considering all the fresh air too. Someone's an influence on you nowadays.

PHIL *takes off his sweater and shirt and sits on the sand, but not close to* JULE.

JULE: I don't want to.

ANNIE: You've let yourself be carried away, Jule. What is it your friends have done? My own ideas are very sympathetic but putting them into practice would be wicked. It means shutting your eyes to other people. Who's told you you can do that?

PHIL: Don't upset yourself, Annie. Come and sit down in the sun. It's quite warm.

ANNIE: You make your protest with some explosive device and that's fine for you and your friends. That proves your heart's in the right place. But someone may be killed who's not interested in your ideas. I've seen pictures in the papers and I can't go along with it, Jule. You see the man's

shock. He hasn't been asked does he want his arm blown off for this cause. He has his wife and children and things to do. He doesn't want to take part.

JULE: Nobody wants to take part in war. Who's asked?

ANNIE: What war? There isn't any war. Who's been telling you you're a soldier?

PHIL: Don't get yourself too excited, Annie. We don't know what your sister's done.

ANNIE: Why don't you tell us then, Jule?

After a moment ANNIE *sits down by* PHIL, *who takes her hand.*

ERIC, *in swimming trunks, comes in at a jog, and jogs beside them on the spot. Throughout he hardly keeps still – he walks about, jogs, does exercises, push-ups, headstands. He is pale and not muscular.*

ERIC: Made some nice friends?

JULE: My sister Annie. Phil. This is George.

ERIC: Your sister?

JULE: I told her how we met each other here on the beach and I'm staying just for now up in your tent.

ERIC: Yes. Yes that's right. We just ran into each other. I've just been running now to get warm.

PHIL: It must be very cold for swimming.

ERIC: Do you mind getting cold?

PHIL: The sea's always a little cold of course. You expect that. But I do like it warmer than this.

ERIC: Most people do. You're in the majority there.

ANNIE: It's only natural.

ERIC: You think what most people believe is bound to be right?

ANNIE: Right for them. They know if they're cold or —

ERIC: So you think the majority of people know what is right for them? And for other people?

ANNIE: That depends what —

ERIC: And suppose you have two candidates and one says swimming only in the first fortnight in August and the other says swimming only in the second fortnight, which one would you vote for?

ANNIE: It wouldn't make much difference.

ERIC: And specially not to those of us who are here in June. Democracy's a wonderful thing.

ANNIE: But that's not —

ERIC: You're not going to say you don't believe in democracy?

ANNIE: I do of course, but —

ERIC: Good girl, so do I. And in those little green men in flying saucers?

ANNIE: Which little green men?

ERIC: Don't you believe in little green men?

ANNIE: No.

ERIC: I thought if you believed in democracy you must be like me and believe anything.

ANNIE: You don't believe anything.

ERIC: I do, I believe in capitalism and revolution. But wait, you say, that is two different meanings of the word believe. One meaning is you think something exists. Example, I believe in green men. The other is you think it's a good thing. Example, I believe in the prime minister. Now of my belief in capitalism and revolution, do both exist, are both a good thing, or does one exist while the other is a good thing and if so which?

ANNIE: It's hard to believe in you.

ERIC: In either sense, yes, I know it is. And what's Jule's sister doing here?

JULE: She came to see me. She's here for the day.

ERIC: How did she know you were here?

JULE: I sent her a postcard, all right? With a picture of the harbour and a postmark.

ERIC: I'm just surprised you want to go telling people where you are.

JULE: I know you're surprised, George. You'd like to see me in a false moustache. There's no secret about where I am. What's the matter?

ERIC: Nothing at all. You just make me nervous. Doesn't she make you nervous to have in the family? Discontented people like ourselves like to learn of violence on the television news. It makes us feel better as we sip our cocoa and sleep all the sounder. But we're not sure we want it in the family.

ANNIE: Of course it doesn't make us feel better.

ERIC: You're not discontented?

ANNIE: Only like everybody.

ERIC: Everybody's discontented. That's the good news. Everybody's discontented like Jule's sister. That's the bad news. What do you do?

ANNIE: I've just been cleaning somebody's house in the mornings.

ERIC: Do they treat their servants well? I bet they let you have a cup of coffee. And you?

PHIL: I work for a large electrical company which produces equipment for various industries and a wide range of domestic appliances.

ERIC: Why it's essential to have a refrigerator is they're now marketing frozen days you can pop in the freezer and live whenever you're feeling short of time. They can't get a good product image for Mondays so they sell them with Saturdays in a double pack. And with what labour do you create yourself?

PHIL: In fact I'm on sick leave at the moment. I had an accident.

ERIC: Car? Motorbike? Plane, train, hovercraft? No, don't tell me. You were just walking along and something hit you. Industrial accident or domestic? Most accidents happen in the home. Just when you feel you're safest – bang, you fall in the fire, you slip on the wet floor, you're electrocuted by your toothbrush. Let alone acts of God like Jule, who go about causing accidents.

PHIL: Industrial accident.

ERIC: Mangled in the machinery?

PHIL: I had a fall.

ERIC: Better now?

PHIL: Thank you.

ERIC: You got plenty of money out of it, I hope. You exaggerated all your symptoms.

ANNIE: The compensation hasn't been settled yet. Phil has a lot of trouble with his back. He won't be able to do the same work. And besides, the pain must be worth something. The company's insurance company say he should be better by now, they don't believe him. Let them try living with him. Pain's something you can't get round.

PHIL: They'll pay. We're taking them to court.

ERIC: British justice will see you all right. I hope you believe in British justice.

PHIL: They won't find any contributory negligence. I'll get the full amount. I won't settle.

ANNIE: It's not exactly the money so much. Phil wants them to admit his back hurts. He wants the judge to find that's so.

ERIC: He wants justice. You've both lost sleep over that back. Shareholders don't lose sleep. Top management don't lose sleep. Money doesn't pay and nor does an old man in a wig saying yes, your back does hurt. They won't care. Get Jule here to make them jump. That's more like justice. Don't you want more than you'll ever get?

PHIL: Accidents happen.

ERIC: They do, yes, they happen to miners and even people like you, but they don't happen so often in the board room.

PHIL: Our safety level is normally very high. There's no point in me losing my temper.

ERIC: Excuse me, I believe you are one of the workers of the world we're waiting for to unite. But now you can't do the same job, is your socio-economic status about to change? Do you feel a difference in your historical role? In what way is it different from a sausage roll? You don't know? Then I won't ask you to buy my lunch. You might as well have fallen to your death for all the use you're ever going to be. Backache's too good for you. *And* compensation? Greedy bugger.

JULE: You can tell him to be quiet and lie down if you want to.

PHIL: Oh no, it doesn't bother me, thanks.

ERIC: Who are you trying to placate? I'm not your father. I'm not your boss. Nor is power growing out of the barrel of my gun.

JULE: Stop jiggetting about, George.

ERIC: She's the one who should strike terror. Not me. I come down here for a peaceful holiday and find myself in bed with a terrorist. Ninety-five per cent of the dead believe in violence. Do they believe it exists or do they believe it's an effective course of action?

ANNIE: But Jule hasn't caused any

deaths. Does she tell you about what she's done? Can you understand her?

ERIC: I set myself limited objectives. Understand myself today. Understand the world tomorrow. Understand Jule the day after.

JULE: George, will you keep still? You get on my nerves.

ERIC: Right, I'll just be at one with nature.

ERIC *lies down abruptly.*

ANNIE: You'd be much better coming home with us.

PHIL: It's nice and sunny now for a snap and we're all here together.

PHIL *half kneels to take a picture.* ERIC *suddenly sits up and lunges at* PHIL, *knocking the camera out of his hand.* PHIL *falls over.*

ANNIE: Here, that's an expensive camera. And mind his back.

ERIC: If he can afford an expensive camera I expect he can afford another expensive camera.

ANNIE: Is your back all right, Phil? (*To* ERIC:) What's the idea?

ERIC: I'm not having pictures. It wouldn't be safe for your sister.

ANNIE: Why not? Jule, what have you done that I don't know about?

JULE: Of course he can take my picture. Of course it's safe.

ERIC: It makes me nervous.

PHIL (*examining the camera*): I don't think there's much harm done.

ANNIE: You didn't have to push him over. Think of his back.

ERIC: Did I hurt your back?

PHIL: Only a little, thank you.

ERIC: What do I owe you by way of compensation? Ten p?

ANNIE: Is your back all right, Phil?

ERIC: He doesn't mind being pushed over. Accidents happen.

PHIL: Come along, I want some smiles.

PHIL *takes a picture.* ERIC *stands well out of the way.*

ERIC: This is definitely not my picture. A happy day by the sea on a day return that returns you unused at the end of the day.

ANNIE: We came by car in fact.

ERIC: I'm not a great one for the family party, Jule. (*He goes out.*)

ANNIE: Put it away, Phil, don't waste film. I don't feel like smiling. Jule's always admired people anyone else would apologise for.

PHIL: He does seem to have more energy than he knows what to do with.

JULE: I've known him use some of that energy to stay awake three nights with a friend that needed someone to stay awake with him. I don't see you doing it. He's feeling the strain lately but I've known him take other people's strains.

ANNIE: How do you mean, lately? If you've only just met him? When did you know him stay awake three nights?

JULE: By lately I mean today.

ANNIE: Jule, how did you get into all this? Have you yourself ever made a bomb? Don't bother not to answer. I know you're not going to answer.

PHIL: It seems to me there are different things. There's indiscriminate terror. That's hard for anyone in their right mind to defend. But how do we feel about assassination? Remember the prime minister of Spain, blown over the wall in his car. There's a regime where things might be different. If Hitler had had an assassin he'd be a hero. I'm not saying I'd do it myself but it is a question. And then there's destruction of property, which again I wouldn't say yes to, but an empty car isn't a human being. You may get bricks and mortar blown down and nobody hurt except by accident. Though whether they're right to risk the accident I wouldn't like to say. It's more dangerous than driving down the M1 and with less excuse. And you can't have everybody with a grievance taking a gun and going after their MP. Where would it end? Not in a democratic country.

Meanwhile the sun has gone in. JULE *takes* PHIL's *sweater and puts it on.*

JULE: How do we feel about assassination?

PHIL: As I say, I've no view. It's not something I'd ever do but then I'm not driven by the circumstances. I think I'd always resort to non-violence.

JULE: On impulse or as a principle?

PHIL: Both, you know. I'm a great believer in things sorting out. There's more goodwill than people like you think. Even in high places I hope for the best.

JULE: Are you a floating voter?

PHIL: Now and then.

ANNIE: Don't talk to her, Phil, she's laughing at you.

PHIL: I can tell.

JULE: You take care of Annie anyway.

PHIL: People like you are very arrogant. Forgive me, that was rude. I've no business.

ANNIE: I could never hurt anyone. I haven't the confidence.

JULE: But why are you crying?

ANNIE: I'm not, I've given it up, same as smoking.

PHIL: She's been on edge all week. I put it down to you. Without blaming you. I just mean my diagnosis. Try breathing slowly, Annie. You can't have any effect on anything so why get worked up? Come on, we'd got you feeling fine. Your sister's got her own life. We can argue about the philosophy of it without getting involved personally. It's no good if ideas make you cry.

ANNIE: It's not just the ideas. It's myself.

PHIL: There's nothing wrong with you.

ANNIE: Everything I do is a mistake. If I could start again, but how far back? Before I was born.

PHIL: Don't feel you have to stay if you don't want. I can take her away to talk in a café somewhere. You may have enough troubles of your own.

JULE: Annie dear, what is it?

ANNIE: Oh no, I despise the way I fuss. I'm not sure talking does any good. Phil usually massages my neck.

JULE: Is it because of me? You mustn't mind.

ANNIE: You may have been at the back of my mind when I chose that day for saying something. It was only yesterday.

PHIL: Saying to who? At work, is it, Annie?

ANNIE: What you need explaining, Jule, is how that couple look. He is the man in the grey car but more often I see him with her. They move as a unit even when they're not together. They're after the same thing, it's one style. The surface has such a polish it's hard to think of them as victims, though what they must have done to themselves to get where they are, because it's all competition in that world. They must have been attractive at the start, the bones are still there. They're well known for a striking couple. They've lived all their life for the company. It's hard not to confuse them with the product. That way they come into every home and you can't do without them.

JULE: You can always resign.

ANNIE: I always do but it comes to the same thing. I'd only have to find another job just as bad and without even dinner with Phil in the canteen. And when I finally couldn't stand it, cleaning a clean house seemed such a treat. I took my shoes off to feel the carpets and nobody said a word. She even gave me her old clothes and I made a lot out of saying no but I took them. They were better than any new clothes we've ever had and there aren't the occasions to wear them. I feel a fool in my own home in silk.

PHIL: But what is it you've said to them, Annie? Something you're sorry for?

ANNIE: What happened is I was using the hoover and she was just sitting. I hoovered all round her. Maybe she was thinking but nothing you could call work. I said, Lift your feet, and ran the machine under her suede boots. She dresses right up in case anyone comes or perhaps just for herself so she won't go down. But what goes on in her head? I wouldn't touch it. She makes her face so you can't see and then gets up to anything she likes. I might not have been there. But her feet moved. All morning I cleaned up that woman's mess. Cigar butts by the basin. Tissues on the parquet. Broken glass in the spare bed. A little party, she said, last night. That was all she said in three hours I was there, and scratched herself. I went in the kitchen and put on the dishwasher to drown her out.

PHIL: You shouldn't let her get you upset.

ANNIE: She doesn't get me, it's nothing she does, she does nothing. It's me that's upset, myself, that's all.

PHIL: Perhaps you should give them notice if they upset you. You could give them a month without putting them out.

ANNIE: Will you let me tell you? You never let me lead up how I like. At twenty-past twelve I was back in there wasting the last bit of time and she was still sitting on that sofa, and he

came in. Oh, she talked then, they had quite a conversation. I dusted round the edges and never a word to me, not a nod, not good morning, not the glance you'd give a budgerigar. They feel perfectly free with me there, they joke, they touch. I would have thought seeing them there was nobody else in the room but that was me.

PHIL: Isn't it always like that, Annie?

ANNIE: That's what I'm saying, it is, always, exactly. If it was just once I could make an excuse. I could say they had a bad hangover. They went out of the room together the way they do. They go on wheels with a very expensive motor so you don't hear it. They glide together. They have profile. So once more it was time I went and I'd got almost to the front door. The smell in the hall is the kind of wax on the wood. Then he did that thing of coming up behind me. I was in no mood. I said to him, Look, I'm sick of blackmailing you all this time, it makes me feel ill. Because it does, doesn't it? Those stomach aches have all been this trouble. I said, Look, I wouldn't tell your wife. Not the abortion, not even that you ever touched me. I can't give the money back, I told him, because it's spent. But I won't have any more. And no more of him in any way ever. So that was good so far, wasn't it, and it was partly with Jule in mind because (To JULE:) I can't see you working in that house.

PHIL: Was he offended?

ANNIE: What he said was — he might have been lying which would be a comfort, to think of him annoyed enough to lie.

PHIL: He said what?

ANNIE: It might have been made up to hurt, because he is a very intelligent man. He said she knew anyway all along. From right at the beginning, before I thought of asking him for money, right back when it started in the office down behind the desk. He told her each night. He says they agreed to give me the money as a way of giving me money because they know I'm proud and wouldn't accept —

PHIL: They may have meant it kindly, Annie.

ANNIE: Do you think I care how they meant it?

PHIL: They can't help the kind of people they are. They're very efficient at a certain job and that's all they know.

ANNIE: But I really thought I was doing something to them. I used to feel good cleaning up her shit because I thought I knew what was what and she'd got no idea. When really I was the one. That's all it is. Whatever you do to them, they can afford it, they include it, they glide. That's all it is that makes me cry.

JULE: But leave them, Annie, tell them what you think. Put a brick through their window. You don't have to take any of that. Why ever get into it? Why get involved with a man like that?

ANNIE: I keep quiet about your men.

JULE: But blackmailing him and cleaning his house, what's it about?

ANNIE: In fact Jule he reminds me of you about sex. I don't think he knows what else he could do to give himself a shock. He's got past the end of his fantasies and does things he hasn't even thought of.

JULE: I'm not afraid to do anything I want anymore, if that's what you mean.

ANNIE: You do things you don't even want to see where it gets you.

JULE: Not anymore I don't, I do what I want. How do you know what you don't like if you haven't tried?

ANNIE: What don't you like? Alsatian dogs?

JULE: No, and I don't like women much. I like men, and only very few, and usually only one at a time, and just now one more than the rest.

ANNIE: Oh, Jule, how do you concentrate? On — what is it you concentrate on? Yourself? I never carry anything right through. I'm always turning off sideways. I can't get into an extreme position. I can't even hate those two enough to do anything about them. Their rooms are full of useful things that are none of them necessary like fondue dishes and matching toilet paper and there's no good reason for getting rid of any of them but it just shouldn't be like that. The company has profit sharing and a pingpong room and its products are harmless and sometimes even helpful, and he was so efficient in bed, Jule, I didn't know myself. But what's the point? I sometimes get the feeling my arms and legs and body and head aren't all joined together. I see my hands a long way away.

PHIL: Annie, Annie, don't be upset.

JULE: But if you can't stand it, Annie, you should —

PHIL: Leave her alone, will you, leave her alone.

JULE: I can talk to her.

PHIL: You upset her, go away.

ANNIE: Don't, don't, oh don't.

JULE: You're the one upsetting her. She cries if we quarrel.

PHIL: I'm sorry if I seem to lose my temper. But please leave her alone to calm down.

JULE: Why should she calm down? There's nothing to be calm about that I can see.

ANNIE: Don't, don't.

PHIL: Annie. (*He puts his arms round her.*)

JULE: I'm going to go and get dressed

before it starts to rain. (*She goes out.*)

ANNIE: I'm sorry.

PHIL: No, I'm sorry.

ANNIE: What for?

PHIL: I can't talk to your sister very well.

ANNIE: You were talking.

PHIL: No, something blocks my chest. I try to get my views into focus and they disappear the minute I squint at them. Was I like that before the accident?

ANNIE: You're no different.

PHIL: It must be what I'm like, I'm afraid.

ARTHUR *comes in to look for the thermos flask. He finds it but stays half-hidden crouching behind the rocks to watch them.*

ANNIE: We're a pair.

PHIL: I won't let you go.

ANNIE: No, I like it when you hold me.

PHIL: It helps me breathe. I feel fine when we're alone.

ANNIE: So do I. We should come to the sea sometimes.

PHIL: We are.

ANNIE: Other times too, with no Jule. I haven't even looked at the sea till now. I'd like us to walk along the shore. Once you start watching the waves it's very interesting. I wouldn't need anything else to do all day.

PHIL: I picked you up some shells, little yellow ones.

ANNIE: It seems crazy to me now, the way I've been with those two, you know. It's over now.

PHIL: It doesn't have to be.

ANNIE: But it is.

PHIL: You've said that before.

ANNIE: But this time it is. I feel different. I hate to be tricked. I hate it if what's going on isn't what I thought.

PHIL: You're not very honest yourself.

ANNIE: I am.

PHIL: You steal things from supermarkets.

ANNIE: Ah yes, but that's just hitting back.

PHIL: I don't like it. You'd be better joining a political party.

ANNIE: You won't be the one who gets caught. You're not honest yourself. You're too quiet. We talk about what's wrong with me endlessly, we know there's lots of things wrong with me. You soak it up. You could be a professional. We've been together three years nearly and I wouldn't know what to tell someone about you. I can't imagine what you think about when I'm not with you.

PHIL: I'm the strong silent type.

ANNIE: Silent.

PHIL: I don't think very much, that's what it is. I do things or I see things. I don't think.

ANNIE: But how do you see?

PHIL: I was living for too many years secretly. You were married five years that I was alone, and I'm older than you. It's hard to lose the habit of being alone. My mother was a mistake.

ANNIE: You wouldn't rather be alone again?

PHIL: You like to hear me keep saying I'll never leave you.

ANNIE: When I think what it's like, because I know, living with someone you find you don't love, and then living with you, every day.

PHIL: Oh Annie, you're endless to me.

ANNIE: I wish it wasn't starting to rain and we weren't on a public beach.

PHIL: But it is starting to rain, isn't it. Where's my sweater?

ANNIE: Jule put it on, didn't you notice?

PHIL: That girl's a nuisance.

> ANNIE *and* PHIL *go off.* ARTHUR *watches them go, then hurries off the other way. The sky has darkened. There is a loud sound of rain.*

> MISS FORBES *comes in, wet with rain, looking for shelter. She is wearing a coat and carrying a handbag and several carrier bags. She shelters by the rocks and mutters to herself.*

MISS FORBES: Oh, damn you, damn you, why do you do it to me? Every time. I won't bear it. I've a right to a fine day like anyone else. Oh, you bastard, dripping down my neck, oh it's not fair. (*She mutters on inaudibly.*)

> JULE *comes in, dressed.*

JULE: Annie?

> JULE *also shelters by the rocks in a different place.*

MISS FORBES: There's not much shelter here.

JULE: It's only a shower.

MISS FORBES: It's no good going on anyway, is it? We'd get far more wet before we could keep dry. But it's so wet here, I don't know why I'm bothering to keep still. I'll catch a cold now and I'd only just got rid of the cold I had the whole winter, the same cold all winter without a single day's break. You might have thought it was ten different colds, but no.

JULE: I think this place is drier. Come over here.

MISS FORBES: Are you quite sure? It's going to mean crossing an open space.

JULE: As you like.

MISS FORBES: At least it can't be worse than where I am, can it. Ohhhhhh.

> MISS FORBES *hurries across to* JULE.

There. There. Well, it's still not what I'd call dry. But it's very kind of you to try and save my day though I don't think I'm in the right place.

JULE: Why, where should you be?

MISS FORBES: On a beach, I've got that much right, but I think it must be the wrong one. I came here years ago and it wasn't the same. I came somewhere years ago. I forget the name. I looked on the map in the right area and this name leaped out at me but perhaps that was from something different. I could have seen it in the paper or heard it on the news. There's so much information you can't keep out.

JULE: Was it a holiday you had here?

MISS FORBES: I had a happy day here once. Or wherever it was. With a man, I need hardly say. And now and then it comes over me. Oh, I could scream but of course I can't. I blame myself, oh, I blame myself. I used to think I'd been too ugly. I accepted that because it couldn't be helped. But no, it was my hesitation that drove him away. It wasn't at all like this beach. There were golden sand dunes. Very very hot sand dunes.

JULE: You've never tried to go back to the beach till now?

MISS FORBES: I've tried, I've often tried. I miss the train. I can't get out of the door to go to the station. But I managed all that this time. I've been taking a very good new pill. Though I don't like pills, I don't trust them. They may not mean well. They won't last. But they got me onto the train and down here. But then look at the rain.

JULE: It's not so heavy now.

MISS FORBES: It's the wrong beach. There wasn't that big stretch of mud.

JULE: It's low tide.

MISS FORBES: But there should be sand dunes, not rocks and cliffs.

JULE: I think there may be some dunes in the next bay.

MISS FORBES: It's too far. I've a drawer at home of things that are impossible. Letters I can't answer, bills I can't pay, library books I can't take back. Oh my family was behind it all. There's nothing you can tell me about myself. You can deal out psychological terms like tarot cards and I'll read my fortune. I had a brother. My father was always dead in the first war. My mother lived on and on. My family burst in my flesh like shrapnel.

JULE: There's not enough rain to worry about.

JULE comes out from the rocks. After a moment MISS FORBES *tentatively follows.*

MISS FORBES: I was so angry last time I missed the train that I left my umbrella in the tea-room.

JULE: The wind's blowing the weather over quite fast. It won't be one thing or another.

MISS FORBES: Are you busy?

JULE: Not exactly.

MISS FORBES: You wouldn't come along with me, would you? To look for the dunes.

JULE: I really ought to find my sister.

MISS FORBES: It wouldn't come over me so much if you were there.

JULE: She'd wonder where I was.

MISS FORBES: Please, I need you to come with me.

JULE: Can't you see I don't want to.

MISS FORBES: Now I must take off my coat. I must take off my cardy. I never can get in agreement with the temperature. I bring everything I could possibly need. I'll put on my jacket. My raincoat won't go over my jacket but my jacket's not waterproof and my raincoat's not warm enough. My jacket can't go over my cardy but my cardy will go under my raincoat.

JULE: Where do you live?

MISS FORBES: Will you come and see me?

JULE: No, I just wondered.

MISS FORBES: I live in Woking. What's it to you?

JULE: You managed to get all this way.

MISS FORBES: Don't ask me things about myself unless you mean it.

JULE: Mean what?

MISS FORBES: I get so angry. I get so angry. I bite myself. I tear out tufts of my hair. And it's not my fault, it can't be.

JULE: Of course it's not.

MISS FORBES: You're nice to me, you don't want trouble. I'm a strong woman.

JULE: But do you ever hurt other people?

MISS FORBES: Only if I'm in love. That hasn't happened to me very often.

JULE: Suppose you had the material to blow something up? What would you do with it?

MISS FORBES: I'd throw it — I'd throw it — No, I'd hold it tight against myself, and there, at last.

JULE: But it's not your fault.

MISS FORBES: Oh it is, it is. I blame myself. I shouldn't have ever said no. He was very good-looking in what I recognised as a dangerous way and he had a wife. My brother would have killed him. I often think of that. And I could never stop thinking of my brother when I should have stopped thinking entirely. Even in the dunes. I blame myself. He was very gentle. But I couldn't stop thinking even in the dunes.

JULE: Perhaps he would have left you anyway.

MISS FORBES: Why have I never been loved too much? So that whatever I do the other person loves me too much and can't stop loving me whatever I do.

JULE: You want too much.

MISS FORBES: Yes, I want too much, that's what I want. You can't help.

JULE: I never thought I could.

MISS FORBES: You won't come with me up the beach because that would be boring for you.

JULE: And I have to find my sister.

MISS FORBES: You make me angry. You'll forget all about me as soon as I've gone. But I'll be stuck with hating you all afternoon, all up the beach. And if it's the wrong beach, what am I to do?

JULE: I'll come with you, just a little way.

MISS FORBES: There's no need to trouble.

JULE: Not far because —

PHIL (*off*): Jule.

JULE: Oh, here they are now. I won't come. I'm sorry.

PHIL *comes in.*

MISS FORBES *waits a moment, then goes out.*

PHIL: We went into a café while it rained. I hope you don't mind. Are you very wet?

JULE: Do you want your sweater?

PHIL: Only if you've quite finished with it.

JULE: I should have said 'please'.

JULE *takes off his sweater, which she was wearing over her own clothes.*

Thank you. Is Annie feeling better?

PHIL: Before we go back to the café —

JULE: Yes, what?

PHIL: I wanted to say. I never told Annie.

JULE: Told her what?

PHIL: About us.

JULE: What about us?

PHIL: I'd like to pretend it didn't happen myself. It's not an episode I'm proud of. But we'd far better face up to it, Jule.

JULE: I'm not pretending. I don't think I remember.

PHIL: All right, lie. It fits with your destructive character.

JULE: Oh, I remember what you mean. At Christmas the Christmas before last, when I came to stay with Annie and you at Christmas.

PHIL: She remembers. Put it like that if you like. You're prepared to talk about it now anyway.

JULE: Nothing much happened, did it? You were drunk.

PHIL: Nothing happened except I came into your room in the night and tried to get into bed with you.

JULE: And I said piss off and you did, as far as I remember.

PHIL: Not straight away.

JULE: What happened then? We kissed each other.

PHIL: You weren't wearing a nightdress either.

JULE: I don't if it isn't cold.

PHIL: And you'd really forgotten.

JULE: I did have the impression when I saw you again that you'd always fancied me a bit but I'd forgotten what gave me the idea. It was all very passing, we were quite drunk, it was Christmas.

PHIL: I've remembered it all in great detail.

JULE: It's nothing to worry about.

PHIL: Yes it is, Jule. I love Annie. It worries me a lot that you're her sister.

JULE: I can't help that.

PHIL: I have feelings for you I'd rather

not have for someone I'm likely to see again. If you'd been no relation that night, I could let it go. I see attractive women all the time. I might do something about it or I might not, but on they go, on I go, our separate ways.

JULE: But we hardly do see each other again. I don't think I've seen Annie and you once since that Christmas. I've been very tied up with the people I'm living with. My family's the last thing I bother to visit.

PHIL: But I'd like to see you.

JULE: You just said you wouldn't.

PHIL: It preys on my mind. I go over and over that night and I ask myself how I could do it. You're Annie's sister. I'm not married to Annie but it's the same, it makes you my sister. It should do. It should rule out that kind of obsession.

JULE: Of course it doesn't.

PHIL: Doesn't it for you?

JULE: Do I have to feel you're my brother? I don't at all.

PHIL: Then perhaps I should just yield.

JULE: How do you mean?

PHIL: Let my feelings take me over.

JULE: But just because you're not my brother doesn't mean I've any interest in you. It might be more interesting if you were.

PHIL: You're saying you don't want me because of Annie. You're right, of course.

JULE: No, because I don't.

PHIL: Why didn't you say so in the first place?

JULE: I did, I said piss off.

PHIL: Not at once.

JULE: A few kisses at Christmas is nothing. I'd quite like to kiss you now but I wouldn't want to go on.

PHIL: Why, what's wrong with me?

JULE: I'm involved with someone else. I couldn't be bothered.

PHIL: That one jogging about?

JULE: No, no, he's just a passing . . .

PHIL: Then what's wrong with me just passing?

JULE: You'd go on thinking about it for a year and a half. I don't want you thinking about me.

PHIL: Because of Annie?

JULE: No, because of the way you'd go on and on thinking. I'm not interested in being your guilty obsession.

PHIL: You mean, you will if I don't feel guilty?

JULE: Go away and tie a knot in it.

PHIL: No, but Jule, I could try to change the way I feel guilty. I know I worry too much. I lived alone with my mother a long time. I got the courage to say something to you about it. I never thought I would. I get a pain across my chest, here, like an iron bar. I can't lash out. You can so you don't know the problem. With you I could —

JULE: No, I don't want to. You make it sound so therapeutic.

PHIL: Yes, Jule, yes.

JULE: No, it's all so heavy. Where's the joy?

PHIL: I think the joy would come.

JULE: Not to me.

PHIL: You make me want to hurt you. It's a terrible feeling. I want to break you up on these rocks.

JULE: But you won't because you'd feel guilty. It might give you a pain in your chest. And you've already got one in your back.

PHIL: And you can jeer but that's lucky for you, isn't it. Isn't it lucky for you I'm the decent sort of person I am? You're proud of being a slut and a murderer. You — oh, you fucking fucking — oh, I hate you —

JULE: I think that's Annie coming.

PHIL: I hate you, I hate hate you.

JULE: Yes, it is Annie.

PHIL: You're saying that to distract me.

JULE: No, it is Annie if you look. (*She waves to* ANNIE *in the distance.*)

PHIL: That's lucky for you, isn't it. I can't face Annie now. This must be like a horrible dream. I forget all my dreams but sometimes when I wake up I think I must have had a horrible dream because I feel — oh, what shall I do?

JULE: Whatever you like.

PHIL: I must look like myself. I must get my face — (*He turns aside.*)

In a moment ANNIE *comes in.*

ANNIE: The café seemed so dreary now it's dry.

JULE: I'm not hungry.

ANNIE: Why don't we make a fire and get warm? There's plenty of wood on the beach if it wasn't so wet. We always used to make bonfires, didn't we, Jule?

JULE: The bigger pieces wouldn't be soaked through if we could get it started.

ANNIE: I could go and buy a packet of firelighters.

JULE: Or paraffin would do.

PHIL: You want to light a fire? I'll get you something. (*He goes out.*)

ANNIE: Look at all the oil on this bit. Will it burn better?

JULE: My feet are covered with oil. This beach is all rubbish if you look.

ANNIE: We'll clean it up with our fire.

JULE: What you are, Annie, is a girl guide.

JULE *and* ANNIE *start building up a fire, with a newspaper of* ANNIE's, *driftwood, etc.*

ANNIE: I'm sorry, Jule, bursting out like that. I feel better now.

JULE: Did you have a good cry? What does that change? Don't cry, don't feel better, and do something about it.

ANNIE: But doing something would just make me feel better. Nothing changes.

JULE: Suppose you killed that man you work for.

ANNIE: That's one of the reasons I can't do anything. You make me think of terrible things I'd never dare. And don't even want to. It stops me thinking of sensible things that might be some use.

JULE: Yes, I'm sorry. I know I do that to you. But what you call terrible things aren't all so impossible. You think you'd stop being Annie. But I haven't become unrecognisable this last year, have I? Look at me. Listen, Annie, there are quite a few of us —

PHIL *comes back carrying a can of petrol.*

PHIL: What nonsense is your sister talking now?

ANNIE: What have you got there? Not petrol?

PHIL: I always carry a spare can in the boot to be on the safe side.

ANNIE: Yes, but you want to be very careful.

PHIL *pours some petrol into an old tin from the beach.*

JULE: So you hurt your back.

PHIL: Yes.

JULE: So you can't work.

PHIL: I might take up something different. I'd like to.

JULE: Why? Does your life seem a bit pointless?

PHIL: There are things I'm interested in.

JULE: So it's all for the best?

PHIL: I wouldn't go that far.

JULE: How long were you lying flat in hospital?

PHIL: Two months.

JULE: And you didn't feel furious and helpless?

PHIL: Only sometimes.

JULE: And Annie in the silver grey car? At about the same time?

PHIL: I'd been home a week out of hospital before she told me.

ANNIE: I couldn't tell you sooner in case it made you ill.

PHIL: It did make me ill.

ANNIE: You were very understanding about it.

PHIL: I was, yes.

ANNIE: You don't put your own feelings first. That's one of the things I love you for, Phil.

PHIL: For being a fool. For just taking everything.

ANNIE: No, for —

PHIL: A fool not to go and smash his face.

ANNIE: I'm the one who talks about violence. I get aggressive about him and you say how good he is at his job, how in some ways it's an honour, how you have to admire —

PHIL: I smile, I smile, my face is beyond me. I can't spit.

JULE: You can.

ANNIE: Jule, don't upset him, he's been ill. I'm going to try and get this lit without petrol. (*She busies herself with the fire. The newspaper burns but the wood is too damp.*)

JULE: You could change the way you feel guilty. You could get rid of that pain across your chest. You could probably get rid of that pain in your back. You could secretly do something to that executive, or another one, the function's the same, they've no faces, and only you would know, you alone, and you would know you felt quite different.

PHIL: Secretly —

JULE: Through the post —

PHIL: A letter to blow his hand —

JULE: Or in the office. You could leave something. Or in the house, where Annie can easily go.

ANNIE *gets up from the fire.*

ANNIE: No, Jule, we don't want to.

JULE: Think how they glide, Annie, all their lives. That woman knew all along about you.

ANNIE: No, Jule, that's something of my own. I mind it myself, in myself, I don't do something —

PHIL: Jule —

JULE: Phil, yes, Annie, listen, my loves. It's not your fault. It's not just what's done to you. It's because you're just things to them, like all of us are just things to them. They produce more and more useless things. And they're just things, the way things are now. And being hurt is all they notice.

PHIL: My face always smiles. I smile even more often than I'm insulted. But I can feel how I could hurt them.

JULE *squats by the fire, adding more paper, nursing a small flame.*

JULE: You smile yes to it all. You must learn to say no.

PHIL: I do say no.

JULE: You must do it then. (*She bends low over the fire.*)

ANNIE: Do what? Nothing violent?

PHIL *suddenly throws the petrol over the fire.* JULE *just manages to get out of the way as it flares up.*

How can you be so stupid, Phil? Jule, are you hurt?

PHIL: Oh to feel how I hate . . . how things blaze up . . . then you'll see the joy you're after.

JULE: Don't turn away from it, Annie.

ACT TWO

High tide. Sunny afternoon.
  JULE in a bathing suit is lying in the sun. ERIC comes in. He is dressed and his long hair has been cut very short. He is carrying a child's bucket and spade.

ERIC: Would you recognise me?

JULE: Yes, of course.

ERIC: I was hoping you'd say my own mother wouldn't know me. But then she hasn't for a long time so perhaps she would again. I must look more like I did at ten.

JULE: I never noticed your face too much in all that hair.

ERIC: Why, what's wrong with my face?

JULE: It's not so much as if you were in disguise. More as if you'd taken a disguise off. There's nowhere to hide your eyes.

ERIC: You're saying I looked like a different person before?

JULE: Slightly?

ERIC: Good, that's all. I don't need to know if it makes me ugly.

JULE: There's nothing to get in my fingers when I kiss you.

ERIC: Do you still want to now you can see my face?

JULE: It still feels like the same face.

ERIC: I'll miss you, Jule. Look, I found a nice bucket and spade nobody was making use of. (*He starts making sand pies.* JULE *idly knocks them flat.*)

JULE: Eric, have you decided yet where you're going?

ERIC: Wide open spaces.

JULE: Strangers stand out more in open spaces. Manchester's where to get lost, or Birmingham.

ERIC: I'd rather be found than hide in Birmingham.

JULE: I'm not sure what it is this trip's for.

ERIC: A new life.

JULE: Finish up your old one first.

ERIC: I want it quiet. I want to get into one of those butter ads and see the cows.

JULE: Sounds more like a holiday than a life.

ERIC: It makes a start.

JULE: But you can't be away long.

ERIC: I can't know exactly when I'll be back before I've even gone, can I?

JULE: Will you go to Wales?

ERIC: I might do.

JULE: Have you not decided or are you not saying?

ERIC: I've somewhere in mind but I like to change my mind.

JULE: You're not saying.

ERIC: Leave it alone, Jule, O.K.?

JULE: Do you think I'll be after you with tracker dogs?

ERIC: I'll just feel better, O.K., Jule, if nobody at all has any idea where I am. And stop knocking the fucking pies over.

JULE: Look, I told my sister I'd only just met you. I called you George. I lie about you without even bothering to think, as if lies are the only way to talk about you.

ERIC: Fine, keep it up.

JULE: You're feeling paranoid so I humour you. I feel I'm being watched myself sometimes, I feel I must be doing something wrong, I must be very conspicuous. I want to keep still. But if you're really planning to disappear you're humouring yourself too far.

ERIC: I don't accept I have to go back to court just because of the bail. My father can afford to lose the money.

JULE: Not because of the bail. Because of all the things we're planning to do. As soon as you came back to us, the police would pick you up then, they're not stupid. You'd just waste time.

ERIC *has stopped making pies. He starts digging a hole.*

ERIC: I don't accept I have to go back.

JULE: Of course you have to.

ERIC: If I choose to go back that's a different thing.

JULE: You'd better choose it then.

ERIC: I'd like to show them we're not so easy. We slip through their fingers. I thought I'd dye my hair.

JULE: And a false beard? and glasses? and rubber ears? and walk with a limp?

ERIC: Yes, I have got some glasses I'm meant to wear for reading.

JULE: Is there something I don't know about?

ERIC: I thought you knew everything.

JULE: Previous convictions?

ERIC: I would have boasted of them, wouldn't I?

JULE: Then why bother running away from a drug charge that isn't even what the police are after? You know that was just to get us in. They didn't find anything they wanted. The only worry we've got is Vin and Rose being kept on the grounds there may be 'more serious charges', and that's just a bluff, it must be. Because what can they use? They're onto us too soon. There's nothing Vin's done. But you hardly need more than nothing for conspiracy. That's what you should be worrying about, not going on the run to make yourself interesting.

ERIC: I will if I choose.

JULE: They'll soon get you, Eric.

ERIC: Do you want them to?

ERIC *moves away.*

JULE *starts making the pile of sand from the hole into a castle.*

ERIC: It's easy for Vin.

JULE: What is?

ERIC: He's been in prison.

JULE: How does that help?

ERIC: He's been living this same life since he was what? Fifteen?

JULE: It's not the same life. He used to get into fights and steal cars. He didn't see what it was about. Anything he does now is deliberate. He knows what's been done to him. He knows who his enemy is.

ERIC: Yes, there you are. That's what I mean.

JULE: Are you making your point? Are you winning your argument?

ERIC: No, listen, Jule. I know you love him. I do too, I'm not attacking him. That's not what I'm saying.

JULE: Now you've talked about what you're not saying. Now you'll talk about what you are saying.

ERIC: Vin talks. You listen by the hour. His mother, his mother, and him, age six, out on the street. Think sometimes when he's on about his father, how that all helps. He lashes out with that child's anger.

JULE: So what are you saying? He's just a psychopath?

ERIC: What it is, Jule, you're too like me. That's why you don't like to listen. We can't stand what's done to other people. Vin can't stand what's done to himself. He's not unselfish and he's stronger for it.

JULE: I can't stand what's done to me.

ERIC: Nothing bad's ever been done to you except in your head.

JULE: I've one life just like anyone.

ERIC: You and I are too well-read. All Vin finds in books is what he already knows. He can read that violence is man recreating himself and that probably is true for him. He never has been anything except through violence. When he learnt some theories he didn't have to change, he just got a better idea of himself.

JULE: So what are you saying?

ERIC: He can read, 'Freedom, the power to act, shrinks every day except for the criminal in the so-called free society.' Lucky him to have been a criminal first and read that afterwards. I have to make myself a criminal in order to act. It's the harder way round, that's all I'm saying.

JULE: It's not all you're saying.

ERIC: What then?

JULE: You're saying you've had enough. Just one little nudge from the police. Didn't you know they meant to frighten us? How can you let them do it?

ERIC: Jule, come on.

JULE: We won't be hearing from you again. Isn't that what it is? Your new life?

ERIC *sits down and helps with the castle.*

ERIC: Jule, all I'm saying is, I want some time. We were all only talking about what we might do. Things have suddenly started moving on. You wanted to get out of that house yourself.

JULE: Yes, but I always knew I was going back.

ERIC: Did you? Every minute of this week?

ANNIE *comes in with three ice-cream cornets.*

ANNIE: I was getting an ice-cream from the van and I saw you here.

JULE: This is Peter. Brother of George.

ANNIE: Yes, I can see the family likeness. Are you twins?

ERIC: No, I'm the elder and better.

ANNIE: Are you camping on the cliffs as well?

JULE: It's the same man, Annie. He's cut his hair.

ANNIE: I liked it better long.

JULE: He's really called Eric Montgomery. He expects you to know the name from the papers. He came down to the sea with me to get away from it all but now he wants to get even further away. I'm surprised you recognised him with short hair because he's in disguise.

ERIC: I don't mind you telling your sister that. Tell her what you like.

JULE: He's a coward.

ANNIE: Have you changed your mind, Eric, about what you and Jule are doing?

ERIC: Yes. Yes, I have, now you ask. That shocks Jule.

JULE: Does the thought of what we might do make you feel guilty, Eric? Tell Annie. She'll know what you mean.

ERIC (*though what he says is often aimed at* JULE *he addresses himself entirely to* ANNIE. *He forgets to eat the ice-cream, which melts*): Jule doesn't have these bourgeois sentiments. She knows only villains are nasty enough to be heroes. Nice people don't make revolutions, they count the dead. All right, if the wretched are violent who can blame them? But I think they're all in other countries. In that house where we were all living I did feel wretched enough. That house, if you'd seen it, the dark stairs, the layers of wallpaper coming off the damp, the house next door, the number of people in it, the rent they paid, the work they went out to, the street they went out into with more houses of too many people, the rent they were paying, the work they were going out to, the children in the street growing up to more of the same, and the next street the same, the next the same, too much ever to grasp, the children growing up to more. Waking up in the morning there was waking up to need to do something impossible. The kitchen window was stuck. We didn't clean it. I'd get up and be thinking how does anyone get through a day? Outside the window all the streets. I thought we were being suffocated. I smashed the window one morning but it just made us cold. I mended it with a piece of hardboard.

JULE: But a few days by the sea in the sunshine and he's a different man.

ERIC (*still to* ANNIE): Are you very, somewhat or not at all happy? Somewhat? If not at all and you wanted to die, you wouldn't ask me to do it for you. Most people are somewhat happy, they'd say they are, I'm not going to tell them they're not. Happy just walking along, liking each other, liking their work even, some of them. Some of them don't. I know all sorts of economic arguments, I expect you've heard them yourself. Say we go on with what we've talked about. What's the most obvious difference it makes? A bit of rubble and perhaps a few people not walking along that were walking along somewhat happy.

ANNIE: You say, what you've talked about. Has it just been talk?

ERIC: Is that a relief? Because of course it would be wrong to indulge in violence. Not 'of course' Annie. But Jule herself knows what's good is very simple times that are happy. We have them. Cooking a meal up on the cliffs when it's getting dark. Making love and talking after. It may be Jule and Vin is something more extreme I don't know about. Vin and me is something very extreme. But do I want it? The way Jule and I are together seems

more what my life might be about. But Vin can't be happy, like that, she'll say, plenty of people can't. They're too put down to make love, they haven't time to look at the sea. Does that mean I can't ever be happy when I can be? If only it was you, Annie, I was asking. Will you come with me, Jule?

JULE: The ice-cream's melting all over your hand.

ERIC *scrumples the cornet in his fist and drops it on the sand.*

ERIC: Don't I get an answer?

JULE: Of course we've been happy. It shows up more compared to how things are. Like feeling most strongly for someone just when you know you won't see him again. It won't stop me doing whatever has to be done.

ANNIE: But, Jule, it is important to be happy.

ERIC: Do you think I mean happy like you? I mean what I meant before I met Vin. I mean starting with changing myself.

ANNIE: You could do with it.

JULE *starts digging a moat round the castle. Apparently aimlessly she throws the sand at* ERIC.

ERIC: Why can't I think of my life as a slow explosion into other lives, not hurting but somehow changing —

JULE: He's going to be a saint now, Annie. Why didn't he shave his head while he was about it?

ANNIE: He still doesn't make as little sense as you.

JULE: You'll explode with a fizz in a little bottle marked Poetry. Powerful men enjoy poetry. It helps them relax after dinner.

ERIC: I just want some time, Jule. I don't know. I want to be somewhere quiet and look at things. I'd like to play some music again some time.

JULE: Is there any address we can write care of? Vin might want to get in touch.

ERIC: No address.

JULE: You can always contact us if you want to.

ERIC: Will you stop throwing bloody sand?

ERIC *digs some sand towards her.* JULE *still throws hers at him.*

JULE: Do you think you're going to want to get in touch?

ERIC: I hope you think of me sometimes, Jule.

JULE: Do you want to hide from us, Eric? Would it be more peaceful for your meditations? Do you want to hide from Vin?

ERIC: Don't think too badly of me. Fuck you.

ERIC, *getting more sand thrown at him, throws more at her again.*

JULE: Of course I think badly of you. It doesn't matter. You'll stay some sort of friend, I daresay.

ERIC: It's for Vin's sake, Jule, I've got to go. You should be grateful.

JULE: What does that mean?

ERIC: It's easy for Vin.

JULE: You've said that.

ERIC: He doesn't get confused. It's sometimes hard under pressure to know what you're doing.

JULE *stops playing with the sand.*

JULE: Eric, what have you done?

ERIC: How do you mean?

JULE: We know each other. Come on.

ERIC: Come on where?

JULE: It wasn't when we were arrested?

ERIC: I didn't say a word. I'm sure I didn't let anything out they didn't know already.

JULE: What did you say?

ERIC: I said I wouldn't tell them anything.

JULE: Anything about what?

ERIC: Anything about anything.

JULE: What did they say?

ERIC: They said to go away and think about it.

JULE: Think about what?

ERIC: Whether I had anything to say. I told them I hadn't.

JULE: So you've been thinking about it?

ERIC: Of course not. I always knew I wasn't going back.

JULE: I suppose they said they'd drop the drugs charge if you could help them about Vin.

ERIC: How could I? We haven't even done anything yet. The worst they could do would be conspiracy.

JULE: What did you say?

ERIC: Nothing. What you say to pigs doesn't count. I might have given the impression I'd think about it but that was just to get them off my back.

JULE *starts to throw small stones, aiming just short of him.*

Anyone might say anything if they were pushed. But you don't keep your word. I'm not keeping my word. I'm not going back. You can't think I'd go and give evidence against the rest of you. I never for a moment dreamt I'd do that. And now I've got to move on, you see, so they won't know where I am.

JULE: What did you say?

ERIC: Stop throwing stones. It's dangerous.

JULE: What did you say?

ERIC: Nothing, Jule, I really didn't.

JULE: Why not come back then?

ERIC: I don't choose to come back. You should be grateful.

JULE: Because if you came back you know you'd talk.

ERIC: I just want to get right out of it.

JULE: Get out of it then.

ERIC *is hit by a stone.*

ERIC: You deserve whatever you get.

ERIC *picks up some stones too.*

JULE: I don't know why you let me know you cut your hair. You'd better not let me know what colour you dye it.

ERIC: You wouldn't all take some revenge would you? It wouldn't be our policy. It's more Vin himself when he's angry that makes me nervous. Perhaps if you didn't mention to Vin about my hair.

ERIC *is slowly retreating.* JULE *starts throwing large stones harder.* ERIC *dodges and goes.* JULE *throws a few more stones down the beach after him. Then she sits in the hole dug earlier by* ERIC *and starts pulling the sand of the castle over herself.*

ANNIE: You won't go to prison, will you, Jule? Because what could he tell? It sounds as if there's only been talk. Is that right?

JULE: Remember how we used to bury each other in the sand.

ANNIE: Because surely everybody talks. I'd like to know you hadn't done anything.

JULE: It doesn't mean I'm not going to.

ANNIE *and* JULE *concentrate on burying* JULE *in the sand. When* JULE's *arms are buried,* ANNIE *goes on covering her, piling sand on and patting it down hard.*

You used to lie on the floor and shut your eyes and scream because someone would always come and kiss you better. They may kiss you now but not better. You should listen, Annie, when it's me telling you. But that's just why you won't listen. You never wanted to play my games. You thought being older put you in charge. But my games were always better. You don't make me worry about what I'm doing. It's not something I go into. But I love the friends I'm with more than you because what we're bound up in is more important than if we always get on. Eric's really gone. And I love you more than them, Annie, and I wish you were with me bound up in it. Even Phil sees the point. Why not you?

ANNIE: It's not a good moment to ask.

JULE: Why, what is it?

ANNIE: Phil told me.

JULE: Phil told you what?

ANNIE: Everything. Unless of course he didn't.

JULE: What everything?

ANNIE: You and him. How could you just never tell me?

JULE: Annie, your man is nice enough but mad. What's he saying? He started raving to me about it too. Nothing happened.

ANNIE: You kissed him.

JULE: Annie, don't be stupid, we were drunk.

ANNIE: You were naked.

JULE: I was trying to go to sleep and he blundered in.

ANNIE: And what?

JULE: And I told him to go away. Does he say anything different?

ANNIE: It doesn't sound quite so cool as he tells it.

JULE: Sodom and Gomorrah. The Vampire. I expect he showed you where I bit his neck.

ANNIE: Did you bite his neck?

JULE: Of course I didn't.

ANNIE: Why wasn't I told?

JULE: There wasn't anything to tell.

ANNIE: If it was nothing you would have mentioned it.

JULE: It wasn't important.

ANNIE: It was to him, it was to me. It should have been to you.

JULE: I'll tell you everything another time. 'Annie, your man just gave me a piercing look.'

ANNIE: We all know you're the world's most liberated woman. We all know you have five men every night.

JULE: Why don't you ever pay attention? You don't care what my life's like, you never really want me to tell you. It's been quite good the four of us living together. It's been up and down. Eric was the one who was most nearly left out but we all need each other. It's Vin he loves more than me or Rose. We all love Vin most is the trouble. Rose was with him first. I admire Rose for a lot of things and one is because she never tried to stop me joining them. Perhaps she knew I'd make no real difference to her and Vin but she can't have been sure. We all got frightened sometimes by things that happened. But we wanted to find out what made us frightened. Why should there be anything frightening about four people who want to understand each other? We've laughed a lot. Eric makes it sound as if that house was some kind of mental home. He was the one who got most depressed. But we laughed a lot. We did at the beginning. We got frightened of where our politics was taking us and what we might do. But it makes sense to other people not only us. It's not so frightening when you're used to it.

ANNIE: I don't understand you.

JULE: You don't want to.

ANNIE: No, I don't want to.

JULE: I don't know what's going to happen to us. You can't think it's all for nothing. I wish you'd see it, Annie.

ANNIE: I can see living with three people, if that's what you like. Nobody minds that. I mind violence.

JULE: Everybody does.

ANNIE: Well, of course.

JULE: And they're meant to mind it.

They stay silent for a time. ANNIE *has finished burying* JULE *by now and only her head shows.*

Maybe I can go on lying here till the tide comes in over me. It's coming quite fast.

ANNIE: I was thinking that.

JULE: Thanks.

ANNIE: You don't ever expect me to hate you.

JULE: Not much, no.

ANNIE: Haven't you ever been jealous?

JULE: Yes, but with some reason. Or is it because I made Phil understand what I'm talking about?

ANNIE: There is a reason if he feels so strongly. I don't care what really happened. What matters is how he remembers it. Why is it a year and a half later I'm told and it mattered to him all that time? You're always more important than me. You climbed the tree too high and broke your arm, and I was obviously right not to climb so high, but you got the attention. You always get attention.

JULE: When Phil and you make love do you usually come?

ANNIE: Why?

JULE: I wondered.

ANNIE: Sometimes. Why?

JULE: Because I'd like you to. You look so sad most of the time.

ANNIE: I hate you, Jule, quite often. Now as well but often when you're not there, when I think of you. It would be a relief to know I was hurting you. I see why people use knives. I've thought that sometimes in the kitchen. I'd enjoy slashing your face and knowing it was too late, that I couldn't be sorry and change my mind. The blood would be pouring out, frightening us.

JULE (*laughing*): I'd better not come and stay with you, had I?

ANNIE: Laugh, then, laugh. How can you laugh?

JULE: It is funny when you keep saying how I've got to go and stay with you to be safe.

JULE *laughs, her head lying right back on the sand.* ANNIE *suddenly throws sand over her face, covering it, and pats it down.* JULE *can't struggle properly because of the weight of sand on her arms.* ANNIE *goes.* JULE *struggles out. She spends some time getting sand out of her eyes and mouth, shaking her hair, slowly brushing sand off her body. It has clouded over and now starts to rain.* JULE *goes out slowly. It rains.*

MISS FORBES *comes in, wet with rain.*

MISS FORBES: No, oh no, no, no, it's not fair. Why on me? Why rain on me? I won't stand it. Rain on me, then, rain on me. I don't care.

MISS FORBES *stands crying in the rain.*

ARTHUR *comes in, holding the newspaper over his head and carrying the deckchairs. He goes and shelters by the rocks. After a moment he decides to speak to* MISS FORBES.

ARTHUR: Excuse me.

MISS FORBES *pays no attention.*

Excuse me, er, miss.

She turns.

If you want to shelter, you can shelter here.

MISS FORBES: It's too late.

ARTHUR: Why too late?

MISS FORBES: I'm soaked already. I'm soaked to the skin. I can feel the water running down my back. I'll never get dry now whatever I do.

ARTHUR: Come on, come on, don't be upset. Come and shelter here.

ARTHUR *comes from the rocks and ushers her to shelter.*

There, that's not so bad, is it. Perhaps there's something else upsetting you apart from the rain.

MISS FORBES *cries harder.*

If you'd like to tell me about it. I don't expect I'd be able to do anything.

MISS FORBES: No, no. It's a private grief.

ARTHUR: It's terrible weather when you're not feeling so bright yourself.

MISS FORBES: You don't happen to know if there's any beach near here that has sand dunes?

ARTHUR: Sand dunes. No, it's all rocky as far as I've walked but I'm not an expert on the area. You could always ask at the police station.

MISS FORBES: It's not worth the bother. I never should have come. What did I hope to get from it anyway? Some sort of thrill I'd be better without. The tide coming in doesn't make it the right beach. I remember a beach with pounding surf.

ARTHUR: Excuse my asking, but would it be a romantic memory?

MISS FORBES: I suppose there's no harm in admitting that. Everyone has them.

ARTHUR: I have a few myself. As we get older we realise that some things may not happen to us again.

MISS FORBES: If only I had nothing to blame myself for.

ARTHUR: A clear conscience is what we'd all like. But you can't have that where romance is concerned.

MISS FORBES: You think I'm wrong to blame myself then?

ARTHUR: You may well be right to blame yourself. But everybody should blame him or herself. You're no different there.

MISS FORBES: That's a comforting way to look at it. Perhaps *he* blames himself.

ARTHUR: If he's worthy of you I'm sure he does.

MISS FORBES: But that makes it worse if he regrets it too. We might so easily still be together.

ARTHUR: Do I take it you're somewhat by yourself in life?

MISS FORBES: I have a brother in the north of England but we don't write.

ARTHUR: Not even a Christmas card?

MISS FORBES: Cards, yes, but without any message except the seasonal.

ARTHUR: That's very lonely. I know what it is.

MISS FORBES: Are you in the same position?

ARTHUR: I'm very much alone.

MISS FORBES: No family at all?

ARTHUR: It's not so much that.

MISS FORBES: Are you parted from them?

ARTHUR: I am in fact married, I regret to say. I mean I'm very happily married so far as it goes. I have a grown up son. But I still think I can say I know what it is to be lonely.

MISS FORBES: Not really lonely, no, you wouldn't know.

ARTHUR: It can be lonely even with two in a bed.

MISS FORBES: Not lonely. You'd hear the other breathing.

ARTHUR: Breathing. Yes. Well.

MISS FORBES: Tell me about your son.

ARTHUR: He's a fine boy, taller than me. He works in a bank and he looks beyond that. He's a member of the National Front.

MISS FORBES: Is that your politics too?

ARTHUR: I was never so whole-hearted. But he's a great one for purity. He has these high ideals for the British people. The foreigners won't do themselves any good by coming here. I'm not saying we ought not to welcome them, just that they've no place in our midst. We brought him up to an ideal of purity. We washed out his mouth a few times and then we had no more trouble. Instant obedience we taught him and it's served him in good stead in his working life. He knows how to obey in his party and therefore he knows how to command. Obey and command, two precious words, that young people today sometimes forget.

MISS FORBES: My brother has always been more of a socialist. He's a trade union man.

ARTHUR: That's not my idea at all.

MISS FORBES: Your son's a fascist.

ARTHUR: That word may not be the insult it's sometimes used as today. It's a proud word.

MISS FORBES: I mean it as an insult.

They stand there. MISS FORBES *holds out her hand but it is still raining.*

ARTHUR: Come, come, let's not quarrel about politics. Religion and politics should never be discussed at dinner and certainly not with a lady.

MISS FORBES: This isn't dinner.

ARTHUR: No, but stuck here side by side in the rain is just like a social occasion, don't you think?

MISS FORBES: I don't have very much social life.

ARTHUR: My own life's very quiet. There's an annual dinner dance that goes with my work.

MISS FORBES: I wouldn't remember how to dance.

ARTHUR: I'm sure you dance very well. You look like someone who knows how. Once you've done it it always comes back.

MISS FORBES: I used to dance.

ARTHUR: I like a dance. An old-fashioned dance where you take your partner in your arms. Not one of those dances the young do where you don't touch each other. I like the kind of dance like a last waltz cheek to cheek, don't you? Highly romantic and nobody takes offence.

MISS FORBES: I have my own memories of course.

ARTHUR: My wife disapproves of everything. I'm forced to go to shops for literature. I can't help it, it's a natural urge, it's disgusting but I can't help that. You're the same, you're no better, you dance, you've had men, you like it, you like it, you'd like it now, you want me to do it now, it's not my fault, you're making me do it, you're making me.

ARTHUR *undoes his trousers.*

touch me, quick, touch me, touch me, touch me —

MISS FORBES *shrieks and rushes away. She trips over some rocks near the sea's edge and falls heavily.*

ARTHUR *hastily does up his trousers.*

Look what you made me do. It's not my fault. It's you. It should be stopped.

ARTHUR *picks up the deckchairs and hurries off.* MISS FORBES *shrieks again. She stays lying where she is and shrieks again.*

MADGE *comes in.*

MADGE: Whatever is it? Oh, you poor dear. Did you slip? You've fallen in a little rock pool, you're all wet. Can you get up?

MISS FORBES: My ankle —

MADGE: Have you sprained it? Let me have a look.

MISS FORBES: Ohhh.

MADGE: It isn't broken but it might be sprained. We can't be too careful. Let me help you up a little bit. You're rather heavy. I don't know if I can — oh — if you hop —

MISS FORBES: I can just put it to the ground.

MADGE: That's wonderful. That's wonderful. We're moving now. I wish my husband was here with a deckchair.

MISS FORBES: I'll sit on the ground.

MADGE: It's very wet.

MISS FORBES: I'm wet through anyway. (*She sits on the ground.*)

MADGE: The rain's stopped again, that's one blessing. Had we better take off your shoe? Is your ankle swelling? Don't cry, dear. It's the shock, I know.

MISS FORBES: It's not . . . it's not . . .

MADGE: Just sit quiet a minute.

MISS FORBES: It's not my ankle. There was a man.

MADGE: A man?

MISS FORBES: He . . . oh . . . he . . . need I say?

MADGE: No, did he really? What exactly?

MISS FORBES *whispers in* MADGE's *ear.*

We must call the police. What did he look like? I saw a most suspicious character earlier, I expect it was him.

MISS FORBES: He looked quite a harmless little man.

MADGE: I can't possibly leave you here

alone. He might come back. As soon as you're feeling well enough we must go to the police. I wish my husband was here. I was just spending a penny and when I came out it was pouring with rain and he'd folded up the deckchairs and was gone. He could run and find a policeman.

MISS FORBES: I'm not sure I want the police.

MADGE: Of course we must get the police. Think of the danger to the public prowling the beach.

MISS FORBES: I would never have screamed like that in the normal way. It was more the surprise, and slipping over.

MADGE: A terrible terrible shock.

MISS FORBES: I don't think he meant to hurt me at all. I expect he was quite frightened when I screamed.

MADGE: Always scream and hit out with a handbag or better still a sharp umbrella.

MISS FORBES: I didn't mean to make such a fuss.

MADGE: You're having a happy time by the sea and someone does that to you, you've every right to make all the fuss you like.

MISS FORBES: I wasn't having a happy time. I was crying and he made me feel better.

MADGE: Why were you crying, my poor dear? What a day for you.

MISS FORBES: I came to the sea hoping for a moment of — great — some great feeling.

MADGE: Yes, yes, that's what I come to the sea for.

MISS FORBES: It's so hard to get out of the house. I sometimes feel the top of my head will blow off. I very much want to relieve the lack of pressure round me. I felt that this place where I'd suffered . . . where I'd been so

happy . . . where in memory I'd been so often . . . but this is the wrong beach in any case.

MADGE: Any beach, any beach, or a coach tour of Scotland would do you good.

MISS FORBES: Scotland?

MADGE: Hasn't Scotland ever occurred to you?

MISS FORBES: I could never do it alone.

MADGE: Perhaps you could do it with us.

MISS FORBES: I'd rather you didn't say that.

MADGE: Why ever not?

MISS FORBES: I'm quite used to being lonely, thank you.

MADGE: But what a terrible thing to be used to. I'm used to my feet hurting but that's past help. You must come to tea with us every Saturday. It's very rarely I meet anyone who cares for higher things as you do. In this day and age we must cling together. Now how's that ankle coming along?

MISS FORBES: A little better I think.

MADGE: Let's go and tell the police.

MISS FORBES: No, the poor man.

MADGE: Whatever do you mean?

MISS FORBES: He probably isn't very happy himself. He said he was lonely.

MADGE: They always say something like that to try and catch you.

MISS FORBES: I think he was lonely.

MADGE: There, there's my husband. He suddenly came out from behind those rocks. What is he doing right down there? Arthur! Arthur! Come here at once. Do you hear me? Come here quickly. We want the police.

MISS FORBES: I'm not sure we do.

MADGE: It's very unpleasant to have to put into words a horrible experience, but you must be brave, my dear, and think of the good you'll do other women. It's your duty.

ARTHUR *comes in.*

Arthur, there you are at last. This poor woman is the victim of an attack. Run for the police, Arthur.

ARTHUR: What sort of an attack?

MADGE: You don't want me to embarrass her by repeating the details. Go and get the police. A maniac is on the rampage.

MISS FORBES: I'm not sure I want to tell the police.

MADGE: Of course you do. It's the shock, Arthur, that makes her say that. Go along.

MISS FORBES: No, stop. I never should have screamed like that. It was just the surprise. I don't think he would have hurt me. He's lonely. I should have understood.

MADGE: It would be compounding a felony to keep silence. I shall inform the police if you won't. Now come along, my dear, can you walk?

MISS FORBES: Just slowly.

MADGE: Why don't we go to the café and have a nice cup of tea to help you get over the shock and Arthur can be finding a policeman.

ARTHUR: What description of your assailant shall I give the police?

MISS FORBES: Oh, he was a very tall man. Thick set and with a lot of dark hair. He was wearing a red pullover and white tennis shoes.

MADGE: That sounds like the man I saw. Very dark, and you could say thick set, I think. He wasn't wearing a red pullover. Perhaps he's changed his clothes. Unfortunately, I didn't notice his shoes. Or there may be more than one maniac at large. Nothing would surprise me. Help our friend to walk along, Arthur.

MADGE *and* ARTHUR *support* MISS FORBES *on either side and they go out.*

The sun comes out.

TERRY *comes onto the beach. He is wearing a dark suit and black tie and shoes. He looks along the beach both ways.*

JULE *comes in.*

JULE: What have you come here for?

TERRY: The postcard had the necessary information.

JULE: I didn't say come.

TERRY: I don't need you to give me instructions.

JULE: You might easily not have found me. I wasn't going to come back on the beach. You would have wasted hours of your time. It's only that the sun came out again.

TERRY: Well, it did.

JULE: You don't seem very pleased to see me for someone who bothered to come.

TERRY: I took the decision not to see you again. But I resented telling you what I thought of you over and over and over in my head so I got on a train to have the satisfaction of being heard.

JULE: I can't think what it is that's upset you.

TERRY: I saw how the paper put it. I know what it means.

JULE: You've known what I think a long time. There's nothing sudden.

TERRY: I thought so this is what I've been waiting for. I knew she'd do something this stupid.

JULE: We haven't done anything yet. They're onto us too soon.

TERRY: What's the difference?

JULE: No, that's true, no difference, because we'll go on.

TERRY: The only difference is you're so inefficient you get caught before you even start. I expect you talk too much.

JULE: Have you come in some official capacity? To say the party disapproves of anarchic counter-productive individualistic violence?

TERRY: No, I came to say you're a shit.

JULE: It's the same thing because you only recognise two kinds of people, communists and shits.

TERRY: Don't pretend you're anything political. If you go on like this you'll be a murderer.

JULE: If I was it might not matter. There are far more deaths that don't worry you.

TERRY: Violence is nothing to do with revolution, it's secondary, it's incidental. There may be violence but it's not —

JULE: If you're killed in the course of incidental violence does that help you feel your dying is incidental? That must have been a great comfort in Russia at the time, knowing your death wasn't important to the revolution, just incidental.

TERRY: If, in the sweep of a huge historical movement like the working class coming into their power, there is some violence —

JULE: But there isn't too much huge historical sweep about our working class at the moment, don't you find that your problem?

TERRY: If in a revolution people get killed I accept that. But I'm not insane enough like you and Vin to think if I go out and kill someone that itself makes a revolution. Who's behind you? What mass of people? Everyone, I suppose you'll say, but they just don't know it yet.

JULE: You do look official dressed like that. Ought I to stand up?

TERRY: Even something the size of Paris in '68 didn't work because it didn't have the working class organised behind it. And what have you got? Not just no organisation but no one at all.

JULE: Terry, it was nice of you to come and see me.

TERRY: Of course, if people are treated violently they react with violence, a few of them, it's surprising sometimes how few of them. One or two slaves kill one or two masters, but that's never the end of slavery. Marx ends the dream of impotent violence that you're still having. The contradictions of society —

JULE: Terry, I'm glad to see you.

TERRY: It's not the damage you do I mind most. It's stupid, it's sad, all right. What I mind is you drive people the other way, we get more law and order because of you, more power to the police, more middle of the road, more shit. All right, you can say, we'll drive them all the way to the right, make them show themselves for the fascists they are, then we can really start. I don't believe that. I can't be glad of any fascist government. I work long hours to organise. And you and Vin and your other lovely friends go out for an evening's fun smashing it up.

JULE: I hope I do. I don't want what you organise. If you ever were in power I'd be the first one out on the streets against you.

TERRY: And I'd have you arrested.

JULE: Of course you would. Tell me some time when the communist party hasn't stood in the way of revolution.

TERRY: You get angry. So what if you get angry? You've nothing to do with anything except yourselves.

JULE: You would have liked my grandmother who once told me she'd never struck a child in anger. Just coldly, you know, as a just punishment. I'd be more proud to say if I'd struck a child that I'd never done it except in anger.

TERRY: Psychopaths don't make good soldiers. It's been established that the best soldiers aren't feeling aggressive when they're fighting, they're quite calm, they do their job.

JULE: I'm sure they do, like Eichmann.

TERRY: It's a different job. That does make a difference. I may not do anything dramatic like Vin but I keep working steadily towards what will one day come about.

JULE: No, you'd never go raping and looting. You'd rape only if ordered. But if ordered, very thoroughly.

TERRY: There was a time when you would have despised someone who talks like you talk now. I can't take you and Vin seriously. He may be a threat to me but he's certainly not to the state. A long sentence is just flattery.

JULE: And what threat are you? You're out of the history books. Everybody knows nowadays there's not that to choose between what you offer and what we've got already.

TERRY: What do you offer? A little kids' gang, what do you offer? What has anything you do got to do with running a country and people living and working in it, and eating? You used to have some grasp of how things work.

JULE: It's only when things stop working that —

TERRY: Only when people stop eating.

JULE: Why should I try and explain myself to you? You won't hear a word, you never heard a word I said in three years. I don't know why you bothered to come if it's only to shout. It's nothing to do with you what I do or what I believe or anything at all about me.

TERRY: No, that's true. It's your life to waste.

JULE: So go home, will you?

TERRY: I certainly don't know why I bothered to come. I forget when I've been away from you how thick and nasty you are. I even had some idea of suggesting you came back, because I'd forgotten how much I dislike you.

JULE: Back to you?

TERRY: I'm not still suggesting it, don't worry.

JULE: Husband and wife again? All that?

TERRY: You could call it what you like. It wouldn't be the same as before. But the basis of it would be that we'd be together. Most of the time only. I was thinking of giving Liz two parents again.

JULE: Can't you manage alone?

TERRY: Yes, very well. She goes to day nursery still all day and she calls it school. She tells me bedtime stories. No, it wasn't for Liz. She's much better off without you.

JULE: Terror's always made you uneasy. You like to think things are under control. They never are and they shouldn't be. You think if you work hard enough at the little jobs, never mind what the little jobs are, everything's bound to turn out all right. If you can't quite grasp the overall strategy never mind, perhaps that's just as well since you might not agree with it, you keep marching, you keep your head down. Your Catholic mum and dad may not like your politics but they can't doubt your faith is as strong as theirs, they did a good job on you those first seven years. You try very hard to be consistent because that's part of having it under control, you read it up, you've learnt the defence of nearly every policy. If nearly everything you believe was chopped off by what your party actually do, you'd grow whole again like a starfish from one arm and a bit of your centre. Why we can't live together is because we frighten each other.

TERRY: I refuse to take an interest in my character. Vin's waging a glorious liberation of himself. I've no interest in that. You've always been critical of what I'm like. If I'm full of inhibitions and fixations I haven't time to be bothered. I work all right as I am and that's what matters. If you can explain that I'm only a communist because I'm neurotic, I'm happy to stay neurotic and stay a communist. There's more important things to be put right than my mind. Afterwards perhaps I'll think about what I'm like, the time may come. And time for sitting in the sun by the sea.

JULE: You could say the same about Vin. If what's happened to him has made him what you call a psychopath that doesn't explain away what he does. It makes him able to do it.

TERRY: You can say what you like about Vin but I'm not interested.

JULE: How's your sex life these days?

TERRY: Secondary.

JULE: Like violence is secondary?

TERRY: Yes, if you like. They're both distractions from work that has to be done. Secondary and confusing.

JULE: You should pay it more attention.

TERRY: I should pay it less.

PHIL *and* ANNIE *come in.*

ANNIE: Jule. We're off now. We're going home. Though if you want to come with us we could wait while you get ready, because I saw George leaving with his tent. Terry? Is it? I didn't realise for a moment because it's so long since I saw you. I didn't know you were here.

TERRY: We both still run round after her as if she couldn't look after herself.

ANNIE: And Liz? How's Liz? Is she here?

TERRY: No, I left her with a friend. She hasn't seen Jule for a time and she's perfectly happy. I didn't want to risk upsetting her.

ANNIE: I don't think I was living with Phil when I last saw you. This is Terry. He used to be Jule's husband. Or still is.

JULE: Getting married was enough of a mistake without getting divorced as well. I don't plan to keep the state informed. It's not as if staying married means we're together. I don't recognise the marriage.

ANNIE: Jule, I'm sorry about just now. Were you all right? You once did that to me when we were children and afterwards I was sick. Phil and I should have our quarrels in private.

PHIL: Yes, I feel I should owe you an apology. I got carried away and quite confused. I exaggerated.

ANNIE: We've been for a walk along the shore and talked it over.

JULE (*to* PHIL): Now you're the person I want to show Terry. (*To* TERRY:) He'd never work with you in the party, he's not convinced by economic arguments. But the mess of his own life convinces him. (*To* PHIL:) Tell him what you told me about the people you work for. Tell him how you and Annie are tied up. (*To* TERRY:) One violent action and they'll be out. (*To* PHIL:) Tell him.

ANNIE: If you mean in a mental way, Jule, changing our attitude, we have done that I think, thanks partly to you. I won't go on working for them again. But as for this other. I don't think Phil would do anything illegal.

JULE: I don't mean mental, Annie, I mean physical. I mean illegal. Phil means that.

PHIL: I did see your point for a while there. As I say, I exaggerated all kinds of ways. About that Christmas time, and also about the couple we were telling you about, who certainly have their faults, but it isn't all exactly them to blame, it's the world we live in like it or not. I can't feel I'd be justified.

ANNIE: She can't really have thought, can she, Terry, that when Phil's back at work she'd have him setting off with an explosive carrier bag?

PHIL: It's not an action I could approve of. It wouldn't bring about what I'd like to see.

JULE: What would you like to see?

PHIL: It's hard to put into words, isn't it? The same things everybody would like to see.

ANNIE: Perhaps like you said, Jule, I should try to be something like a teacher. Something exhausting and worthwhile.

JULE: I said exhausting.

ANNIE: That sort of thing.

JULE: Terry believes in doing things that are exhausting. They give you a great impression of being worthwhile because they keep you so busy.

PHIL: Excuse me asking, if it's an impertinence, but would you be in mourning? Seeing the tie.

TERRY: Yes, that's right. I've just come from a funeral. I decided which train I was going to catch and didn't leave myself time to change.

ANNIE: Who was it, Terry? No one close I hope.

TERRY: It was my father.

PHIL: I'm very sorry. Perhaps I shouldn't have said anything.

TERRY: He's had a weak heart for some time.

ANNIE: He was a nice man.

PHIL: Once your parents have gone it brings it home to you that you're

next. In my case I felt that.

TERRY: Yes, so did I.

ANNIE: Our parents have a lot of worry over Jule. You couldn't write to them, Jule, could you?

JULE: I might do.

PHIL: Well, we must be off and hope the traffic's not too heavy.

ANNIE: I feel better for some sea air. It blows away the cobwebs. Nice to see you again, Terry.

PHIL: Don't forget, Jule, anything we can do.

PHIL *and* ANNIE *go.*

TERRY: Is it much better for you with Vin? Sexually. Than me.

JULE: No.

TERRY: Why not?

JULE: I don't think he notices the other person so much.

TERRY: That sounds a bit limited.

JULE: No one's saying he's some amazing being.

TERRY: I can't think where I got the idea from then. Certainly not from meeting him.

JULE: What is better with him is what I'm like myself. I don't feel I have to try and be something I'm not.

TERRY: You don't have to with me either.

JULE: Oh but yes, you know how it was. There were things you expected a wife to be like.

TERRY: I've got over that.

JULE: I can't get over it. I can't trust you. I'm sure you'd mean to leave me room to move but you couldn't do it. I couldn't do it, it's probably my fault, I'd go back to being like I was. I'd be pretending.

TERRY: So what it comes down to is Vin is better.

JULE: Not exactly Vin. I like what we're all like. We don't crowd each other.

TERRY: So you'll stay with him.

JULE: You like to think I only believe in what I'm doing because of Vin. You think I'm some sort of gangster's moll. But I don't think his way because I love him. I love him because we think the same way.

TERRY: I'm not sure which you mean to be worse.

JULE: Even if in some ways I like you better, I can't come back and switch to your ideas.

TERRY: I had the impression you liked him better.

JULE: I wish Annie thought the same as me. I wish you did. You can't leave politics out of it yourself. You know you hate me for what I'm doing.

TERRY: But I still came to ask you to live with me again.

JULE: Thinking quite differently from you?

TERRY: There's still plenty of things we both oppose.

JULE: We'd agree to abolish the monarchy and not vote for the three major parties. But it's a bit beyond that. I want to live with the people I'm working with.

TERRY: Do you think I wouldn't find it hard too? I remember what it was like.

JULE: There you are. All our effort would go into quarrelling. We'd never get anything else done.

TERRY: Spend our lives cancelling each other out? Of course I don't want that.

JULE: I've more to do than loving another person.

TERRY: Yes, so have I.

JULE: If I can leave Liz, I can leave you.

TERRY: I know you can, you already have done.

JULE: But now and then all our lives we can meet —

ANNIE *comes back.*

ANNIE: Jule, I just came back to say goodbye. And I wish —

ANNIE *and* JULE *kiss.* ANNIE *goes.*

JULE: What's all this about your father?

TERRY: I came straight from his funeral. I couldn't come before. If you'd taken a proper look at me you might have seen.

JULE: Has he been ill long?

TERRY: He'd been having some trouble with his heart. But it happened quite suddenly the day it happened. He wasn't too good ever since Mum died.

JULE: Your mother died? When did she die?

TERRY: The end of last year.

JULE: You never told me.

TERRY: It didn't seem anything to do with you.

JULE: Was your father very lonely?

TERRY: They were close. The way it is. He's not good at getting his own dinner. He wasn't meant to get excited because of his heart. I'd go and see him and we'd make some toast because toast has always been a thing we've both liked, when I was little, and we'd talk of this and that. But after a bit we'd get embarrassed. We'd have to take the dog for a walk on the heath. Because all we wanted to talk about really was to quarrel and I wouldn't in case I gave him a heart attack and he wouldn't — perhaps less for his heart than because I was holding back. But in his mind you could always tell he never could let my communism go. I got it from him, that's what he minded most, from him talking about the thirties when I was small. He wore himself out all his life for the union and it never seemed to me to be enough. But he couldn't forgive me because of being a Catholic. He always took Stalin very much to heart, Hungary, Czechoslovakia — all my life he always had the latest newspaper cuttings that showed how badly Russia was behaving. Right up until we started being careful because of his heart.

JULE: So how did he die if you were so careful?

TERRY: There was nothing much we could talk about that wasn't upsetting. If we started on a football match we'd soon be avoiding the stadium in Chile.

JULE: You would have found things there to agree about.

TERRY: We were good at spotting ways back to our differences.

JULE: So how did he die?

TERRY: We took the dog for a walk as a distraction and it ran in the road under a car. I didn't know how to deal with this thing which was partly a mess on the road and partly a head I knew looking at me. It must have been mostly unconscious. So a vet disposed of it and so on. His heart attack was on the way home. He died luckily quicker than the dog.

JULE: Did he say anything?

TERRY: No last words to sum it all up if you mean that.

JULE: No, I meant anything.

TERRY: He hasn't got a lot of family so the funeral was quite small. I hadn't felt at all like crying till I saw his brother, who looks quite like him. I saw he wouldn't be alive for long. Or myself. Or you.

JULE: Some men never seem to cry but it never surprises you. Remember how we often couldn't sleep. Not over something that had happened to us, but we would have argued so late about why it happened and how it could have been different, that we felt right in it. We'd be really angry at whoever let it happen, even something that was over years ago. You sometimes cried.

TERRY: We've no trouble finding things we both think are wrong. It's doing something about them that comes between us.

JULE: Will you stay tonight?

TERRY: Yes. Will you come back with me?

JULE: No.

They go on sitting on the beach. The sun is shining.

Objections to Sex and Violence

I've just read this play for the first time in nearly ten years. It seems so long ago it's quite hard to say anything about it. I feel a little as if I were writing about a play by someone else, though with inside information.

I started thinking about it towards the end of a three-month journey in north Africa with my husband and children in 1974, and wrote it during the next three months when we lived on Dartmoor. We came back to London at the end of the summer and I sent the play to the Royal Court. It was directed by John Tydeman, who'd directed seven of my radio plays in the late sixties and early seventies. It opened in January 1975. It was the first play I'd had on the main stage of the Court. *Owners* had been done in the Theatre Upstairs in 1972, directed by Nicholas Wright, and I had already written *Moving Clocks Go Slow*, which was done as a one-night show in the Theatre Upstairs later in 1975 by John Ashford.

I don't much like the title. Though I wasn't happy with it at the time, I preferred it to my alternatives, *Day Return*, and *Bread and Circuses*, which I'd probably choose now. The trouble with the title now is that it suggests quite a different set of ideas, developed by feminists, of the links between male sexuality and violence, which wasn't my starting point at all. Jule's sexuality and violence (not violent sexuality) are subversive, and the other characters have different objections to them both.

The Angry Brigade bombed the Post Office tower in 1972, Patty Hearst's kidnapping was in the papers, I think, the summer I wrote the play, Baader-Meinhof hadn't happened yet. I've looked through the notebooks in which I wrote it to see where I started from and how the situations of the play gradually emerge, and am left with a strong sense of what I was thinking about in the early seventies, of how immediate and pressing ideas about the anarchism, revolution and violence were. Among the notes groping towards characters and events are notes on what I was reading, Reich on Aggression, Hannah Arendt on Violence, with quotes from Marx, Fanon, Sartre; Eric's quote about 'the power to act shrinks every day' is by Pareto at the turn of the century, via Arendt. Most of the IRA bombings in England hadn't happened when I wrote the play, and it's hard to unthink them and see the play without them. Miss Forbes originally came from Guildford — the Guildford pub bombing happened between writing the play and its production and I changed the place to Woking as it would have looked like a deliberate reference, and similarly I took out Eric's line about Birmingham.

Something else I found in the notes also has a topical reference: 'Mary Whitehouse and man in raincoat as married couple — both with same ashamed attitude to sex — they think of themselves as different but in fact identical.'

So reading the play now it strikes me as very much of its time, but a lot of the issues are still live ones. On the whole I enjoyed it more than I expected. It's funnier than I remembered. The characters mostly talk too much — I was aware of this when I wrote it, but I remember being slightly alarmed by a knack it seemed to me I was getting of mocking my characters in the way they talked and defining them too tightly, and I wanted to give them more rope, take them more seriously. What seems to have happened is a difference in style, with the seaside postcard couple Madge and Arthur at one extreme, and Annie, say, and Terry with more freedom. The most vivid characters to me reading it now are Phil and Miss Forbes.

Fire regulations made it impossible to throw petrol on a fire on stage, so the end of Act One was changed slightly with Annie knocking the petrol can out of Phil's hand.

Caryl Churchill

Caryl Churchill

Stage plays

Owners (Royal Court 1972). Owners in property and relationships; a comedy. A woman property developer finds what she's capable of.

Moving Clocks Go Slow (Royal Court 1975). Sci-fi play.

Objections to Sex and Violence (Royal Court 1975). Terrorism and seaside.

Vinegar Tom (Monstrous Regiment 1976). Seventeenth century witchhunt; songs about women now.

Light Shining in Buckinghamshire (Joint Stock 1976). How the English Revolution didn't happen.

Traps (Royal Court 1977). An impossible object.

Floorshow (Monstrous Regiment 1977). Sketches and lyrics for cabaret about women and work.

Cloud Nine (Joint Stock 1979). About sexual politics in colonial Africa and present-day England.

Three More Sleepless Nights (Soho Poly 1980). Short play. Two couples try to change.

Top Girls (Royal Court 1982). About the life of a successful woman executive.

Fen (Joint Stock 1983). About a village in the Fens.

Softcops (Royal Shakespeare Company 1984). About control and punishment.

ROSE'S STORY

Rose's Story was first presented by the Drama Society at the Polytechnic of the South Bank on 25 January 1984 with the following cast:

SISTER JONES	Jenny Baker
MR JOHNSON	Everton Francis
ROSE JOHNSON	Lola Henry
BERTIE	Michael Hinckson
WPC	Debbie Jenkins
SISTER ENNIS	Diana McDowall
SISTER THOMPSON	Ruth McDowall
MRS JOHNSON	Diana Phillips
ELAINE JOHNSON	Hazel Samuels
LEROY WILLIAMS	Ainsley Sewell
DOCTOR	David Seymour
SOCIAL WORKER	Doone Smith

Stage Manager Colette Noe
Lighting by Brent Oldfield
Directed by Grace Dayley
Designed by Ron Hobbs

The action takes place in the DOCTOR's surgery, at the flat, and at ROSE's parents' home.

Time: The present

Act One
Scene 1   ROSE at the DOCTOR's surgery
Scene 2   ROSE back at the flat with LEROY
Scene 3   ROSE at her parents' house

Act Two
Scene 1   ROSE at her parents'
Scene 2   Back at the flat with LEROY
Scene 3   ROSE at her parents'
Scene 4   ROSE at her parents'

The words of the hymns, 'Kneel at the Cross' and 'Precious Name', which are sung during the course of the play, are printed at the end of the script.

Many thanks to all those involved in the production of *Rose's Story*. To Anne Smith and Donal Brennan for sending out publicity material. To Deborah Robinson and Sharon Toppin for their typing services. Special thanks to the social science students who encouraged and supported me during rehearsals. This list would not however, be complete without acknowledging the influence of my son Clive and my sister Heather to whom I owe a special debt, as without them this production would not have been possible.

ACT ONE

Scene One

As the scene opens, ROSE JOHNSON *is sitting opposite the* DOCTOR *in his surgery – Doctor Pattabhi is an Asian Doctor around fifty years old.*

DOCTOR (*sorting through the papers on his desk*): Well, Miss Johnson, you are definitely pregnant . . . Do you want the baby?

ROSE: Of course I want the baby. (*Boldly spoken.*)

DOCTOR: How can you be sure? You've hardly given this vital piece of information time to lodge in your mind. Do you realise a baby will change your life completely?

ROSE: Well, I've thought of nothing else for the last four weeks. Believe it or not, I've actually thought about the alternatives, like having it adopted, fostering it until I'm older, or even sending it to my rich Auntie in Jamaica. I have decided, however, to have the baby and keep it. I just know that I can manage. I'll just have to.

DOCTOR: But you're only . . .

ROSE (*interrupting boldly*): I know I'm only fifteen, not old enough to know my own mind. I have my whole life ahead of me. I have not yet finished school. What will my parents say? What will my friends say? I do realise there will be problems. Just because I'm pregnant doesn't mean I'm totally stupid.

DOCTOR (*patronising tone*): Maybe you'd like someone to talk this over with, someone who is qualified to advise. I'm only a GP and I have no specialised knowledge of these situations. I'll go and see if the receptionist can organize something.

Exit DOCTOR.
ROSE *turns to audience.*

ROSE: Jesus Christ, Look 'pon me now . . . Now they are going to start categorizing me, I'll be on this list, that list and the other list, I'm already on the list for running away from home.

By the way my name is Rose and this is *my* story . . . As you have heard, I'm pregnant, yeah, fifteen years old and pregnant. (ROSE *looks down at her tummy and then looks back at the audience.*) Let me tell you how it all started . . . My parents, hum, yeah my parents, you see, they are Christians and you know what these Christians are. I grew up a loner in a house full of people, people who did not know and who did not want to know. My parents, well, we'll forget them for now. My elder sister, Jennifer, she is into her books and getting to University. I don't think she's all here some of the time. My brother Patrick, him, he's only interested in his little job at Sainsburys and buying pretty clothes. Elaine, my younger sister, now she is the devil himself, she don't put up with shit from nobody, parents, teachers, nobody! She used to get beaten nearly every day, she is so hardened to it now that I don't think it matters anymore. Me now, I was the quiet one, the one who could be shoved around and told to do anything, (*Shakes her head.*) no, boy, no I was no trouble.

You know . . . it was a miserable existence, nobody outside that house could understand. It was church, school, church, school and more church, school.

There was young people's meetings and prayer meetings in between, but basically church and school was the only . . . no, no, is the only thing I know, we couldn't even watch television, . . . yeah, tell me in this day and age which child cannot watch television . . . well I couldn't . . . not until two months ago when I ran away from home with Leroy. Leroy, sweet

Leroy. He came to live next to my home about eighteen months ago. I've been seeing him ever since . . . on and off . . . About a week before I ran away from home, my parents found out about him, you see I'd been sneaking out to see him all that time and they only found out because of busybodies and church busybodies at that. After they knew, I think I went to hell and back. I was watched and scrutinized, scorned, beaten, no one could ever imagine what it was like, they even timed me when I was sent to the shop. (*Tears coming to her eyes.*) How are they going to take this? I think I'll be better off dead, God knows . . . It was just as well that they didn't know that Leroy only lived next door cause that would have been a turn up for the books . . . so after thinking of ways to commit suicide, yeah, a fifteen-year-old thinking how to commit suicide. It wasn't the first time, anyway, I'd thought of it before when I was much younger, this time I decided to run away. I just couldn't take it.

Hey, I just remembered a recitation we used to say at Sunday School, it's called 'Wits' End Corner', and that's just where I was. It went something like this:

'Are you standing at Wits' End Corner
Christian with a troubled brow?
Are you thinking of what lies before
    you
And all you are bearing now?
Does the world seem all against you?
And you're in battle all alone?
Remember at Wits' End Corner
Is just where God's power is shown.'

Well, I'd pray to this invisible God often enough, no direct answer came, so I suppose it was his way of answering by putting the idea of running away to me. It may have been the devil, but I prefer to think it was God.

The way I did it though was so sneaky, no one knew: I pretended that I was ill when they were going to church, when they came home, I was gone. (*Smiling a little.*) I must admit a smile does come to my face when I imagine the horrified look on their faces when they realised that one of their slaves had absconded, and this time she had taken her clothes . . . Oh boy . . . Yes that's right, this wasn't the first time . . . I'd left for a day or weekend before. But this had been the longest I've been away. This time Leroy and I have a place to stay, with his friend, and now . . . well now speaks for itself . . .

DOCTOR *re-enters the room.*

DOCTOR: Miss Johnson, are you all right? You seem miles away.

ROSE: Um well, Doctor did you find out anything?

DOCTOR: I'll send the local midwife round to have a word, maybe someone from the Social Services who knows about girls in your situation, will be able . . .

ROSE (*interrupting*): What do you mean girls in my situation? Just don't classify me with anyone else, right!

DOCTOR: I'm sorry Rose, but I'll have to inform the Authorities. It's my duty.

ROSE: I suppose this is just the beginning of informing this, that and the other . . . I think I'll leave now. (*She gets up to leave.*)

DOCTOR: Not so fast, young lady. You'll need a prescription for Iron and Vitamins.

After all, if we're going to have a baby we must do the basics (*Writing prescription.*) like looking after ourselves. (*Mockingly said.*)

ROSE *takes the prescription and proceeds to the door. When she reaches it, she turns, facing the DOCTOR.*

ROSE: Thank you once again, for all your help, Doctor.

Exit ROSE *from surgery.*

Scene Two

ROSE *arrives back at the flat,* LEROY *is sitting there when she goes in. When he sees her he jumps up and runs towards her.*

LEROY (*swings* ROSE *round*): Well, whappen I man a go be a fada?

ROSE *walks across room and sits down on chair.*

ROSE: I'm pregnant so it does seem like it.

LEROY (*claps his hands*): Great! We can start planning, we can buy . . .

ROSE (*stands up*): Hold on a minute. I don't think you realise the implications of what I'm saying. You are going to be a father with responsibilities. (*She stands up.*) You can't sit around here all day smoking weed and playing music. Do you think it's going to be easy? . . . Doctor Puttabhi said I should think about the alternatives open to me. You're only interested in your little ego trip – not about whether or not I'll be able to cope or whether I actually want this baby . . . Look, Leroy there is just no question about it, you'll have to get a job. You were saying buy, buy what without money?

LEROY: Look, Rose, when is this baby actually due?

ROSE: In about eight months time . . . but that doesn't change anything.

LEROY: Cho man, noh hassel me, yu noh se seh me turn man. Plenty time did deh fe go look work . . . right now I man a go have a lickle youth . . . Praise an tanks be to Jah . . .

ROSE: All you're worried about is turning man, well, you have to face the facts, *men work*. I'm only fifteen so I can't work, plus I want to continue with school. Now it's more important to get qualifications, 'cause a job in Woolworths is not going to keep me and the baby and even you by the look of things . . . I want to give my child the best . . . What about my mother? How am I going to tell her? she'll probably disown me. What am I going to do when my belly starts to show? What'll I tell my church and school friends? . . . Oh my God, those church people . . . OH NO.

LEROY: Noh worry bout dat man, mek we go celebrate. (LEROY *puts on a record and starts dancing round the room.*)

ROSE (*shouting over the music*): You just don't have the faintest, do you? You think it's all celebration and showing off that you turn man.

LEROY (*shouting over the music, jokingly said*): Well, having a baby is no problem, of course yu belly we get big but dat's all . . . me we fine a job, man.

ROSE *walks to the record player and takes the record off,* LEROY *turns and gives her a dirty look.* ROSE *walks over and stands in front of him.*

ROSE (*with charm*): Leroy, what about that YOPS scheme that the job centre send you on. Why don't you go? You'll need qualifications to get a job, to look after this baby. With all this high unemployment and being black it's hard enough, and you're not helping the situation by sitting here smokin'. I hope you realise that cigarettes and splif will have to go. That's one way of saving money without sacrificing too much . . . Smoking isn't good for babies anyway.

LEROY: Splif will have to go noh? . . . Noh go on soh Rose man, me know how yu feel . . . Yu feel well, (*Smiling.*) – pregnant in it?

ROSE (*sucking her teeth*): Fucking hell,

Leroy man, how can you joke at a time like this? You just don't understand, do you? You think it's going to be roses, celebration, and weed. Well, it's going to be hard. Knitting, nappies and stretch marks . . . as you don't seem to have anything constructive to say I think I'll phone my mother . . . the sooner I get it over with, the better, I mean she'll have to know sooner or later.

LEROY: Yu sure yu whan fe tell yu mada soh soon?

ROSE *walks over to the telephone, glancing back at* LEROY *but he doesn't answer, she picks up the receiver and dials her mother's number.*

ROSE (*under her breath*): Jesus Christ, what am I going to say?

MOTHER: Hello! Hello! Who is dat?

ROSE: It's me, Mummy.

MOTHER: Me who? Is dat you, Rose?

ROSE: Yes Mummy, it's me.

MOTHER: What's de matta, Rose? Where are you? Why are you doing dis to me . . . Lard hah mercy, is wha happen now?

ROSE: Mummy, I'm . . .

MOTHER: Me hope seh yu know seh de police a look fe you. Yu still wid de good fe nottin Leroy? Lissen gal, yu tink seh yu is woman but mek me tell yu someting, yu fada naw go fegive yu fe weh yu a do to im . . .

ROSE (*interrupting quietly*): I'm pregnant, Mum.

MOTHER: Wha? Whey yu a seh to me?

ROSE: I'm pregnant, Mother.

MOTHER: Yu mean to tell me seh yu pregnant; me can't believe this, yu sure, Rose, my baby ah go hah baby? . . . No . . . Mek me sit down, Rose yu mean to seh yu pregnant? After me grow yu up inna Christian home. God knew me try fe teach unnu right from wrong, an dis is how yu repay me?

ROSE (*crying*): It's not a matter of right and wrong, Mummy. I'm pregnant, I'm sorry if I hurt you, I didn't mean to.

MOTHER (*also crying*): Lord know, me try wid you children, an out ah all my children — not you, Rose, not you.

ROSE: Mummy, I'm sorry, I'm truly sorry.

MOTHER: Rose, is whey yu deh? Me seh is weh yu deh? Me know all bout de good fe nottin Leroy, im is dere?

ROSE: I can't tell you that or you'll send the police round.

MOTHER: Rose, I haven't had a good night's sleep since yu lef. Yu mean to seh yu couldn't tell nobody weh yu deh. Yu sister gone to University widout knowing wedda yu dead or alive. Yu neva tink bout dat, yu noh hah no consideration fe yu one annada, jus come ome, me chile . . . jus come ome.

There is a knock at ROSE's *door.*

ROSE: I'll have to go now, Mum, there's someone at the door. 'Bye, Mum, I'll call you tomorrow. (*She hangs up the receiver quickly.* LEROY *jumps up to answer the door.*)

LEROY (*joking*): Noh tell me seh de police reach yah already. (*He runs to the door and answers it.*) Oh, Bertie, it's you, me soon come mek me get me jacket.

ROSE (*walks quickly to* LEROY): Look, Leroy don't tell Bertie yet, OK?

LEROY: Of course I a go tell im.

ROSE: Just don't tell him, OK?

LEROY: OK den, Rose I won't, (*Gives* ROSE *a quick kiss on the cheek.*) Me noh deya now.

ROSE: Goodbye, Leroy. Have a good time.

Exit LEROY. ROSE *goes over and sits back by the phone, wiping her eyes a little and looking intently at the phone.*

ROSE (*facing the audience*): I seem to be at Wits' End Corner yet again. My mother is mad and Leroy has gone raving. I just don't know what to do . . . Maybe I should go and see Mummy, yeah . . . I'll phone and see. (*She turns to the phone and dials once again*).

ROSE: Hello, Mummy.

MOTHER: Rosie, is dat you again?

ROSE: Yes, Mummy.

MOTHER: Rosie, come ome me whan fe look after yu. Me noh want yu fe have it ard out dere . . .

ROSE: Will Daddy be going to work tomorrow?

MOTHER: That's right, me chile, yu come tomorrow when im deh a work.

ROSE: OK, Mummy, I'll see you tomorrow around one o'clock.

MOTHER: All right den, Rose, see you tomorrow.

ROSE: Bye, Mum, see you tomorrow. (*She hangs up the receiver, and sits, with her head in her hands.*)

Scene Three

ROSE *arrives at her* MOTHER's *house. She rings the door bell.* SISTER THOMPSON *opens the door.*

SISTER THOMPSON: Hello, Rose . . . (ROSE *steps in the front door.*)

ROSE: Hello, Sister Thompson, where's Mummy?

SISTER THOMPSON: Go sitting room, chile, yu Mada a wait fe yu. (*She shuts the front door; they both walk into the sitting room where* SISTER ENNIS, SISTER JONES *and* ROSE's *mother are praying. When they see* ROSE *they break off. The mother beckons* ROSE *to come in with her hands.*)

MOTHER: Kneel down, Rose, mek we pray fe yu.

SISTER ENNIS *starts to sing 'Kneel at the Cross' and the others join in,* ROSE *takes off her jacket and kneels down reluctantly. While the others are finishing the song* SISTER JONES *begins to pray.* SISTER JONES *puts her hands on* ROSE's *shoulder.*

SISTER JONES: Oh merciful Fada, once more we approach thy mercy seat. Look down in your tender mercy and loving kindness upon dis chile. She has strayed from the pathway of righteousness. She has succumbed to the evils of the world.

But, because we know dat Satan is like a lion seeking who he may devour we ask you to give her, Fada, a special anointing of the Holy Ghost, so dat de devil won't tempt him to do wrong and kill this prodigal chile. We beg you, Lord God, to bring her back to the fold. For dis we ask in Jesus name.

SISTER THOMPSON: Thank you, Lord.

SISTER ENNIS:
MOTHER: Amen.

ROSE (*looking towards the audience*): Jesus God. Sister Thompson got bad breath, yu see.

SISTER THOMPSON *helps* ROSE *up from her kneeling position, and guides her over to one side of the room.*

SISTER THOMPSON: Sit down, Rosie.

ROSE *sits down and* SISTER THOMPSON *sits beside her.*

Yu mada tell me bout de situation. Mek me gi yu a word of advice. Dem man out dere, dem is all trousers, dem noh hah notten fi gi yu. Tek my silly advice, come ome to yu mada an fada, dem truly care fe yu. Me wan tell yu someting bout myself. When me get pregnant wid Joseph, me haffi run lef me mada yard. Me go weh wid de man, im noh good so me lef im. Meantime, me pregnant me meet a man a town, im treat me good so me stay wid im. After me hah de baby, all im want is me body an bam me get pregnant wid Pauline. After dat now, me careful. Me work ard fe come a Englan' an get money fe look after dem . . . now when me come a Englan' me meet anada man an Bam! me get pregnant wid Junior. Today, all me do is serve God an left man alone, 'cause me hah tree pickini, wid tree different man, an none a dem noh good. Soh yu see girl, jus trus God an lef man alone.

ROSE's *mother comes over and sits down beside* ROSE. SISTER THOMPSON *turns to* ROSE's *mother.*

SISTER THOMPSON: Me just a gi Rosie a word of advice, Sister J, me hope seh she we tek some a hit.

MOTHER (*pointing towards the kitchen*): Yu whan lickle soup, Rose. Yu look like yu naw eat. If yu noh want it now tek it wid yu.

ROSE: No thanks, Mum, I must go now, Leroy is waiting for me at home. (*She stands up, moves slowly towards the door. The* MOTHER *also moves towards the door, dipping in her pocket.*)

MOTHER: Yu hah money, Rose? When me a go see yu again? Why yu living? . . . Yu naw tell me notten . . .

ROSE: I'll come back tomorrow, and explain everything.

MOTHER (*being persistent, putting her hands on* ROSE's *shoulders*): Where are you living, Rose, why can't you tell me? Me is yu mada, yu know, yu mus trus me.

ROSE: Look, Mummy, I must go but I'll be back tomorrow. I'd thought we'd have a chance to talk today but . . .

MOTHER: Me we try an sort out tings wid yu fada, seeing as yu naw go tell me where yu live . . . but maybe yu should tell me, yu know. Suppose yu tek sick or someting. Me know seh de good fe noting Leroy couldn't manage.

ROSE: I'll see you tomorrow, I promise I'll come back.

MOTHER: Mek sure yu come back, 'cause there is a lot of tings to sort out.

ROSE: How is Elaine and Patrick, Mum? Can I go up an say Hello to them?

MOTHER: Well, Patrick at school. But Elaine upstairs, but me noh tink seh yu should see her yet, yu see she don't know yet.

ROSE: Do you think I'll contaminate her? Pregnancy is not catching, you know!

MOTHER: Me did kno seh dis good behaviour was too good to be true. Me did wonder when yu was going to start yu bareface cheek again, Rosie, yu seh yu haffi go, well, me we see yu tomorrow.

ROSE: Goodbye then, goodbye everybody.

ROSE *puts on her jacket and exits.*

ACT TWO

Scene One

The next day, ROSE *goes back to her mother's house, in order to have a talk with her* MOTHER *and sort things out.*
    ROSE *rings the door bell and her sister* ELAINE *opens the door.*

ROSE: Hello, Elaine. (ROSE *steps inside;* ELAINE *shuts the door.*)

ELAINE: Hello, Rose, come in. God, haven't you lost weight. Mummy and the . . . no, no, and a friend of yours is waiting in the sitting room.

ROSE: Not that lot again, today. I suppose they are going to ask God to wash away my sins as well as my baby.

ELAINE: Oh no, it's not them today. It's your friend from the local nick. Good luck . . .

ROSE: The nick? . . . Do you mean . . .? (ROSE *walks hesitantly towards the sitting room, she turns to* ELAINE.) But . . .

ELAINE: Go on in, she's been waiting a while.

    ROSE *walks into the sitting room, there is a female police officer.*

WPC: Come in, Rose. Have a seat.

    ROSE *goes over and sits by the window, as far away as possible.*

ROSE: Well, Mummy? . . . What is this, what is she doing here?

MOTHER: Well, me haffi inform dem seh yu return, as me did beg dem fe look fe yu when you did run weh. When me tell dem, deh yu come back, dem seh dem wan fe talk to yu, so dem sen dis police lady fe . . .

ROSE: I see . . .

WPC: Well, then, young lady, I'd like to speak with you.

ROSE: What about?

WPC: About where you've been. Have you anything to say for yourself?

ROSE: I have nothing to say to you, pig.

MOTHER: Yes, Lard, she start; look, Rose, yu mussie whan dem fe trow yu in jail or someting.

WPC: I'll deal with this, Mrs Johnson, thank you.

MOTHER: Me we leave unnu to it, den.

WPC: Well, Rose, where have you been?

ROSE *sucks her teeth.*

WPC: Who have you been staying with? I could have you sent away; I hope you realise that there are places for people like you . . . Where have you been . . . So you're not going to answer?

ROSE: You've got the message . . .

WPC (*patronizing tone*): Now, Rose, be a good girl and tell me where you were. (ROSE *is still silent.*) You know that you have to tell me sooner or later. (*Getting angry.*) There are too many young children running away from home. Now I want to know where you've been, and who you've been with . . . Well . . . you might think you're being clever, well, you're not very clever and wasting police time. That's a very serious offence, withholding information is also serious; very serious indeed. Do you think that the police have nothing better to do than to deal with silly little girls like you?

ROSE: If you've quite finished, Miss Police Woman, let me tell you something. I, Rose Johnson, don't have to tell you anything. Now, why don't you just go back to your little station and help beat up some youth, because you're not going to get anywhere with me.

WPC *comes over and points her finger in* ROSE's *face.*

WPC: Look, my girl, I can get information out of you if I choose to pursue this matter.

ROSE: Go ahead . . .

WPC: I suppose I should just caution you not to do it again, and be grateful that you're not roaming the country making a nuisance of yourself.

ROSE (*sucks her teeth*): Jus kiss me arse, yah, bout roaming de country, yu full a fucking shit.

WPC: I don't really see any point in pursuing this any further. But I do think that you're an abominable child.

ROSE (*smiling*): Who cares what you think?

WPC (*moves towards the door*): Thank you for the tea, Mrs Johnson, I'll be getting back to the station now.

MOTHER (*appears from kitchen*): No! No! officer, thank YOU. Tea was no trouble.

ROSE: She noh even drink de tea, but she a seh tank yu.

ROSE *goes over and looks into the tea cup.* ROSE *sees the* WPC *out and returns to the sitting room.*

Why? . . . Why, Mummy, did you let these kinna people come here? . . . bouy. (*Shakes her head in disbelief.*)

There is a knock at the door, a tall elegant lady enters the room.

ROSE: Who is dis now?

MOTHER: Hello, you mus be Miss Pickford, who me talk to on de phone yesterday, come in, come in an have a seat.

PICKFORD: Hello, Mrs Johnson. (PICKFORD *turns to* ROSE.) Hello, you must be Rose.

ROSE: Umm . . .

PICKFORD: Well, Rose I'm Sue Pickford, your social worker. (*Takes her file out of her bag.*)

MOTHER (*pointing at* MISS PICKFORD): Rose, Miss Pickford is going to help you, soh me we leave unnu to it.

Exit MOTHER. PICKFORD *takes a seat.*

PICKFORD: Well, Rose, your mother has told me a little about the situation. She is very concerned about the way you're living; she has brought me in because she wants to make sure that you get all the help that you need. She has explained to me about your father, and how he would feel about you returning home. After a fairly detailed talk with your mother, she thinks that the best thing is for you to be taken into care, in order to sort out what you're going to do with your life, the baby, and your exams. Have you any thoughts on the matter?

ROSE: Well, I would really like to sort out things with Leroy, if possible, so that I can go back to school or college after I have the baby.

PICKFORD: So you are definitely having it?

ROSE: Of cour . . .

PICKFORD: Have you thought about the difficulties ahead if you decide to have the baby and keep it? I think you should seriously consider having an abortion.

ROSE (*angry at this suggestion*): Ab . . . who?

PICKFORD: You don't have to have the baby, if you don't want it, you know.

ROSE (*confidently spoken*): Well, I want it.

PICKFORD: Think before you answer, Rose. You are young, you have your whole life ahead of you. You must consider how you are going to manage. You have no money, no home, no support whatsoever. Be realistic, ask your parents for their consent for an abortion. Believe me, I've seen girls like you before and this almost always proves to be the best possible solution. What does your boyfriend . . . (PICKFORD *looks down at her file.*) Leroy, is it? . . . What does he think?

ROSE (*looking directly at* PICKFORD): I don't know why you are asking me what he thinks, I'm the one who's having the baby — not Leroy, plus why should I want to have an abortion, I don't want to kill my baby before it's had a chance to live, would you have an abortion . . . Well, would you?

PICKFORD: Right now we're not here to talk about me, but about your problems, I'll also need some information about Leroy. How old is he? Does he have a job? Well, does he realise that he could go to jail for this? After all you are a minor.

ROSE (*cuts her eye at* MISS PICKFORD): Me naw anser no stupid question.

PICKFORD: Okay, back to this baby. You could have it adopted.

ROSE: Look, I've told you, Miss Pickford . . . adopted by who anyway? . . . some middle class white people who can't breed, an feel seh dem is doing my baby a great favour? . . . Yu mussie crazy, or in Leroy's words you're tired of living.

PICKFORD: I think you're getting things out of proportion. You could have the baby fostered, then you could visit on holidays and at week-ends.

ROSE (*laughs mockingly at* PICKFORD): Hum . . . me neva know seh baby hah haliday . . . Dis mussie someting new.

PICKFORD: You know, you're not helping the situation by being rude and clever.

ROSE: Who clever, me clever, no me noh clever or me wouldn't be here talking to you. Yu noh see yu is de clever one. Yu have a job where yu can drive roun in a yu lickle Renault a tell people wha fe do wid dem baby weh dem noh even have yet.

PICKFORD: Well, one day you will have it, my girl, and you will have to face facts then. What about school?

ROSE: Well, I'm going back to my education. I don't care what anybody says about school — girlmother and all that . . .

PICKFORD: How will you do that? (*Mocking* ROSE.) Will you take it to school with you?

ROSE: Funny, funny, I have thought about that and I do have some idea of how to go about it.

PICKFORD: Some idea indeed . . . your father has stated most emphatically that he will not have you back here. A mother and baby home would be the best solution to this problem. There you could continue with your education and even take your exams. I can't see any other way around this problem . . . Your school will also have to be informed.

ROSE (*interrupting*): Why not just go to Speakers' Corner and inform the whole country? So at least that way you save your breath, I know what I'm going to do with this baby . . .

PICKFORD: If I'm thinking what you're thinking, forget it. There is no way you can go on as you are without getting some sort of help. I don't see how you can go back to your school, and look after a baby.

ROSE: All dis thinking and stinking forget what? What am I thinking? . . . So you are a mind reader as well . . . You think you've got this thing all sewn up, don't you . . . Well, I might have to go into a home, I might have to live on the streets, but just let me tell you this. I'm not going to kill my baby, I'm not giving it to any white couple who can't produce and I'm definitely not going to sign it over to the council, like my parents are thinking of doing to me.

PICKFORD: Well, Rose, if that's how you feel, I don't see that there is much I can say to convince you. But I'd like to see you tomorrow. By then I should have some idea of what's going to happen to you. It will also give you a chance to speak with your father about the situation. He'll have to consent to anything that you decide to do.

ROSE: Look, Pickford, I'd rather not have to see you again. I think we've said all we have to say to each other. You said you were my social worker, I suppose you don't want another illegitimate child roaming around now, do you? It's all, get an abortion, Rose, do this, Rose, do that, Rose. Have you got any children, MISS PICKFORD? Do you know what it's like to have an abortion? Would you have an abortion?

PICKFORD: Well, Rose, whether or not you'd like to talk to me or see me doesn't matter, as you have no choice. Your father has made it clear that you cannot stay here.

ROSE: Why is everyone making such a big deal out of this coming home business? If I'd liked it here in the first place I'd have stayed. Plus I wouldn't want my baby to grow up the way I did.

PICKFORD: Rose, I'll have to go now as I have another client, but we'll talk tomorrow, all of us. That way I can find out more about the mother and baby home and everybody will have a chance to air their views.

ROSE (*resigned to the fact that there isn't much she can do*): Yeah.

PICKFORD: Tomorrow then, at six o'clock sharp.

PICKFORD *gets up, puts her file into her case and walks towards the door. ROSE sits there just looking at PICKFORD. MOTHER enters the room.*

MOTHER: Goodbye, Miss Pickford, an tank you very much.

PICKFORD: Goodbye, Mrs Johnson, goodbye Rose. (*Exit PICKFORD.*) I'll find my own way out.

ROSE: Well, who's next Mum? The FBI?

MOTHER *gives* ROSE *a dirty look; she hurries out, calling after* MISS PICKFORD.

MOTHER: Miss Pickford, Miss Pickford, hang on a minute.

Scene Two

Back at the flat with LEROY. ROSE *walks into the room.* LEROY *is sitting there, reading his* Sun *newspaper and smoking.* ROSE *walks into the room, stops and looks at* LEROY (*hands akimbo*). ROSE *drops her bag and continues to walk across the room.* LEROY *realises that something is wrong so he puts down his newspaper and looks at* ROSE.

LEROY (*lightheartedly*): Wa happen, Rose? What did the glory bound sisters have to say today?

ROSE: Today it was the Police and the Social Services actually, trying to convince me to get rid of the baby . . . By the way, Leroy, I may have to go into a home.

LEROY: Home? Wha kinna home?

ROSE: For DISTURBED or PREGNANT CHILDREN.

LEROY: But yu noh disturb . . . jus pregnant. Tell dem fe go bout dem business. Yu noh hah fe go inna no ome if you noh whan go.

ROSE: Yeh, well, that's what you think, but unless you can come up with an alternative, like getting a JOB, Leroy, you know, maybe something nine-to-five so that we'll have some money coming in each week, I will have to go into a home.

LEROY *takes a puff of his cigarette.*

LEROY: Where me fe get job from? Me noh have no qualifications, me only kno' how fe hussle an stretch me lickle dole money. Yu noh see Bertie — him hah tree an him noh work . . . Well, not often.

ROSE: LEROY, that's Bertie, and while we're on the subject of Bertie, I would just like to add that I think you should stop keeping company with that person. He is much older than you for one thing, and he is a bad influence for another. In fact, the only brains that Bertie's got are in his balls!

LEROY: Stop keeping company wid im? How yu fe tell me who fe keep company wid? Me a man, yu know. Yu come in jus like yu madda bout bad influence. A de same ting she would a seh bout me a bad influence pan yu. Anyway, how de fuck yu know where Bertie brains, deh?

ROSE: Cho Leroy, stop roun' up yu mouth man, yu know seh Bertie naw defen' notten.

LEROY: Aa gal jus lef me 'spar'. (LEROY *now pointing at* ROSE). Yu ever hear me say anything bout yu an yu lickle froozy-tail fren' dem?

ROSE: So you would rather I got rid of the baby as well, would you? Seeing as yu noh whan no froozy-tail 'youth' as you call it.

LEROY: Cho Rose man, yu kno seh me noh hol' wid dem tings deh. People who do dem tings is cemetery belly, dem is worse dan murderers to bumbo.

ROSE: Alright! Alright! Don't overdo it. I'm going to have the baby, home or no home, Bertie or no Bertie, froozy-tail or no froo . . .

LEROY *comes over and kisses* ROSE *in order to shut her up. He sits on the settee beside her with his arm around her shoulders.*

LEROY: Never mind Rose, man, everything we be all right.

ROSE: Leroy . . . does this mean that you actually decided to join the happy throng of sardines in the tubes every morning? Does this mean you have seen sense and realised that nappies, knitting needles and baby-grows don't get delivered along with the baby?

LEROY: Rose, is weh yu tek me fa? Yu really tink seh me would a mek yu an my lickle youth suffa. No . . . Me naw promise notten, but unnu won't starve, unnu we hah everting unnu need . . .

ROSE: But yu naw promise notten . . .

LEROY: How me fe mek promise, suppose me go out a street and get knock down tomorrow, suppose . . .

ROSE: Suppose you learn your Green Cross Code!

LEROY (*smiling*): Yu a joke . . . Tomorrow me we go a Job Centre go se wah Thatcher have on offer.

ROSE: It seems I'm not the only joker around here, and I have the least to joke about. Leroy . . . I hope you're serious about getting a job, because before long I'll need maternity clothes.

LEROY: Maternity clothes, an notten naw, show yet . . . yu can really be depressing, yu know, Rose. Don't you realise that having a baby is not as depressing as yu mek out.

ROSE: Well, it's best to look at all the problems. Be realistic, I'm only fifteen, I can't work and you never know what will happen in the future . . .

LEROY: I know what you're driving at . . . me and Gloria, yu tink seh me would a leave yu fe a tramp like Gloria?

ROSE: Yu didn't tink she was a tramp last time.

LEROY: One moment of weakness an yu we neva mek me feget it, will you?

ROSE: Yu mean one month of weakness, and the only one Rose found out about. It was only because me did feel sho shame, when yu was down on yu knees in the launderette a beg forgiveness. Me jus' had fe fegive yu fe save me face.

LEROY: Fe save yu face . . .? Yu did well-an-want me.

ROSE: Well, whedda me did want yu or not, I've certainly got yu now, haven't I . . . Get us a drink, Leroy.

LEROY (*gives* ROSE *a long hard look*): Okay, I'll get your drink, but don't expeck me to run roun' behine yu for de nex nine months, because as yu keep telling me, I'll have to get a job. (*Jeering.*) Get a job Leroy. Get a job Leroy.

LEROY *leaves the room to get* ROSE's *drink. In the meantime,* ROSE *is sitting there rubbing her stomach.* LEROY *returns with the drink.*

ROSE: Thanks, Leroy. Turn on the telly, will you?

LEROY: ROSE . . . don't mess, me is not yu slave, yu know. (*He walks over and switches on the television set. They sit together.* LEROY *has one arm around her shoulder, the other resting on her tummy.*)

Me can't fee notting, when dis baby ya go start fe kick?

ROSE (*smiling*): Fool . . .

There is a knock at the door. LEROY *gets up to answer it, while walking towards the door he turns to* ROSE.

LEROY: No, no, don't get up, your Majesty, I'll get it. (*He opens the door.*) (*Excitedly.*) Bertie. (*Fraternity hand shake.*)

ROSE (*under her breath*): Speak of the devil.

LEROY: Come in man, we jus done talk bout yu.

BERTIE: Wha unnu a chat bout me seh? Hello, Rose.

ROSE (*drily*): Hello, Bertie.

BERTIE: Well, wha unnu a seh bout me.

LEROY: Wait little, man, mek me get yu a drink. (LEROY *goes off to get a drink.*)

BERTIE (*turns to* ROSE): Well, Rosie. Wha wrong wid Leroy? We a celebrate someting?

LEROY *returns with the drinks, he gives* BERTIE *a can of Special Brew, and opens one for himself.*

Wha bout Rose?

LEROY: Rose noh fe drink . . . (BERTIE *gives* ROSE *a knowing look.*)

BERTIE: Rose noh fe drink?

LEROY: Yeah man, dats right, today, today, today I Leroy Williams a go be a fada. (LEROY *is laughing enjoying himself.*)

BERTIE: I an I don't believe it. Is true, Rose, yu mek Leroy?

ROSE (*interrupts drily*): No an angel did it.

LEROY: Bertie . . . is where we a go tonight?

ROSE: Tonight you are helping me to pack my bags . . .

LEROY: No badda start, jus noh badda start . . .

ROSE: I have to be home tomorrow. I can't stay here with you. Look at you, you don't want to sit down and talk about this thing properly, don't you think there will be enough time for celebration later?

BERTIE: Rose is right, yu kno, Leroy, there is lots of talking to be done, after all, Rose is young, very young and parents can bring in the police an all dat sort of ting.

ROSE: They already have.

BERTIE: Yu see deh now.

LEROY: Police, yu mussie mad, any one a dem babylon weh tink seh dem can hol I fe dis dem is wors dan crazy.

BERTIE: Look, me noh know Rose fada, but me can tell yu seh, him we whan fe see yu go a jail, especially like how im a Christian hum . . . me kno seh if it was my daughter . . . bouy.

LEROY: Yu can col up a man spirit ee, Bertie, wha yu did do when Shirley did get pregnant wid Joseph?

ROSE (*turning to the audience*): Shirley is the nut who lives with him, cooks, cleans and produces children.

BERTIE: Me neva hah no trouble me P. Yu see, Shirley parents cool. Dem noh gi I no hassel, dem jus show I seh Shirley was I an I responsibility an I an I been working on building sites on an off ever since.

LEROY: How long is dat?

BERTIE: Arm . . . let me see now . . . nearly seven, eight years.

LEROY: Eight wha? Me noh inten fe work pan no building site all my life.

ROSE: Oh no, it's not the building site. You don't intend to work full stop.

BERTIE: Leroy man, yu we haffi mek some attempt fe sho Rose parents seh yu can tek care a Rose or yu noh know wha we happen to her and de youth.

LEROY: Me noh haffi show nobody notten, Me is LEROY WILLIAMS an nobody don't push me aroun an tel I wha fe do, (*Pointing at* ROSE.) Not even you, Rose Johnson.

ROSE: Look, Leroy, I know you think that you're something great but the rest of the world doesn't realise that yet, so you will have to show them, won't you? (ROSE *gets up and walks towards the stairs.*) Anyway I'm going to pack.

LEROY: Well, go pack den.

ROSE *gets to the stairs and turns to* LEROY.

ROSE: There will be a meeting for all concerned at my mother's, if you're interested.

LEROY: Cho man, go pack an shut up.

ROSE *goes on up the stairs.*

BERTIE: LEROY WILLIAMS. LEROY WILLIAMS, I an I is yu good, good, spar. But me haffi tell yu seh yu we haffi humble yourself if yu noh whan Rose lef yu high and dry . . . me a tel yu.

LEROY: Alright, alright, don't go on. I di tink seh dis was suppose to be a happy time, instead everybody's getting at everybody else, even yu, carefree Bertie.

BERTIE: I an I tink seh yu should go talk to Rose. Remember united yu stan divided yu fall. At least you an Rose should stick together. Lissen man, yu kno yu a me p. but right now I an I haf reason wid yu. An show yu seh yu haffi gawn betta dan so. In the eyes of the law, Rose is still a youth, Jah knows dat can cause a whole heap of trouble for de man. Me is not a bouy, me see nof nof tings, happen to my spar dem out deh all a go a jail because dem neva have nobody fe reason wid dem. Das why I an I a show yu seh pride goweth before destruction an a hearty spirit before a fall. Whe yu a man, put away childish tings start fe tink like a man! Me now go tell yu seh a easy ting fe live wid woman, Jah no sometimes yu jus whan fe leave oman an youth behind, and be free of all your responsibilities. But Jah has seen seh it's time fe bless you wid a youth, so look after Rose, care fi her, she a go need somebody fi stan by her. Yu haffi show her some positive vibes. Sho her seh yu a man.

LEROY *stands and pushes back his chair roughly, vexation on his face, goes up to* BERTIE. BERTIE *stands and faces* LEROY.

LEROY: Jus watch ya. (*Pointing in* BERTIE's *face.*) Me no need none of your ras clath advice, me is a man.

BERTIE: Yu a man! No! Yu is a bouy. Mek me show yu how yu is a bouy, instead of yu a look bout Rose, yu a tak bout raving. A fe yu duty fe see Rose reach her yard an see wha her parents dem a defen. She neva do it by herself! An a soh dem a goh look pan it, yu tink dem a goh respeck yu anymore when she turn up wid her bags in her hands BY HERSELF!! If yu was a man, yu would know seh yu haffi reach on down deh wid her, show dem seh yu not a good fe notten, one suit, dryup skin, hallup bouy!!!

LEROY: Jus keep yu bumbo seed advice to yu ras claut self, yu come in like a lickle GIRL . . . to ras!

BERTIE: Man, cool. (*Sensing that* LEROY *is angry.*) I an I a go site de man more time, remember wha I an I seh, tek care a Rose, Jah know she a go need yu. (*He walks to the door and turns to face* LEROY.) I an I a go site de man later.

Exit BERTIE.
LEROY *sits facing the audience, a solemn look on his face, his anger gone.*

LEROY: Yu see me trial now, Rose appresure me fi fin job, Bertie turn gainst me, an Jah kno all me whan is to be free.

Scene Three

The next day ROSE *arrives at her* MOTHER's *house, baggage in hand.*

MOTHER (*opens the door, takes* ROSE's *bags*): Hello, Rose, come in, me child.

ROSE (*steps inside and takes off her jacket*): Is daddy at home?

MOTHER: Yes, im upstairs soaking im foot.

ROSE (*as she walks into the sitting room*): Oh my God, what am I going to say to him, all hell will be let loose now. (*She goes into sitting room to join* ELAINE.)

ELAINE: Hello, Rose, how are you today, Mummy has told me everything. Do you want to have the baby? I wouldn't mind having a nephew around the house . . .

ROSE: Well, it won't be around this house, I'll tell you that much . . .

MOTHER *enters.*

MOTHER: Yu naw go see yu fada? Him know seh yu is here.

ROSE: No, Mummy, I'd rather wait here for Miss Pickford.

MOTHER: Look, Rose, you haffi face yu fada sometime, after all, im is yu fada.

MOTHER *walks towards the door, the* FATHER *enters, towel in hand.*

FATHER: Hello, Rose. (*He stands up looking at* ROSE, *hands akimbo.*) Rose, is how yu soh skinny? De bouy Leroy noh feed yu?

ROSE: Daddy, please . . .

FATHER *sits down.*

FATHER: Yu pregnant, don't it?

ROSE: Yes, I'm pregnant. (*Boldly spoken.*)

FATHER: Lard God, me ask de gal if she pregnant an she seh yes. She noh hah de decency fe lie to me Yu soun proud a weh yu do. Yu should be ashamed of yuself. Me hope seh yu remember seh yu did baptise in Jesus name . . . (*He starts drying his foot.*)

ROSE: If I'd said I wasn't pregnant you'd have called me a liar. I tell you the truth and you still go on. Anyway, I'm asking you for nothing. All I want is to have my baby with the least trouble possible.

FATHER: Yu seh yu naw ask me fe notten, but yu mada seh Miss Pickford fone an seh if yu haffi go inna home, me haffi contribute.

ROSE: Well, you would have had to look after me if I'd been at home . . .

FATHER: Yu kno seh yu mada a loose money cause a yu, she haffi sen back de chile benefit book, umm . . . yu soh braisen wid yu wrong doin. Tell me, Rose, is wha yu expeck from life now? Yu we hah six pickini by de time yu is twenty, yu noh tink bout dat.

ROSE: No, I've not thought about that, because I don't intend to have six children.

FATHER: By de way, Leroy ah go marry yu?

ROSE: I don't want to marry him. He might not even be around in six months.

FATHER: Him might not be around hoh. Rose, me mus admit me did expeck more from yu, me neva expeck seh yu could a come let me down like this.

ROSE: I haven't let you down. If I've let anybody down, it's myself, not you or anybody else.

FATHER: Rose, I really don't know what I can say to you. You don't seem to want to hear. Yu madda seh Miss Pickford ask her fe consent fe yu fe have abortion. If yu was tinking of dis, forget it, because the scripture seh 'Nation shall rise up against nation, there shall be wars and rumours of war, Children will be having children'. Soh is jus revelation a come to pass: Yu hah de baby an suffa wid it. Me naw tek yu back in a dis house wid no pickini . . . Where Leroy deh? (*Goes over to* ROSE *and shakes her.*) Where him is? (ROSE *looks up angrily.*) Yu naw answer me, me tell yu mada seh anybody whe tink anytink bout you, would a come home wid yu, an stan up like a man . . . Well, tell him seh if I ever catch him a naw spare de rod and spoil de chile. If yu wasn't pregnant, me would a fix yu business to.

ROSE: Oh yeah . . . I hope you know that there are laws against this sort of thing, and the police will have to lock you up.

FATHER: Back home de whole family would a catch him and horse wip him. Him would a haffi lef the country. Rose, yu mus have a good talk wid Jesus bout dis, if yu did a only trus God an lef the pleasures of de worl behind, it would a serve yu betta. Yu did tink seh de bright lights out dere was a enjoyment and fun, but God mek yu fall pregnant so yu can learn seh, dat the pleasures of the flesh is not always de best ting. Soh Rose, is what a go become a yu now? Wha yu a go do wid yu life? Me can't tek yu back inna dis house wid de belly, it wouldn't be right. Me haffi face de worl an preach de Gosple, soh my house haffi be in order before me can stan up before my breathren . . .

ROSE: But dad . . .

FATHER: No badda, but daddy me . . . the scripture seh, Let your light so shine before men, that they me see your good works and be led to glorify your father which is in heaven. Today I have to let my light shine for Jesus. I can't condone weh yu do an expeck fe lead God's children, I mus shine fe Jesus.

ROSE: So you think that by carrying on this way you're letting your light shine. The Bible also says 'forgive that we shall be forgiven' . . . So if you feel I've done a wrong against you you should be ready to forgive me.

FATHER: God may fegive yu, but I will neva . . . yu tink seh me want any bastard chile come in here come call me grandad.

ROSE: Who cares . . . the child might not even want to know you.

FATHER (*walks over to* ROSE *and points in her face*): Yu start, yu mada tell me seh yu still as facety as ever but me naw tek yu non a hit, pregnant or not. (*He gives* ROSE *one slap across her face,* ROSE *rubs her cheek and looks at him angrily.*)

ROSE: If I was as indecent as you mek out, I wooda gi yu one box in here today yu wooda shit weh yu neva man. Why don't you just go to prayer meeting, go beg forgiveness for your evil works?

FATHER: Yu tink seh yu can come tel me wha fe do inna me own house, me a go a prayer meeting now but me an yu we have it out later. (*Exit* FATHER.)

After the parents have gone to the prayer meeting, ROSE is alone in the sitting room and ELAINE enters.

ELAINE: Now we'll have a chance to talk.

ROSE: Umm . . .

ELAINE (*goes over and sits beside* ROSE.) Are you all right, Rose?

ROSE: Yeah sure.

ELAINE: Where did you live? You're lucky that Daddy never kill you. You should have heard him last night. He was giving me warnings, upon warnings . . . about fornication, the wrath of God and heavens knows what . . . this whole business is horrible . . . Rose, aren't you scared to death. If it was me I'd be worried sick, I mean, suppose Daddy won't sign the papers and you have to roam the streets at night with the baby . . . remember how much trouble him did give just to sign the school journey form?
(ELAINE *starts to sob and* ROSE *puts her hand around* ELAINE's *shoulder.*)

ROSE: Don't cry Elaine, because I've realised that I will have to become somebody in my own right, no longer listening to everything people try to push down my throat. Do you remember a time when I was the quiet one who never answered back, I used to get trodden on all the time, people could dump their shit on me left, right and centre . . . I know this may sound really silly, but me getting pregnant, is not such a bad thing. I now answer back because I've got to . . . I can't really afford not to . . . Elaine, look at it this way, all this means is that Rose is growing up and I'll have to learn to hold my own . . . the only person I can let try to dump their shit on me now, is the child I'm having . . . so cheer

up; things will sort themselves out . . . as for . . .

ELAINE: Yeah, as for Leroy, he's rubbish, even you must realise that now, I mean, where is he?

ROSE: You're fucking right about that. (ROSE *is angry about* LEROY.) Leroy is a child, all the big man talk, well, I can see now that he's as full a shit, just like all the people he talks about.

ELAINE (*dries her eyes*): Rose, I'm sorry, but I'm just frightened for you, what are you going to do?

ROSE: Have it, and keep it, with or without Leroy. I will probably have to go into a home, but . . .

ELAINE: It must be hard to make a choice, but at least your mind's made up. Just don't let anyone try to change your mind . . . If only Jennifer was here, she'd know what to do. They always look up to her. She wouldn't allow them to put you in a home. It must be horrid to live in a place like that with all kinds of nasty people, I'd . . .

ROSE: But Elaine, I can't live here; if I could I wouldn't have left in the first place. Mummy and Daddy don't understand that we weren't born in the 1920's and can't relate to their norms and values. I definitely have my own idea of how life should be . . . Daddy thinks I'd want to have an abortion, but how wrong, how wrong he is . . . I now feel that I have a reason for living . . .

ELAINE: You should have gotten some protection . . .

ROSE: What! When Mummy and the doctor are so close?

ELAINE: I suppose that would have been worse than getting pregnant, because as Daddy always say 'Things done in darkness shall be revealed in light'.

They both laugh.

ROSE: Elaine . . . do you remember the time when we were gonna take those pills?

ELAINE: Yeah, things were dread then.

ROSE: Well, I never feel like that anymore, I never feel like killing myself. I know it's going to be difficult, according to Daddy, children having children, and all that. But I'm prepared to face anything life throws at me. I'm not saying I'm not scared, I was shitting bricks coming down here, but now I'm determined to make a go of things for me and my baby . . . as for Daddy and his Christian ideas about sending Leroy to jail, well, I'm not saying where he is or anything, so if they can find him good luck to them . . . things like that are not right.

ELAINE: Daddy can't do that, man. Him is a Christian soldier of the Lord, and God won't hold with him if he does that.

ROSE: But Daddy don't care, all he cares about is money and reputation and crap like that.

ELAINE: Rose, you'll just have to show the lot of them, Pickford and all, that you're strong and that you can cope . . . anyway, you know what to tell her if she comes with anymore negative vibes, tell her . . .

ELAINE: Fe go fuck dry up shit a
ROSE: roadside.

They both laugh.

ROSE: Look, fun and games aside, since I left here I've seen some things which make me wonder. We always thought we lived in the real world, that we knew about life, well we have been well and truly sheltered, we know nothing. I've seen people out there husselling to make a living, thieving to survive, moving from squat to squat with no permanent address. Sometimes I wonder if I'll be like them, if I have this baby. All alone in the big wide world with no one . . .

The ringing of the telephone interrupts.

ELAINE: I'd better get it, it may be Frank.

ROSE: Who's Frank?

ELAINE *picks up the telephone receiver.*

ELAINE: Hello. (*Pause.*)
Yes. (*Pause.*)
Yes. (*Pause.*)
She's here. (*Pause.*)
Okay, Miss Pickford, goodbye.

ROSE (*getting up from the chair*): Let me . . .

ELAINE (*hangs up the receiver*): Sorry, too late, Miss Pickford will be here tomorrow, she hasn't managed to sort things out yet. She'll be here around four o'clock . . . (*Joking.*) for the big show down.

ROSE: It's gonna be the big shame up, more like, she's gonna see how ignorant Daddy really is. I'd better phone Leroy and tell him to get down here, not that he's gonna be much help. But it's better than facing the firing squad alone.

ELAINE (*yawns*): Look, Rose, we can finish talking in bed. Come, let's go up, it will be just like old times and you've got a big day tomorrow, so let's get some rest.

ROSE: Yeah, I'll phone Leroy in the morning.

Arm in arm they go up to bed.

Scene Four

MOTHER *and* FATHER *are in the sitting room with* ROSE, *all seated.* FATHER *is drinking tea out of a large mug, with his bible in one hand, flicking through the pages.* MOTHER *is sitting there with her knitting.* ROSE *is looking out of the window.*

ROSE: When is dis woman coming?

FATHER; Jus sit down an keep yuself quiet, me noh really whan fe here your mouth.

MOTHER: Cho, Daddy man noh badda start.

FATHER: Noh badda start? When me start yu we know.

MOTHER: Rose . . .

ROSE *takes no notice.*

Rose . . .

ROSE *turns round.*

ROSE: Yes?

MOTHER: Is not 'yes, Mummy' no more? Yu phone Leroy an tel im fe come down here?

FATHER (*angrily*): Come where?

ROSE: Yes, M U M M Y.

FATHER: A den me a go start, dat good fe notten rascal, if im ever set foot inna me yard today . . . hum . . . Is where dis Pickford she deh . . . the bretheren soon reach here fe prayer meeting.

ROSE *comes away from the window.*

ROSE: She's coming now.

ROSE *sits down near the window. There is a ring at the door and* ROSE's *mother goes to open the door.*

PICKFORD; Hello, Mrs Johnson, may I come in?

MOTHER: Good evening, Miss Pickford, come in, come in.

PICKFORD: Is Roseline here?

MOTHER *points towards the sitting room.*

MOTHER: She's in there wid her fada, go on in.

PICKFORD *enters the sitting room.*

PICKFORD: Hello, Mr Johnson. (*Hands outstretched to shake* MR JOHNSON's *hand, but* MR JOHNSON *just sits there with his mug of tea, but shuts his bible.*) Hello, Rose.

FATHER: Umm . . .

MISS PICKFORD *sits down, and takes out her file.* MOTHER *enters the room and stands by the door.*

MOTHER: Would you like some tea, Miss Pickford?

ROSE: Here she goes again offering people tea, anybody would believe she name Mrs Tetley.

MOTHER *gives* ROSE *a dirty look.*

PICKFORD: No, thank you, Mrs Johnson, I've just eaten.

ROSE: See it deh she noh whan yu tea.

PICKFORD: Look Rose, I know that you consider your childish remarks clever, however, this evening we are here to talk about you. Not whether or not I want tea.

ROSE: Yu sure yu don't have a degree in mind reading or . . .

PICKFORD: Well, Mr and Mrs . . . wouldn't you like to sit down, Mrs Johnson?

MOTHER: No, Miss Pickford, me is quite all right.

PICKFORD: Well, we'll carry on. Firstly I'll run through the situation as it stands, and the various possibilities. We'll then discuss it and see what would suit Rose best. At the moment Rose is only seven or eight weeks pregnant. This gives us one option which we wouldn't have if the pregnancy was at a more advanced stage.

ROSE: A B O R T I O N, here we go.

FATHER: De girl go weh a defile her body, she naw have no abortion, Miss Pickford, all life is sacred. But me noh whan notten fe do wid dat baby.

PICKFORD: If I may continue. Rose, you have stated, emphatically that you don't intend to have an abortion, and I also know the views of you, Mr and Mrs Johnson. Considering all this, I suppose we had better look at some other alternatives. Seeing that Rose is determined to keep this baby, she could have it fostered out until she's finished school.

ROSE: I've already told you, Pickford, no bloody way.

PICKFORD: Well, the only alternative is a mother and baby home.

FATHER: Is wha dat?

PICKFORD: If you hold on a minute I'll explain. Mother and baby homes were set up in the early sixties, some even earlier, just to cater for people like Rose, who are unmarried and wanted to have their babies and keep them. Today they mostly cater for girls under eighteen, who need a place to stay until they have their babies and to learn how to look after babies. Most mother and baby homes have a school room, or are attached to the local secondary school, so that girls can continue with their education.

ROSE: Oh my God, prison.

PICKFORD: No, Rose, it is not a prison, you are free to come and go, as long as you obey the rules of the house.

MOTHER: Well, she might as well be free because there is no worse trouble than the trouble she's already in.

PICKFORD: Believe me, Mrs Johnson, Rose is an ideal case compared with some of the juveniles I have to deal with. We are only talking about a mother and baby home not Borstal.

FATHER: Soh is weh yu saying, Pickford, we should be grateful. All dem place . . . unmarried mothers home, weh yu a tak bout . . . dem shouldn't exist, fornicators like Rose should pay fe dem wrong doings.

PICKFORD: If I could just continue . . . there are, however, no vacant places at present in any of the . . .

FATHER: Well, she naw stay yah.

PICKFORD: You have made your feelings quite clear, Mr Johnson, I would appreciate it if you'd let me continue . . . I am suggesting that Rose goes into a short-stay home until there is a vacant place in a mother and baby home in London. I'm sure you'd want to stay in London, wouldn't you, Rose?

ROSE: Well, ye . . .

FATHER: Me noh partial whe she stay as long as she is out ah my sight.

MOTHER: Cho Daddy man, mek Miss Pickford seh wha she haffi seh.

PICKFORD: If everybody is agreed, that's all really. The formalities of signing these papers is all that's left to be done.

FATHER: Jus gi me de papers, me we sign anyting.

There is a ring at the door.

ROSE: Lard God, Leroy.

ELAINE *who is standing in the passage opens the door.* LEROY *is at the door, he comes in without acknowledging* ELAINE.

ELAINE (*puts her head round the sitting room door*): It's Leroy.

LEROY *does not wait to be asked in. He just enters the sitting room. As he does this,* MR JOHNSON *stands up.*

LEROY (*takes a puff of his splif*): So dis is de conference chamber.

MOTHER *moves forward, sniffing as she approaches* LEROY.

MOTHER: What's dat you're smoking?

FATHER: Yu noh see seh de bouy ah smoke ganja inna me house . . . Put it out . . .

LEROY: OK, Deacon Johnson. (LEROY *walks over to the window and stubs out his splif; he holds the rest of it in his hand.*)

MOTHER: Look, Missa Leroy, the conference is over. Rose is going into a home and dats dat.

LEROY: Soh, I noh hah no seh inna dis ting?

MOTHER: Is yu birth her? Me seh if is you birth her?

FATHER: If me had my way yu would a neva have annada seh inna anything again.

LEROY: Stop roun up yu mouth, ol man. Rose a come wid I man. Get yu bags, Rose.

FATHER *gets angry and grabs after* LEROY; LEROY *steps back, and* MOTHER *comes and stands between them.*

FATHER: God fegive me but me a go kill yu, me a go kill yu. (*Shouting.*) Me a go kill you.

LEROY *is backing away and grinning at the* FATHER.

PICKFORD (*shouting*): Gentlemen, please, there is no need for this. Let's talk about this sensibly; attacking Leroy is not going to help. It serves no purpose and we should listen to what he has to say.

MOTHER *pushes* FATHER *back into his chair.*

MOTHER: Yes, Daddy, sit down, mek we sort out dis ting.

FATHER: Leroy, whatever yu name, me just whan tell yu seh if me see yu a road an lick yu inna yu head yu dead . . . dead . . . dead.

LEROY: I man noh fraid fe dead, Jah know.

FATHER: Yu noh fraid noh.

MOTHER: Dat's enough, let's get back to the matter in hand . . . Daddy, you sign de papers dem.

LEROY: Sign wha papers . . . Rose, dem a sign yu over to the council, dis is wha dem come a Englan fe do, if dem was back home no council wouldn't de deh fe dem fe sign yu over to . . . Tell me now, you social worker lady, you . . . yu believe seh is a good ting dese people a do? . . . yu noh believe seh dem should see reason, is noh good someting when yu see black pickini inna home like seh dem parents noh know betta.

PICKFORD: Leroy, I'd like to help but Mr Johnson is determined . . . he wants Rose out.

LEROY *moves towards the door.*

LEROY: Well, Missa Johnson, I man hope seh yu know weh yu a do because it is not easy someting fe live wid pan a man conscience. Rose, me tek Bertie advice, me come down here me try fe show yu parents seh me willing fe shoulder some of the responsibility but dem determin fe lock yu up inna institution. Yu tek care ah yu self an de youth, Jah know seh I man would a try lickle more but yu fada head hard like a rock stone . . .

FATHER *gets up and goes for* LEROY. LEROY *backs away,* MOTHER *stands between the two of them,* LEROY *takes out his matches and lights his splif.*

ROSE: Leroy, you really tried, didn't you. Look what you're doing, provoking Mummy and Daddy. How can you proclaim to love me so much, when you don't have any respect for my mother and father. Bertie didn't tell you to come down here and show me up. All you have succeeded in doing is showing them that yu is a good fe notten, one suit dry up skin, hall up bouy! You haven't said anything positive since you came. All you have done is shout off your mouth, even a blind man can see that you're not defending anything . . . JUST GO, LEROY.

LEROY: No get me angry, Rose Johnson, me a go weh now, but I man we site yu more time.

ROSE: Goodbye, Leroy.

Exit LEROY. PICKFORD *is sorting through her papers.*

PICKFORD: If you'd just like to sign here, Mr Johnson . . .

FATHER *goes over and signs the paper.*

Well, Rose, you're now my responsibility. I'll come later to take you to St Mark's House. You'll stay there until we can find you some suitable accommodation in London.

MOTHER: Soh is up to yu now, Rose, fe behave yu self an noh gi de people dem no trouble.

FATHER (*looking towards the heavens*): My God, My God, why hast thou forsaken me.

MOTHER: Daddy, now is not de time fe dat, is time to talk to Rose and give her some advice.

PICKFORD: That's a good idea, Mr Johnson.

MOTHER: Yes, Daddy.

ROSE: I like the way everybody's talking about me going into a mother and baby home, a children's home and all sort of things. It seems to be taken as read that I'm going. Who said I'm going, nobody has actually said, is this what you want, Rose . . .

FATHER: At this stage, chile, noh badda expect me or yu mada fe ask your permission, it's not a matter of what you want, yu mada a dead of heartache, an me haffi slough out me guts a London Transport, fe pay fe yu, rude and facety pickini.

ROSE: All yu care bout is money, money, money. If you'd spent more time worrying about us and less about church and money, things would be better. Do you know why I ran away? Do you want to know? You've got your priorities all wrong. You don't think about the hell you put us through in this bloody house . . . I mean, I should be unhappy about going into a home, but I'm not, I can't wait to get away.

FATHER: Yu still have yu foul mouth, yu tink seh me could a talk to my parents like dat, dem would a sling me out without a morsel of bread.

MOTHER: Daddy, yu sign her over to the council, soh let dem do the worrying now.

PICKFORD: Rose, I'll need some particulars, like confirmation of pregnancy, and your expected date of delivery in order to sort out things with the mother and baby home. When you get in touch with Leroy, could you ask him to contact me at the office, so that I can ascertain any area in which he might be able to help.

FATHER: Help? Lard hah mercy . . . It would a easier fe go a hell an get help from de devil himself . . .

MOTHER: Be that as it may, Miss Pickford is only trying to help.

PICKFORD: There isn't much left to be done, until later when I come to take Rose to St Mark's House.

There is a ring at the door. It is SISTER THOMPSON, SISTER JONES and SISTER ENNIS.

ELAINE: Hello, hello, come in.

SISTER THOMPSON: Thank you, Elaine. Is Daddy here?

ELAINE: They are inside.

SISTER JONES: Praise de Lard, Brother Johnson, Praise de Lard Madda. (*Looking at* PICKFORD.) Good evening. (*Looking at* ROSE.) Hello, Rosie.

SISTER THOMPSON: Praise de Lard, everybody.

MOTHER: Praise the Lord, Sisters.

SISTER ENNIS: Praise de Lard, (*She gets down on her knees to pray.*)

PICKFORD: Well, I'll be leaving now. (PICKFORD *stands up.*) Goodbye all, see you later then, Rose.

Exit PICKFORD. ROSE *starts to get up to leave.*

ROSE: I'll go too.

SISTER ENNIS: No, Rose, you sit down, De Lard sent me with a message for you, with all the trials and tribulations you will have to face out dere, lissen to the words of this song.

SISTER ENNIS starts to sing 'Precious Name'. At the end of the first verse everybody joins in with the chorus. Whilst they are singing ELAINE brings ROSE's bags in.

MOTHER (*still crying*): Rose, we off to prayer meeting now.

They all exit, SISTER THOMPSON goes over, tears in her eyes; she kneels down in front of ROSE and holds ROSE's hand.

SISTER THOMPSON: Rose, me chile, tek care a yuself and as the song seh, Take de Name of Jesus with you . . . Goodbye, me chile. (*She gets up and goes out with the others.*)

IN UNISON: Goodbye Rose.

ROSE: Bye everyone.

Exit all the SISTERS and the MOTHER and FATHER. ROSE walks back and stands talking to the audience:

I never thought it would be like this, me going into a home. I always thought those places were for bad children or for those without parents. Leroy, as for Leroy, I thought, he'd get a job, settle down, the baby would bring us all closer together. Instead it's driven us apart. Mummy and Daddy still don't understand me, they are still blind to their faults. I mean, fancy bringing in the Police, Social Worker, who know nothing about me, making decisions that I can't really do anything about. I just did not expect things to end up like this. I don't really know what I expected but not this, and the church people know my business. It's no secret anymore, I'll have to face school friends, and family . . . Rose Johnson is finally growing up . . . But a bloody home of all place. But there was no point creating about that, cause I couldn't stay here, Leroy is no good, so I had no choice but to accept. God knows it's . . . (*There is a knock at the door, PICKFORD puts her head through the door.*)

PICKFORD: Come on, Rose, it's time to go.

ROSE picks up her bags and moves towards the door.

ROSE (*at the audience*): And this is where the story *really* begins.

Curtain.

Kneel at the Cross

Kneel at the cross,
Christ will meet you there,
Come while He waits for you;
List to His voice,
Leave with Him your care
And begin life anew.

(*Chorus*):
Kneel at the cross
Leave ev'ry care —
Kneel at the cross
Jesus will meet you there.

Kneel at the cross,
There is room for all
Who would His glory share —
Bliss there awaits,
Harm can ne'er befall
Those who are anchored there.

(*Chorus*.)

Kneel at the cross,
Give your idols up,
Look unto realms above —
Turn not away
To life's sparkling cup;
Trust only in His love.

(*Chorus*.)

Precious Name

Take the name of Jesus with you,
Child of sorrow and of woe —
It will joy and comfort give you,
Take it then where'er you go.

(*Chorus*):
Precious name,
O how sweet!
Hope of earth and joy of heav'n,
Precious name,
O how sweet —
Hope of earth and joy of heav'n.

Take the name of Jesus with you,
As a shield from ev'ry snare —
If temptations 'round you gather,
Breathe that holy name in pray'r.

(*Chorus*.)

Oh! the precious name of Jesus;
How it thrills our souls with joy,
When His loving arms receive us,
And His songs our tongues employ!

(*Chorus*.)

At the name of Jesus bowing,
Falling prostrate at His feet,
King of kings in heav'n we'll crown Him
When our journey is complete.

(*Chorus*.)

Rose's Story

I first began to write about my experiences during my early teens. Much of what I wrote centred around my life in England comparing it with stories I had heard about life in Jamaica. It was, however, during my pregnancy, living in a Mother-and-Baby-home, that I realised that every pregnant teenager's experience was unique. This prompted me to write about the Mother-and-Baby-home. It then dawned on me that how I came to be there was much more interesting. The notes I made then, formed the basis for *Rose's Story*.

Rose's Story started in earnest after I had seen several unimpressive black productions. The mediocrity of these plays puzzled me as I wondered how such worthless nonsense could attract what limited funding there was. I concentrated on writing the story in script form, but as I was inexperienced, I asked Caryl Phillips (a playwright) to read it. He suggested several ways of improving the script structurally, as well as a monologue to give an insight into Rose's background.

This final version was completed in the summer of 1983, when I proceeded to try and interest black and fringe theatre companies in producing it. Although the responses were encouraging, no suitable offers were forthcoming. Determined, however, that this play should have a 'life', together with Tracy Gibbons and Alex Addo, I set up the Drama Society at the Polytechnic of the South Bank, in London.

From the outset the production seemed dogged with problems. Firstly, we had to adhere to restrictive student union legislation on advertising and publicity for the play. Hence Paulette Ward's article in the December '83 issue of *RightOff*, South Bank's own publication, notifying everyone about the play, not to be missed. Secondly, rehearsal space was a problem; it proved almost impossible to cut through red tape. After approaching the Director of the college, Michael Collins (Accommodation Assistant) was given the authority to provide us with rehearsal space, and to ensure that the main auditorium was available for the production.

Notwithstanding, we pressed on. Madeline Kingsley, a freelance journalist arranged with the *Times* newspaper to do a feature on the play, its origins and the production. But that was not to be; the *Times* chose to strike at this crucial time. When it was finally back in production students would buy the paper searching for even a brief mention of *Rose's Story* but there was none. Undeterred, rehearsals took place and lines were painstakingly learnt. A great deal of time, effort and mental strain had by now been put into producing this play so whatever problems lay ahead, *Rose's Story* had to be staged.

Sexism aside, the women in the cast surpassed themselves. Men were difficult to come by and proved even more difficult to keep, especially when the going got rough. This could have been linked to the actual content of the play, as nearly 50% of the women in the cast were unmarried mothers and could probably make analogies with their lives and thought it important to see the play produced, and hear the reaction to what happened to Rose.

The play ran for only three nights due to another industrial dispute, this time at college. When it was finally performed we had superb audiences both in quality and quantity. Audience reaction was overwhelming. *Rose's Story* had struck a chord with most people, whether they were teenagers, parents or intending social workers. The most common cry was, 'Only one criticism. It was much too short'.

Spare Rib March 1984 Issue reviewed the play rather critically: 'An acknowledgement of the difficulties Black people (with or without qualifications) face, when trying to get a job would have been welcomed in easing the stereotype of Black workshy Leroy, Rose's lover presented.' This play, however, was not about the unemployment situation, Leroy happened to be unemployed, without qualifications, and thirdly black, not the other way round. The significance being it could happen to anybody irrespective of race, colour or creed.

As a result of this production, The Royal Court Theatre offered me an option for twelve months, during which time they hope to produce the play in the Theatre Upstairs. I feel that the publication of *Rose's Story* will increase the number of productions.

And finally, to all you would-be Rose's . . . *be positive.*

Grace Dayley

BLOOD AND ICE

Blood and Ice was first performed at New Merlin's Cave, London, on 27 February 1984, with the following cast:

MARY SHELLEY	Sue Britten
CLAIRE CLAIRMONT	Georgia Allen
SHELLEY	Paul Jeary
LORD BYRON	Paul Mulrennan
ELISE	Pauline Little

Directed by Joanna Proctor
Designed by Sian Wolchover
Lighting by Wendy Davies

ACT ONE

Scene One

The ghostly nursery. There is a large, staring-eyed rocking horse, greys and blacks or dull dun-coloured; bleached-out, similarly unreal toys, perhaps a bit out of scale; a ship in a bottle (or a model ship with unfurled sails); a china-headed doll with frightwig hair, unclothed to show the stuffed cloth slump-body with the attached china lower limbs and arms.

MARY alone, in a cold circle of candlelight, is reading her Frankenstein, *surrounded by packing cases and nightmare toys.*

MARY (*sings*):
Oh we'll go no more a-roving
So late into the night
Though the heart be still as loving
Though the moon be still as . . .

(*She speaks.*) Bright, and cold. And lonely. (*She closes the book. She opens a shutter and is hit by moonlight.*) My element. I swim in it and I do not drown. I dream in it. Swimming, dwamming, dreaming . . . drowning. Sleeping in a dead man's bed. Not yet thirty and I'm sleeping in a dead man's bed.

Last night I dreamed, I dreamed we were back in Poland Street, I found my little baby, my firstborn, it was not dead but — cold merely. Shelley and I rubbed it before the fire and it lived! Awoke and found no body.

No Shelley.

Cold. Must sleep. Must sleep soon.

The Dead Hour. Bring out your dead. No!

Mary, Mary quite . . . quite dead.

Sleeping in a dead man's bed. Don't think of him.

When they found him washed up, his eyes, his face, all parts of him . . . not protected by his clothes were eaten away . . . they only knew him by — in his pocket they found . . . All washed up.

Sometimes I wake up. Cold. Bathed in a moon sweat. And I rub myself slowly to life again. (*Pause.*) The Dead of Night.

Don't think of him. (*Writes quietly, candles flicker, thinks, writes, scores out, writes, slams the book shut.*) It has gone dead in me. My heart's not in it.

SHELLEY's *voice disembodied, barely audible.*

SHELLEY'S VOICE: Mary!

MARY, *frightened, lifts the candle, the shadows are shown up as empty.*

Mary!

BYRON'S VOICE: Mary!

She looks round, sees no one.

MARY (*smiling*): There were three of us.

CLAIRE'S VOICE: (*a giggle*): Mary! (MARY *stops her ears.*)

MARY (*silencing her*): There were *three* of us! There was Shelley . . . and Byron . . . and me.

She snuffs the candle, throws off her dark shawl, and the light comes back up. Rich, late afternoon sunlight pours in and we find MARY at nineteen, laughing exasperated, in filmy white dress in the middle of the room and, bursting in with the light, young SHELLEY, wrapped in a lace tablecloth, damp-haired, seaweedy, laughing, puzzled.

Shelley, how *could* you . . .?

SHELLEY: Swimming, Mary. I want to learn to swim.

MARY: Walking naked across the terrace, all tangled up with . . .

SHELLEY: I forgot. I forgot they were coming.

MARY: You did not! You only wanted to outrage . . .

SHELLEY: What does it matter, Mary?

MARY: What does it matter? It matters to me! She was a great friend of my mother's *and* Mrs –

SHELLEY: Old humbugs, pretending to be shocked!

MARY: I thought Mrs Gisborne would have an apoplexy!

SHELLEY: And the other old goose! Lord, I thought she was going to burst her goitre. Such a becoming shade of purple she turned.

He laughs, delighted with himself. MARY unsuccessfully fights a battle with laughter. SHELLEY comes back to her and hugs her. They kiss.

MARY (*laughing, loving him*): Thank goodness they've gone! They didn't stay a minute after your grand apparition, though! It was make excuses and off before they'd drained their first teacup. Oh Shelley, how could you have!

SHELLEY: I covered myself! Just as soon as I saw you had company to tea. I had two choices. I could brazen it out, or hide myself behind the maidservant. So I –

MARY: What Elise must have thought, I cannot imagine!

SHELLEY: Oh, so not content with fretting over the old dowagers, now we are to agonise over the imagined offence to the servant girl! Well, at least we don't have to worry about what the neighbours will say.

Sharply MARY pulls away.

MARY: It's *his* influence makes you so careless of the regard of others!

SHELLEY: No, Mary, you know I never cared for the world's approval. Not in such . . . silly and private matters. And neither did you! The Mary I met . . .

MARY: Did not go deliberately out of her way to offend elderly ladies in such . . . silly and trivial ways!

SHELLEY: I covered myself. Dodging behind the maidservant, swaddling myself in her apron strings, I twirled around and, sleight of hand, snatched out the topmost tablecloth like a conjurer ere she put down the tea things and sat myself down, decently draped in dimity and lace, to adequate small talk amid the tinkling cups. I do not see how you can begin to complain of me!

MARY: We'll never see them again. I was surprised enough when they called in the first place. You know how our position makes us vulnerable to . . . Of course Maria Gisborne was an acolyte of Mama's, certainly she is of more liberal opinions than most middle-aged, matrons, but . . . it was kind of her to call.

SHELLEY: Kind! Now don't you think Mrs Gisborne might just have been moved by curiosity, not to speak of the passing expectation of perhaps a glimpse of our illustrious . . . no, *infamous* neighbour?

MARY: It was kind of them to call.

SHELLEY: So, they can certainly tell all the English Community that no, they never saw so much as an eyelash of Lord Byron . . . (*He runs to the terrace door and, looking offstage, flashes, his tablecloth outstretched like a cloak.*)

. . . but they saw every inch of Percy Shelley, the whole natural man!

Mrs Gisborne! Maria! Look at me, am I not a pretty sight? Look what the sea threw up! What? You've never seen a naked man in all your sixty summers, course not, I'm not one to believe all the old gossip! Am I not a Bonny Titan with seawrack tangled in my hair? What! Smelling salts, she's fainted, smelling salts? Come here, *I'll* give you a sniff of the sea. (*Spins round, blushing as ELISE enters from the terrace with tea things and exits again, other side.*)

Didn't I charm them? I tried to be charming for your sake.

MARY: Go and change! (*Laughing.*)

SHELLEY: Come with me, Mary.

MARY: I have to feed William!

SHELLEY: Kiss me. (*They kiss.*)

MARY: Oh, you made me shiver! (*They kiss.* ELISE *enters, stands.* MARY *sees her first, breaks.*)

Yes, Elise?

ELISE: Monsieur Byron's man, Madame, he come and say the boat is launched you 'ave to go and sail, he say.

SHELLEY: It's ready? At last, Mary, we must try sailing together. Come and —

MARY: I must feed Willmouse!

SHELLEY: Mary! (*Pleading look.*)

MARY: You go, you know you want to.

SHELLEY (*whispering*): Tonight! I'll make you shiver, Mary. (*Exits.*)

Lights change, twilight. ELISE *turning to go.*

MARY: Elise . . . is William ready to be fed?

ELISE: He's still sleeping, madame.

MARY: You're sure it's not time? . . . Elise, do you think he's settling properly, is the climate agreeable to him?

ELISE: It's not . . . it is not very different from England, Madame? Since you arrived it has been cloudy, and chill enough, sometimes . . . stormy too, most evenings. Not very different from your English June, I think?

MARY: Of course it will get hot.

ELISE: Yes, Madame.

MARY: It will get hot, although I hope we can keep cool here by the lake, but Elise . . .

ELISE: Oui, Madame?

MARY: You will tell me, won't you, if William should seem fretful in any way way?

ELISE: Yes, Madame. (*Pause.*) Is that everything, Madame?

MARY: Yes, you may go.

She begins to, is stopped by.

Oh Elise! (*Pause.*) You must have thought Mr Shelley's behaviour somewhat strange?

ELISE: No, Madame.

MARY: Tell me, are you at home here, Elise?

ELISE: But of course! Here, Madame you are the strange one, no? Switzerland, it is my home. I am at home here, yes, naturally.

MARY: No, Elise, I meant . . . (*In a blurt.*) You must not be surprised at anything Mr Shelley does, he is . . . I think you know we are not . . . he is not bound by normal conventions, he cares nothing for them, neither of us do! But he is a good, good man, he is against all viciousness, and cruelty, and tyranny and ownership. What is nakedness compared to . . .

Pause. ELISE *is withholding.*

ELISE (*shrugging*): It's only nature, Madame.

MARY: Thank you, Elise.

ELISE *begins to go again.*

Oh, Elise! Elise, in the packing today, that arrived from England there is such a pretty dress, but I'm sure, since I've had William, it won't fit me properly.

ELISE: I'm sure I can alter it, Madame, I've some talent as a seamstress.

MARY: Silly! No, I meant for *you*, Elise. It will be . . . Yes, I'm sure it will be very becoming.

ELISE *curtseys.*

ELISE: Thank you, Madame. (*Exits.*)

Lights up on mirror stand with mirror each side. CLAIRE is having her hair brushed out by ELISE. She is in a filmy petticoat, having lacing pulled in at the back.

CLAIRE: Tighter! Lace me nice and small, Elise. Make me beautiful!

MARY comes in similar filmy chemise with her hairbrush.

MARY: Lord, Claire, even to look at you makes me short of breath.

CLAIRE: Tighter, ow, you're pinching!

MARY begins to brush her hair, on the other side of stand, tilting the mirror. CLAIRE tilts it back, ELISE begins to brush CLAIRE's hair.

One hundred strokes! Elise! You're tugging! Give it me. Go get my dress ready.

ELISE goes to the edge of the light where we ought to just sense her waiting resentment. She stands stock still with armful of frou-frou, leaving, in a sort of tableau: MARY and CLAIRE alone together by the fire and candlelight. As if under a spell they begin to brush out their long hair slowly with silver hairbrushes, each other's image.

Do you not think we are somewhat alike? *Oui*? Yes, Mary, we do resemble each other after all. Oh, not in colouring, no, but in bearing, in —

MARY: How could we, we are not —

CLAIRE: Not in blood, no. But we are closer perhaps than sisters, *oui*? Haven't we always shared everything?

MARY: Since we were three years old.

CLAIRE: You love to write. And I love to write. You found a passionate poet to be your lover. And I —

MARY: Came with us.

CLAIRE: Mary! *Tu n'est pas gentil*! What else could I do? (*Pause.*)

You are such a scarlet lady, Mary. And now I am scarlet too! We are two very —

MARY: My mother would have been utterly —

CLAIRE: Oh, she was scarlet too! (*Pause. Looking into the mirror of* MARY.) Mary found herself a young and a beautiful and a passionate poet to be her heart's companion. And Claire found herself a . . . not *quite* so young, but quite as beautiful and as passionate a poet to be hers!

MARY: It really is too vexing! You behaving like a . . . maidservant! Why, this morning at dawn I was looking out of the casement, and I saw you running through the gap in the hedges back through the garden to the kitchen quarters, all disordered with your hair loose, losing your shoe like Cinderella —

CLAIRE: Mary, where is the harm?

MARY: You know very well what is the harm! There can be but one outcome!

Pause.

CLAIRE: So the servants see we too have a little blood in our veins . . .

MARY: Servants! That maid presented it back to you with such an ironical little bob of a curtsey, '*Votre soulier, Madame*', and the most insolent smirk on her face.

CLAIRE: Probably jealous. All England would be jealous of me if they knew. All the ladies in England, at least!

MARY: Jealous! To see you make a fool of yourself, throwing yourself at a man just because he's a scandal — oh, and a Famous Poet!

CLAIRE: I love him. And I know he loves me. Such a scandal though! Imagine! Peacocks, packing cases all over the quayside, monkeys escaping from their cages, a piano dangling in mid-air. And the ladies! All the ladies weeping oceans into their cambric handkerchiefs, pressing *billets-doux* on him, sending little black pageboys to shower him with locks of their hair. Do you know, Mary, some ladies even cut off —

MARY: There can be only one outcome of all this, Claire! Byron is not — he is married already, Claire.

CLAIRE (*laughing*): And you are an hypocrite! (*Pronouncing it 'Ippocreet' Frenchly.*) Byron loathes and detests Annabel with all his heart. Byron has far less truck with Annabel Algebra after only a month or two's parting than Shelley has with his Harriet after nearly three years!

MARY: What do you mean by that?

CLAIRE: Nothing. Only —

MARY: Harriet is the mother of his children. He cannot leave her destitute, his children bereft — I would not for a moment wish him to. Harriet is . . . (*Gentler.*) Claire. Claire, it is just that — I am afraid for you.

CLAIRE: Well, save your fear for yourself!

MARY: Claire. Claire, don't let's quarrel. I . . . I cannot bear it when we do.

CLAIRE: No. Don't let's quarrel, Mary. You are so good, of course you are not jealous. I was silly! Of course Shelley must care for Harriet. Oh, Mary! (*Kisses her.*) I want to love *you*, and Shelley and little William, and . . . oh, Mary, I feel as though my heart could burst. The moment I met him, that very first instant —

MARY (*bursts*): Would you mother a fatherless child?

CLAIRE (*wavers, won't answer*): Mary, you do not know how cruel my life was, *vraiment*! You had Shelley to be your protector, I had no one . . . I told Byron, I wrote to him . . . once or twice . . . and told him what his poetry meant to me, how reading it had transformed my whole drab existence and that made him responsible for me — for the Creator should not shun his Creature . . . and I, I arranged that we would be free and unknown and we could return the following morning! Well, did not your Mama defy

convention so? I am sure she thought it shameful that women must simper and sit in the chimney corner and make mim-mouths and wait for men to decide to kiss them? I am sure she looked forward to a time when woman as well as man may freely state her desire . . .

MARY: Of course! But . . .

CLAIRE: But what? Everything your mother ever thought, everything she wrote — Your mama wanted that women should be free.

MARY: Do you want to be a mother? Because that will certainly be the outcome —

CLAIRE: And if it happened? Perhaps it has happened already. *Peut-être.* There is no stronger bond between a man and a woman than the making of a child. It is only nature, Mary. (*Pause.*) I think . . . perhaps . . . it may have happened already. Oh — I'm sure *not* — don't let's quarrel! You said so yourself. We mustn't quarrel. We must be happy here — the lake, the high Alps — we are a million miles away from tight little *Angleterre.* Did our luggage arrive yet?

MARY: What?

CLAIRE: Our baggages. Lord, I'm sure it seems such ages ago we packed it, and I was in such a lather of excitement — I cannot think what we'll find when we open it! Isn't it exciting?

MARY: You know I do not interest myself much in fashions and frippery.

CLAIRE: Did you pack the blue, *ma favourite*?

MARY: I can't remember . . .

CLAIRE: I was always jealous of that dress. Quite green over the blue! A happy dress — you wore it always that summer when I was the little bird that carried messages between you and Shelley and you walked together in the graveyard. May I borrow it? I'm sure it'd fit me, *oui*?

MARY: I gave it to Elise.

CLAIRE: Elise? Lord, Mary, I think you love Elise better than you love your own sister. But then I'm not your sister. You do keep reminding me.

MARY looks at CLAIRE with all her old childhood spite and CLAIRE is transformed in her eyes (and therefore in ours) to the little stepsister of those days.

CLAIRE: Your papa said you were to love me because I'm to be your sister now. *My mama says —*

MARY: No!

CLAIRE (*in her adult voice, picking up a hairbrush casually*): What's the matter, Mary? (*Absently, adultly winding up a curl.*)

MARY has become her child-self too.

MARY: That's mine!

They go into childhood routine, both of them.

CLAIRE: It's mine! My doll!

MARY: Mine!

CLAIRE: My ball!

MARY: Mine!

CLAIRE: My book!

MARY: It's mine! My hair-ribbon!

CLAIRE: Mine! Oh, keep your old hair-ribbon. I'm prettier than you anyhow!

MARY: I'm cleverer than you.

CLAIRE: I'm prettier! (*Pause.*) How can blood be a river?

MARY: No!

CLAIRE: Your mama died! I heard Maria tell Cook your mama died giving birth to you. Rivers of blood she said.

MARY turns away upset, gathering at her skirt. CLAIRE points to MARY's shift.

CLAIRE: Mary! Mary! What's the matter? Mary, you're bleeding, your shift is all covered, what is it?

MARY (*coldly fascinated*): Great . . . gouts and spatters . . . crimson trickle, tickling . . . a thin dark red line running . . . scribbling as if a quill was dipped in blood and scribbled . . .

CLAIRE: What is it? Mary! Mama! Mama! Come quick, Mary's bleeding. Mary's dying!

MARY slaps CLAIRE hard.

MARY: Be quiet! It's nothing wrong. I read about it. It's normal. It does not hurt. Didn't your mama tell you? She should have told you what to expect. Stupid Claire. Claire's a baby! It's happening to *me*. (*Taunting.*) Claire is *beside* herself and it's happening to me! It's the moon. I am a woman now. It is my age.

During this last, SHELLEY has laughingly, lightly sneaked in and crept up behind MARY with a blindfold to grab her with, unaware of the atmosphere he stands behind her smiling, finger to his lips signalling to CLAIRE who helps him by attracting MARY's attention. She has just tied, choker fashion, a thin red velvet ribbon round her throat.

CLAIRE: Look at me, Mary. Look! Do you not think this is fetching? It is my latest fashion . . . oh rather an *antique* one to be sure, but then something genuinely flattering is surely *à la mode* for all time! (*Pause. Whispers.*) The brave beldams of the French Revolution affected it. It is called 'à la victime'. Don't you love that, so witty, such a piquant bit of stylishness. Oh, only a fashion, Mary, but I'm sure the gentlemen will love it!

SHELLEY grabs MARY and ties on the blindfold and SHELLEY and CLAIRE begin an at first childish and innocent 'blind man's buff' calling 'Mary!' in different voices, dodging under her arms, giggling. MARY spinning round, grasping, stumbles towards, stops at ELISE who has been standing silent at the edge of the feast, like a disengaged, contemptuous onlooker. MARY *feels all down* ELISE's *face and shoulders and breasts.*

MARY: Claire??

Then she feels the armful of frou frou petticoats and screams slightly. CLAIRE *and* SHELLEY *laughing aloud.*

CLAIRE: You're getting colder!

MARY (*spinning round*): Claire!

CLAIRE: Getting cold – er! That was only the maid, Mary, and she's not *in* our game!

MARY (*grasping*): Shelley! (*Desperate.*)

BYRON *limps in silently.* MARY *bumps into him and hugs him.*

MARY: Shelley! Oh free me –

BYRON *kisses her cheek lightly and unties her blindfold.*

BRYON: Easily! But it's only me, Mary . . .

MARY *looks confused, turns away.* CLAIRE *rushes up to him.*

CLAIRE: Byron! Where have you been. I was waiting! When my Albe says he will come over with the poem he wishes me to transpose and make a fair copy for him then I *do* expect him to come . . .

BYRON: But I didn't. Such a fine sail we had, eh, Shelley? We'll get you your sealegs yet, Shiloh! I was born with them. (*He limps arrogantly across the room.*) It's dry land I find difficult, except when I have strong drink taken and am half-seas-over. Well, ladies, how have you been whiling away the idle hours? Apart from rouging and titivating and bathing in asses' milk and waiting for your sailor boys to return?

CLAIRE *twirls around before him.*

CLAIRE: And don't we look pretty? Albe, don't you admire my necklace?

BYRON: Very diverting, yes. Not so

bonny as that gee-gaw you wear at your throat though, Mary. (*Touching it.*) And who is this?

CLAIRE: That's Mary's famous mama!

BYRON: The writer, eh? She was bonny, but not so bonny as you.

MARY: I do not resemble her, she –

BYRON: No, she was all russet – fire and earth. You're more water and air.

MARY *turns away twitchily.*

MARY: And where's Polidori? He doesn't join us this evening?

SHELLEY: Pollydolly says he won't come. I think he's jealous. Really, Albe, I think he's like a petted child sulking because he's lost his bosom companion. He wouldn't sail with us, Mary – I think he wanted us to wheedle and cajole, well I wouldn't! He's free to choose and I think he'd rather lose his friend than share him.

BYRON: He says he's busy writing. (*Laughing.*)

MARY: He has never refused to join us before . . .

SHELLEY: The wild eye, the pale brow, the fevered scratchings and scribblings! (*He laughs.*) A harsh mistress he's taken up with, the Muse, she'll lead him a merry dance, if she don't desert him like she has me these days and nights . . .

CLAIRE: Shall I go, Albe? I'll charm him into joining us. I'll tell him it won't be the same without him.

BYRON: Without his French volume of ghost stories more likely! Lord, but there are some stirring tales in that book of his – oh, after what you read aloud to us last night, Mary Godwin, all the long night through I slept scarce a wink. Yes, after our . . . little *soirée*, our cozy little *conversazzione* of the supernatural . . .

SHELLEY (*in a mock sepulchral voice*): Once upon a time there was Byron and

Mary, and Claire and Shelley. It was a dark and a moonless night and —

BYRON (*breaking in*): — All night long I was quite unmanned and unnerved by thoughts of a light pale little girl with silken hair and the strangest stories to tell. All I could see was Mary, Mary . . .

SHELLEY *is laughing,* MARY *is held in thrall but horrified,* CLAIRE *is pouting, jealous, but when she goes to try and flirt with* BYRON, *wind round him, is shrugged off.*

SHELLEY: See Mary, you are a witch, cast quite a spell on poor old Byron here!

CLAIRE (*pouting*): Albé . . .

BYRON *had never flinched from Mary.*

BRYON: Ask poor Pollydolly! I had to summon him in the middle of the night and he had to adminster me the strongest draught to make me . . . lie down and get me to sleep. (MARY *is released by* BYRON. *He turns to* SHELLEY.*) Poor* Pollydolly indeed, honestly, Shelley, I pick me as travelling companion a physician — hoping he can at once apply the pharmaceutical leeches *and* keep the human ones at bay — and what does he do but decide he should forsake his doctoring and take up competing with *me* at the scribbling. Ah, the Literary Life! And truly, Claire, I think he *is* a little jealous! Since I found myself such . . . congenial neighbours and stimulating companions I have had little time for Pollydolly. (*He kisses* CLAIRE *lightly, sarcastically.*) I fear we have begun to tire of one another. Oh, is it not the way of all human intimacy? — Even the best of marriages, you know yourself, Shelley, grows tedious to the combatants. And even the firmest friendships come unstuck . . .

SHELLEY (*quoting from his own poem, sincerely too*):
'True love *differs* from gold and clay
To divide is not to take away.'

BYRON: Pretty lines! Are they part perhaps of a new production? I thought the Muse had deserted you, Shiloh. Obviously she's furnishing your imagination with some fine fictions —

SHELLEY: Well, I have —

MARY: It's *true*! Because . . . because Shelley loves me it does not mean he must stop loving Harriet, I should be wrong to wish him to!

SHELLEY: I explained, I explained it all to Harriet very calmly. It was difficult to be calm — logical — because it was a time of such turmoil and pain — oh, for Mary and me too — all-hell, confusion, yet Harriet could not seem to credit that it pained anyone else but Harriet, Harriet, Harriet! Oh, she knows that my attachment to her is unimpaired, our connection was never one of passion and impulse —

BYRON: Like your connection with lovely Mary —

SHELLEY: Harriet *must* know how I desire to be permanently and truly useful to her — I think if she would only consent to meet with Mary she would become her friend, she would see what —

BYRON: Honestly, Shelley you do take the Bath Bun and the biscuit too! (*He laughs.*) I'm afraid you're not for this world, Shiloh! Love is all on account, debits, debits, precious few credits, and always less in the coffers than one thinks there is — a sudden running out and not a ha'p'worth left is the common way to the inevitable bankruptcy. The worst of Annabel's lies and slanders is I'll see her in Hell — if only she'd keep a virtuous silence she'd gain the Other Place, and eternity were not too long a time I'd never see her again! . . .

SHELLEY: There could not have been devised anything more hostile to human happiness than marriage.

BYRON: I'll drink to that — if the maid will hurry up and bring the decanter . . . (*He polishes off the last drop.*)

SHELLEY: And abolishing marriage would never lead to promiscuity — whatever those terrified prudes and Tories and superstitious churchmen might think.

BYRON (*bored, placating*): Of *course* it wouldn't . . . Are we going to dine soon, all that mountain climbing has given me such an appetite!

SHELLEY: All connections between men and women will be natural . . . and right — because choice and change will be possible — even desired by both!

BYRON: Lord, Shiloh, I'm not much of a one for such airy platonics. I am a simple man. Ladies, I am as ditchwater dull and tethered to the earth as clodhopper Caliban.

SHELLEY: — And you wallow in it! Oh yes, you are — at your brutish best — as happy as a pig in the proverbial . . . acorn wood, rooting and snouting out every pigmast tidbit. You'll gobble up the last little golden nugget!

SHELLEY *as if bored with being so serious himself rushes around making pig-noises, grunting and snuffling, he grabs* MARY *and nuzzles her neck. All laughing.*

BYRON: Shelley here, though, he's a different kettle of nightingales. Oh, we only have to look at him and we dissolve. He's all Light and Grace, is Shiloh! He's Ariel, a pure spirit moving through the changing air, fashioning liquid verse into new forms for freedom. How he will flame and amaze! And how about you Miranda-Mary? Won't you write up a revolution — like your papa, Mary — Godwin was ever one for writing up a storm of Brave New Worlds, wasn't he?

SHELLEY: *And* her mother.

BYRON: Oh yes, the lady she has hanging round her neck. The writer!

MARY: Yes, that 'Hyena in Petticoats' as all you male writers were pleased to call her.

BYRON: Would I have been so ungallant? I'm sure it was blustering Tories and outraged matrons who waxed vitriolic, and zoological. No, she was an excellent lady I believe although I never read —

MARY: — Then you should!

BYRON: Really? You think Mary Wollstonecraft could teach me something? How about you, Mary? I'm sure you could astonish me. Aren't you a writer too? Mary Godwin?

MARY: No, I don't want —

SHELLEY: Mary writes very well. Oh, you do, Mary. When you've a mind to. That novel you began, that promised —

BYRON: Novel?

MARY: I did not complete it, it was worthless.

SHELLEY: Now, how could one with a parentage like yours write anything worthless?

MARY: I don't want to be a writer.

BYRON: Never mind your parentage — oh illustrious to a man . . . and a woman . . . though I'm sure they were, but what of the *company* you're in? There's *Mad* Shelley and *Bad* Byron . . . and *Sad* Polidori next door scribbling away like a dervish and muttering 'Vampyre, Vampyre' — why, even Glad-eyed Claire is lusting somewhat over cuttlefish-ink and quill-pens, eh, Claire?

CLAIRE: Well, I am sure I cannot decide between the literary life and a theatrical career. Naturally I would want to avoid the disgusting drudgery of provincial theatres. *Naturellement!* Intolerable! I should wish to commence on the boards of the Metropolis. *Certainement!*

MARY *glares witheringly at her.*

Lord, if looks could kill . . .

BYRON: Laudable ambition, Mademoiselle Clairmont . . . However, let us stick to the Scribblitature for the present, eh? Listen, I'll set us a little contest. We shall all try our hand, shall we? Why should we content ourselves with translated, traditional horrors — all bookish and stilted. Home-grown ones are the best. Are they? Now that Pollydolly has deserted us, can we beat his last midnight confection? Who's going to write the most terrifying tale?

Black and up again on:

CLAIRE: Well, I for one, I have begun one!

BYRON: Of course you have. (*A mutter.*) It'd be too much to hope, would it, that of eighteen had nought but fertile imaginations . . .

CLAIRE: In fact I worked on it so late and long I made myself shudder. (*Giggles.*) Didn't I? Shelley?

BYRON: Yes, I'm sure you did. And how about you, Mary? Did you begin?

SHELLEY: Well, all I will say of mine — it's scarce begun to tell the truth — but I will say it is something about a dream!

BYRON: And how about you, Mary?

MARY (*shivering*): I don't think we should play with such dangerous elements.

SHELLEY: Dangerous? Ach, Mary, you sound as superstitious as a milkmaid on All Hallows Eve. There is no *darkness*, there are no forces of evil outside of us. The darkness is in men's minds, Mary. Once we let the light of reason sear through —

MARY: The sweet light of reason! Oh, Shelley, I do not want to write of horror, and fantasy, and sickly imaginings. My mother wrote *A Vindication of the Rights of Women.* And I am to pervert my imagination to writing foul fairy stories which do not have anything anchoring them to real life? —

SHELLEY: A diversion, Mary. Fun! You should try it. You seem to be in need of diversion at the moment.

MARY: And how can I write when William screams all day?

SHELLEY: Let the nursemaid . . .

MARY: He needs me. Every child needs his mother.

SHELLEY: Write a story, Mary. You know how good your fragments are. Try a story. Look out of the window. Think of our situation. Does it not inspire you? It does me.

MARY: And all you can do with this inspiration is . . . to raise the devil.

SHELLEY: Come here, I'll show you how to raise the devil. (*A whisper, a kiss.*)

MARY: Don't always try to kiss me when I'm trying to talk to you!

SHELLEY: And don't, please Mary, always talk at me when I try to reach out and kiss you. (*Pause.*)

BYRON *catches this and we see a flicker of satisfaction in him.*

BYRON: Trouble in Paradise! Well, dear friends, and shall we eat dinner soon, I'm ravenous. Where's the maid? She's forgotten to fill up the decanter. Elise! Elise!

Lord I am so hungry I could eat a Scotch Reviewer. Roasted. Couldn't you? Oh, I forgot, the Shelleys are Utopian vegetarians who won't gorge themselves on anything bloodier than an orange, eh?

ELISE *enters, is looked at voraciously by* BYRON, *handed the empty decanter imperiously, goes again.*

SHELLEY *sees* MARY *angry with him, outraged at* BYRON's

proprietorial attitude to her servants and tries to placate her, to change the subject.

SHELLEY: Ah Mary, I wish you would come with us. Come tomorrow. You would love it, to be at one with the wind and the water . . . Today we were right *inside* that storm, it was — can you imagine — it was like being one of the angels of rain and lightning.

MARY: I am afraid to sail.

SHELLEY: Nonsense, Mary, you want to . . . Remember back there in St Pancras Graveyard we used to blow bubbles and sail paper boats, and plan how we would sail . . .

BYRON: Graveyard? That does not sound the most romantic spot for a courtship, still —

CLAIRE: That was Mary's secret place. Her mother's grave. She would frighten me, tell me how her mother would come and haunt me. If I ate the last of the strawberries say, or crossed her in any way she would say she was going to ask her dead mama to put a spell on me. I never went there. (*Shudders.*)

MARY (*heartfelt*): There, I could be perfectly alone.

CLAIRE: Alone until you began to encourage Shelley to accompany you!

SHELLEY: And I needed little encouragement! (*Kisses* MARY.) You know, Byron, I was half in love with Mary before I even met her. I'd go to Godwin's house . . . how I worshipped Godwin, his politics, his reason! — Since my hellish harried schooldays he was my only hope for the future. I got a whipping once for reading Godwin! And now he was *my* friend, he'd invite me to his house —

CLAIRE: You used to bring Harriet!

SHELLEY: Sometimes . . .

CLAIRE *turns to* MARY.

CLAIRE: *You* were away in Scotland then. *My* mama found you unmanageable!

MARY: I was just fifteen! She sent me away!

SHELLEY: . . . and Godwin, all puffed up with pride at his clever Mary, would show me letters she'd sent, sketches, I knew you before we met, Mary! I could not wait to see the daughter of this excellent man I wished was my father!

CLAIRE: That would have made Mary your sister!

SHELLEY: Mary is my soul's sister, aren't you, Mary?

CLAIRE: If she was your *real* sister you could not —

BYRON (*laughing*): Not without being *the* storm in every teacup in Albion — and you may take that from the horse's mouth!

SHELLEY: And if she were my 'real sister' I could not love her any more, nor do I see any reason why — were she my 'real sister' — I should love her any *less*, or modify the least expression of my love. Where is any possible harm between those that truly love? Ladies, Wollstonecraft said: 'Make brothers and equals of your husbands and lovers'. Shelley says: 'Make husbands and lovers of your brothers and equals' — if you so desire. Let love know no limit!

BYRON: Bravo, Bravo, the Snake! Well, Shelley, you do truly have a trickier tongue than the serpent in Eden.

CLAIRE: Monsters.

BYRON: Pardon, Mademoiselle Clairmont, but I do not think that a *sequitur*, quite . . .?

CLAIRE: The reason sisters can't make love with brothers. Imbeciles. Monsters. The rotten fruit of incest — I remember listening all agog under the table one day and heard Cook tell nurse about a scullery maid whose own father . . . She brought out a babe with two heads, if Cook's to be believed!

SHELLEY: As if there were not an innocent, small and almost imperceptible precaution by which such consequences can be avoided.

MARY: But it does not always work!

SHELLEY: It's not quite foolproof, but Mary, I predict —

BYRON: 'If woman be a slave, can man be free?' You said it, Shiloh, in your poem, and here's a new slant to it: Ladies, *you* have to liberate yourselves from the enforced labour of the childbed, so that we men need no longer be the slaves of our unsatisfied lusts! Lovely! We'll have sweet young ladies of seventeen, Duke's daughters, walking down Mayfair to the milliners sporting their vinegar sponges on silk ribbons dangling from their waists, like the Libertines for Liberty the French Revolution spawned.

CLAIRE: Sponges! Vinegar . . . I do not see how such a thing can be *imperceptible* . . .

BYRON: Nor I, Claire — the only time I ever had a tart try it out on me it stung like the very clap, let's have none of it. Unnatural. *Godwin* would not approve of it, Mary.

MARY: He approves anything which will make men and women equal.

SHELLEY: Yes but not for his daughter! Godwin espouses Free Love for every maiden in England but not for his own Mary. When you and I eloped together it was, 'Oh my daughter! Oh my ducats!' — especially as he could no longer borrow, borrow, borrow from the Vile Seducer!

MARY: My father is not — he is not — he has not been able to live every best political ideal in his own life. But he wrote a great book. Just one, out of all his writings, but it is a great book!

SHELLEY: Oh yes a truly great work.

BYRON: Poor Mary — Mary. Wearing her mother round her neck and her father on her sleeve.

SHELLEY: Albe, I defy anyone to read that book and not be filled with the hope . . . no, the *certainty* that as sound politics diffuse through society — as they inevitably will — freedom and justice for both men and women then must be universal.

BYRON *laughs.*

BYRON: And do you think I have not read Godwin's Great Work, *Political Justice*! Well I have read it, when it was fashionable — long before you, Mary, were into schoolroom pinafores I had seen that silly book for the euphoric bombast it was.

ELISE *enters with the decanter.*

Elise, come help us, we need you to demonstrate. Elise, come here!

ELISE *curtseys.*

ELISE: Lord Byron?

BYRON: What do you do, Elise?

ELISE: Sir?

BYRON: For a livelihood, Elise. Who are you?

ELISE: Mrs Shelley's maid, sir.

BYRON: A maid?

ELISE: Yes, sir.

BYRON (*indicating* MARY): Well, Mademoiselle Maid, and who is this?

ELISE: Mrs Shelley, sir.

BYRON: No, indeed, it is not! This is — a great man. A . . . philosopher, let's say.

ELISE: Sir?

BYRON: No one reads him, of course. Can you read?

ELISE: Yes, sir.

BYRON (*amazed*): You can?

ELISE: I'm . . . learning, sir. A little each day. Mrs Shelley, she helps me when William is asleep, and Mr Shelley, sir.

BYRON: He does?

ELISE: In the afternoons, sir. *Quelque – fois . . .*

BYRON: A maid who can read!

ELISE: And write, sir. Mrs Shelley help me to form my letters . . .

BYRON: Perhaps we shall have dogs on two legs next, entering the House of Lords, and pissing on its portals, perhaps.

SHELLEY: Better than the wolves and vipers and crocodiles that we have to contend with currently!

BYRON (*clapping hands*): We digress! Elise, who is this?

ELISE: A . . . philosopher, sir.

BYRON: And who are you?

ELISE: A maid.

BYRON: His maid.

ELISE (*very uncomfortably*): Yes, sir.

BYRON: And now I have to decide which one of you to save.

MARY: Byron, this is an abuse – Elise, don't be alarmed, this is but a game of our neighbour's, he –

BYRON: Wishes to demonstrate a philosophical argument of Godwin's. And do you know who Godwin is, Elise?

ELISE: He is Mrs Shelley's father, sir.

BYRON: Indeed. Mary Godwin's famous father. And now we shall examine his concept of justice, ladies, gentleman! You are both in a burning building and I have to decide which of you to save. Can't you feel the flames catch at your petticoats, lick at your ankles? (ELISE *looks down, is silent, angry, impotent.*) Can't you feel the thick smoke choke you? Elise, can't you. Answer me, girl!

ELISE: Yes, sir.

BYRON: Now I am concerned with justice. Godwin's justice. There is an old maxim, everyone's heard of it although only you, Claire Clairmont, seem inclined to put it into practice around here: that we should love our neighbour as ourselves.

CLAIRE (*going to his side*): Albe!

BYRON: Stand back! I'm on the track of justice. You, philosopher, and you, chambermaid, are presumably of equal worth, you are both of you *men*, are you not? No, let me rephrase that. (*Laughing.*) You are both of you human beings, are you not? And entitled to equal attention . . . in the natural world at any rate. As a general principle? Yes? No? And yet Godwin says I must save –

MARY: Well, I understand why my father advocated the saving of –

BYRON: *You!*

MARY: Yes. There is the consideration that the common good of all mankind for all time will benefit from my work. So save me.

SHELLEY: Bravo, Mary!

BYRON: Ah, but suppose this mere maid were my wife? Or my mother? Yes, or my sister? Certainly I should want to save my beloved sister before some old philosopher.

MARY: *My* wife, *my* sister, *my* mother! What is so magical about the pronoun *my. My* sister may be a fool . . . or a harlot . . . If she be, then what worth is she lent by the fact she is *my* sister?

BYRON: Where's your heart, Mary? Hear that, Elise. Are you listening, Claire, she'd consign her own sister to the flames. But I don't know I believe her. I think it's Godwin's daughter wishing to convince us – and her papa – that she has her *head* in the right place!

MARY: I believe what I say. And . . . more. Suppose I were myself Fenelon's maid I should *choose* to die rather than him.

BYRON: Ah, so you won't grant life to the maid. Elise, tell me who are you going to save. Yourself, or Mister Philosopher?

ELISE: I . . . I shouldn't like to say, sir.

BYRON: Come, Elise, you are among *friends*, you can tell us what you think.

ELISE: What would you like me to say, sir?

BYRON: Tell us the truth. Who would you save?

ELISE: I should save myself, sir.

BYRON *bursts out laughing.*

BYRON: Thank you, Elise, that was what I wished to hear, you're a good girl Elise . . . and a bonny one . . .

ELISE: May I go, madame?

MARY: Yes, Elise.

ELISE: Madame, I did not mean . . . I hope I did not say the wrong thing, madame?

MARY: You are a good girl, Elise.

ELISE: Thank you, madame. (ELISE *goes.*)

MARY: It was wicked of us to use her so.

BYRON: Why? She is but a maid. You have bought her time, and her attention, so —

MARY: But I have not bought the right to abuse her. I ought to act towards all creatures with benevolence.

BYRON: Benevolence by all means, Mrs Shelley. Nicety costs nothing. But recognise that where you are pay-master, benevolence is yours to bestow . . . or to take away.

SHELLEY: Peddling in human flesh . . . a vile and a universal thing. To be born poor may be translated: to be born a slave. Byron, consider the lot of the poor working people. In the new hells of our cities, the mechanic himself becomes a sort of machine. His limbs and articulations are converted into wood and wires . . . Surely they must rise up —

MARY: But Elise is not my puppet. It is my duty to educate her, enlighten her.

BYRON: So she can see the justice of her giving up her life for you! No she is *not* your puppet, Mary. Thank God we may own the body but, although we stuff the head with Latin, Algebra *and* platonics, we cannot own the heart. (*Pause.*) Nevertheless, if I am honest, and I think I am, I must admit that possession of the odd body does all but suffice. For me. But then I am no Godwinite, I won't tyranise the world by force-feeding it freedom.

CLAIRE: Albé, *qu'est-ce que c'est?* You are not yourself tonight. I don't like these games, I wish Pollydolly was here.

BYRON: Well, he's not. So we have to otherwise divert ourselves. If Pollydolly's deserted us, and deprived us of his deliciously depraved volume of ghostly stories, his . . .?

MARY: Fantasmagoriana.

BYRON (*slowly*): Fantasmagoriana. Well, if we're to do without it tonight — have none of the lovely Mary reading aloud to us — what was that climax last night Mary? . . . 'And when the moon . . . what? . . . And by that . . .'

MARY: . . . 'Blue and baleful light' . . .

BYRON: . . . 'he saw that in his arms he clasped but the pale, pale ghost of her he had deserted.' Oh Shelley, does she not make your flesh to creep and your gorge to rise? Oh, I know she does mine! (*Pause.*) Ah, Mary, but can you make your own story?

MARY: I don't want to.

BYRON: Can you win the wager? I think perhaps you can. Who knows, you may find the damps and darks surprisingly agreeable. I sense you have a talent for it. Am I not right, Shelley, doesn't she? I sense it. I smell it.

A tense pause, broken by –

CLAIRE: Albé, shall I go fetch mine? Shelley said I had made a thrilling start.

BYRON: Yes, yes, Claire. Later. (*Pause.*) Well, Shelley, can you come down from those airy and evanescent clouds long enough to terrify us among the dark and rat-infested dungeons of the human soul?

SHELLEY (*pleasantly, refusing to be goaded*): I hope so. As I said, mine is something about a dream, and, although a tale of horror, somewhat allegorical –

BYRON: Yes, I'm *sure* it is.

SHELLEY: I don't mind admitting that it is a little influenced by Coleridge, but my tale is more . . .

BYRON: . . . Allegorical. Yes. Worse people though to be 'a little influenced by' than Coleridge. (*Quoting flamboyantly.*)

'Blue, glossy green and velvet black. They coiled and swam; and every track Was flash of golden fire!'

SHELLEY (*laughing, continuing*): Oh happy living things! No tongue Their beauty might declare; A spring of love gushed from my heart And I blessed them unaware!

Byron, do not admit that at last we have found a great poet we agree on! (*They embrace companionably.*) I knew our tastes were not so dissimilar. We approach the same shimmering point always and I think you exaggerate how different are the routes we take.

BYRON: Not *very* different were the routes we took these last few days, Shiloh – that was a long climb we had of it, up mountain and glacier after the source of the Arve, no wonder Polidori has had to lard our arches with linament – ladies I am sure we reek like racehorses!

SHELLEY: Oh Mary, you should have been there. Mont Blanc – perfect pinnacles glistening – utterly inhuman . . . and we stood today in that awful ravine where naked power, dressed as a river, pours icy out of the rock and down . . .

BYRON: Mary, your lover is a little mystical for me. Two worlds, he says! He sees *through* things – watch out, Claire, for the Man With the Marvellous Eyes! (*He shields his own eyes with imaginary X-ray binoculars and CLAIRE runs and shrieks as if her dress were suddenly transparent, hiding breasts and sex, laughing.*) He can see through your dress, and your petticoat, and your chemise and –

SHELLEY: Byron, today you accused me of . . . dissolving things . . . in my writing . . . and I know it is a danger – sometimes – Mary takes many a lyric to task –

MARY: – Not often, Shelley! –

SHELLEY: 'Vague shapes!' Oh you *do*, Mary, and I'm glad of it – but Albé, I don't want to melt away what's real –

MARY: Yes, you *do* – to reform – to *trans*form!

SHELLEY: But I want to describe what's clearly there – the invisible, palpable, currents and pulses of the air – oh I can see wires and bonds between us four that are finespun as filigree and structured as a spider web, and stronger than blood, or Manchester iron – or those bee-line cables of delicate smells that chain-haul the insect to the nectar.

BYRON: Gossamer, blood, pig-iron and stink – four very very different things.

SHELLEY: Wrong! The same. The same secret strength of things flows through them all, which governs thought and tides and love and planets in their courses.

BYRON: An architect of air! An engineer of the atmosphere! Perhaps Coleridge would've approved — while he still had a mind to yeah or nay anything, before he utterly addled it with opium. He did have his moments though, Coleridge — at least he's not so tedious as Watery Willy.

SHELLEY: God, but Wordsworth is boring! I told you Byron, our tastes agree!

CLAIRE: Albé, Coleridge used to come to Skinner Street to dine with us! Mama Godwin could not *bear* him.

MARY: Nor he her!

CLAIRE: Such a ragbag, so ill put together, his neckchief awry, and long a stranger to soap and water, and his great-coat all powderstains . . . buttoned up wrong!

MARY: He read us the Ancient Mariner. From the manuscript. While he still worked on it.

CLAIRE: We often had such guests. Albé you would have enjoyed our company then, such intellects!

MARY: Followers of my Mama would come, and Papa would have me parrot great passages of her writings off by heart . . . (*Laughing*.)

CLAIRE: And followers of your father!

MARY: For them I'd recite even *longer* passages from my Mama's works. (*To* CLAIRE.) If *your* Mama's bland puddings and termagant tongue did not drive them off then my quotings did!

BYRON: Well, I don't know that I'd have given a fig for the philosophy . . . but I should have given an arm and a leg — the sound one — to have heard Coleridge — you mean he'd come to take tea and stay to spout poetry? Perhaps I'd have been afeared of his glittering eye!

CLAIRE: Oh no, it was *so* exciting, Albé.

MARY: *Your* mother insisted we were to get to our beds. (*Deepens voice.*) 'Like one who on a lonely road Doth walk in fear and dread.'

CLAIRE: 'I'm sure, Mr Coleridge, the girls are much enjoying the pretty rhymes, say *thank* you, young ladies! . . .'

MARY: 'Doth walk in fear and dread . . .'

CLAIRE: 'Young ladies, it is very late. Mr Coleridge, I must insist!'

MARY: (*sucked into her own fear*): '. . . doth walk in fear and dread And, having once turned round, walks on And turns no more his head Because he knows a fearful fiend Doth close behind him tread.'

SHELLEY (*alarmed*): Mary! (*Goes to her.*)

CLAIRE (*laughing*): 'I must absolutely insist my daughters get their beauty sleep!' Silly Mama! — Oh, but we hid ourselves behind the sofa and made sure we heard him out!

MARY:
'. . . Nor shapes of men, not beasts we ken —
The ice was all between.
The ice was here, the ice was there,
The ice was all around;
It cracked and growled, and roared and howled . . .'

BYRON: '. . . Like noises in a swound!'

CLAIRE: Albé! Mary! Albé, don't encourage her. She's trying to scare me!

MARY: 'Is that a Death? And are there two? Is Death that woman's mate?'

CLAIRE: Mary! Mary, stop it. I swear you do make me shudder sometimes. I felt — Albé, what do they say? — a goose walk over my grave. (*Shakes her.*)

SHELLEY: Mary!

CLAIRE: She's frightening me! Mary! Don't, Mary! (*Begins panic-breathing.*) Shelley! Stop her ...

MARY:
'Her lips were red, her looks were free,
Her locks were yellow as gold;
Her skin was as white as leprosy,
The Nightmare Life In Death was she,
Who thicks man's blood with cold.'

SHELLEY *has fit of hysterics and hallucination, screams.*

SHELLEY: Mary, stop. Don't look at me so. Mary! You're naked, Mary ... cover yourself ... your breasts! Eyes, Mary, you have eyes for nipples. Don't stare at me. Piercing. The eyes in your breasts are staring me down, piercing me to the very soul ...

SHELLEY *rushes from room,* CLAIRE *in pursuit following him, calling him.*

BYRON: The Lamia! Eyes in breasts, like a vision from Coleridge's Christabel! He reads too much.

MARY: Shelley! (*Goes to follow.*)

BYRON: No, Mary, let Claire. You are not the right person. You are the subject of his ... Waking Nightmare.

MARY: I must go to him.

BYRON: No.

MARY: He's ... too much brandy. I'm sure I —

BYRON: Too much imagination. Let Claire see to him. (*Forbids her movement with a look.*) Claire will calm him. You have quite an effect on us poor men, Mary. Too much ... imagination. You know last night I slept very badly. I lay myself down on my solitary bed — solitary because I had expressly forbidden Claire to follow me — not that forbidding Claire is guarantee of aught else than redoubled pursuit — and oh I tossed and turned, tossed and turned ...

MARY: I must go to my husband.

BYRON: Ah! I thought — strange, but I thought poor Shiloh had a wife already, I thought he and I were at least bound in brotherhood by such sore trouble and strife, by similar debts and divorcements. (MARY *stands, tries to break.*) Mary, Mary, don't scuttle off like a man-handled maid-servant! Don't spurn my company. The Lord knows I have had enough of ostracism in England. (*Mock wounded.*) Well. Well, I should have honestly thought it impossible to scandalise Shelley the Antichrist's lady. The Queen of the Ménage à Trois!

MARY *holds the slap of this remark and turns angry rather than victim.*

MARY: Claire is not, and never has been, my Shelley's mistress!

BYRON: Mary, I did not mean to suggest she was! The Lord forbid! I would not wish that Albatross on poor dear Shiloh! No, all I meant ... was not What's His Name your dear friend, Mary, oh and Shelley's closest friend, his dearest ... were not you and he ...

MARY: Hogg was a brother to me.

BYRON: Ah *fraternal* love! I have heard of such things. (*Self-mocking.*)

MARY: Shelley would never tell you such a ...?

BYRON: Hush, hush, no of course not! (*Pause.*) Claire did, didn't she — now it was not unkindly meant, oh, don't break my confidence to you and chide her ... It was in an unguarded, not to say an unclothed moment —

MARY: You cannot know how cruel you are! He was Shelley's friend. Shelley and I do not believe in — I wanted to show Shelley I felt as he did about freedom —

BYRON: Goodness, Mary. Lord above, what's to get in such a tush about? If you loved Hogg, what's to shock? Surely it was nothing but the Revolutionaries declaring Independence from the Laws the rest

of us humble mortals have to live by —
or some of us frolic to claunt! Surely
it was merely the embracing of your
own Published Principles, Mary
Godwin.

MARY: How could a libertine like you
understand, how could you even
conceive of . . . A Noble Experiment
like that . . . if it had worked would
have . . . it *was* a *noble* experiment.

BYRON: The dissection of the affections!
Profane tinkering! The analytical
anatomical dismantling of the human
heart!

MARY: We wanted . . . a new way to live.
Can't you understand that?

BYRON: Oh yes . . . intellectually I can
conceive of it, Mrs Shelley. But there
is something . . . hideously unnatural
in such a cold-blooded put-together
passion, is there not? I cannot believe
it can have been a very pretty thing in
practice. And I'm all for practice . . .
(*Pause.*) making perfect.

Did not sheer imagination, if not that
infamous, excellent, inherited
intellect, tell you the obvious? That
just a little finger on a hair trigger
could set the whole machine a-tick —
and it would be a little . . .
unreasonable to expect it all to die
down again.

MARY: A new way to live. We had to
try . . .

BYRON: Mary, Mary, I'm a simple soul
at heart! None of your rational splits
between the heart and the head for
me. None of your cold-blooded
laboratories of Sexual Relations, just
the head and the heart, body and soul.

MARY: — You have no soul!

BYRON: The healthy mind in the
healthy body! (*Limps flamboyantly
across stage, full of self-hatred and
pride.*) But I *do* have a soul, Mary. A
blackened burned-out cinder of a soul
perhaps — may it rot in hell. And it
has done, it has done. Don't say

you've swallowed Shelley's fallacy of
Freethinking. So you're free to agree
with your Atheist, allowed to assent
to uniting yourself with your
Dissenting angel. But *I*, Mary, am, like
all blasphemers, a True Believer! A
libertine who breaks the code, but is
good and glad it exists to rupture. The
Lord knows, were it not for legitimate
married love there would be not a
convention worth outraging!

MARY: You are a heartless seducer!

BYRON: Not heartless, just . . . faint-
hearted sometimes. Where it could
really . . . make a difference. (*Intense
on* MARY, *then breaks it and
throwaway.*) Oh, I do tumble the
occasional dollymop, that I do freely
admit, do the odd bit of hobnobbing
below stairs, and below the greasy
petticoats of scrubbing scullery-
wenches — I'm not snobbish! But it's
all just to kill time, Mary. No Mary, it
is not that I am half-hearted in my
love affairs. Just that recently — well
you know all about *that*, all England
knows all about that — recently I
have been rather half-witted about
who I choose, but do we ever really
choose, who we truly love?

MARY: Your sister . . .?

BYRON: *Half* sister Mrs Shelley! But,
yes, *I love my sister Augusta.* Too
much to subject that love to the
warpings of platonics. Frustrated love
perverts, produces monsters!
(*Suddenly angry.*) But as for you,
Mary and Shelley and Hogg and Claire
with your frigged up intellectual
notions of passions!

Oh, it is not love which is dead in my
heart, Mary, but hope. (*Pause.*)

Like all highly coloured comedians I
do take a dim view of the World!

MARY: And that is your real sin, Lord
Byron. (*Pause.*) You do . . . give up . . .
too easily. (*Meaning with her. Pause.
She is not taken up on this almost-
offer, so withdraws it by going*

suddenly brisk.) Pessimism! It is unforgiveable! How can you, in a century which has given us Arkwright . . . and Owen . . . and Watt.

MARY:
BYRON: The French Revolution!

BYRON: And the Terror, the heads bouncing into baskets, the Jacobins, the Girondins, the Sans Culottes – that means No Drawers, Mary – the Wild-Eyed Women, the Men rouged like strumpets, flaunting their rosettes, the Ruin, the Rot, the Reaction! Did not Sweet Shelley's Second Honeymoon straddle the charred and blackened corpse of La Belle France? Or didn't he notice? Didn't you, Mary-Mary?

MARY (*shuddering*): That village . . . where the Cossacks . . . nothing but roofless houses and blackened spars and charred stubble . . . people with bones sticking through their flesh . . . marauding bands . . . rags of army . . . the rats . . .

(*Pulling herself together.*) Our eyes were wide open! My Shelley is no sleepwalking dreamer. He does understand the World and Exactly How it Works very well. Very well indeed. He was the first, the only one of his generation quickly to see through Napoleon – and still he does not give up hope! (*Pause.*) My mother, did you know she travelled to France during the Revolution, she lived in Paris all during –

BYRON: That Blood Bath!

MARY: Yes and *she did not despair.*

BYRON *laughs bitterly.*

BYRON: Mary Wolstonecraft's Cookbook. 'You cannot make an omelette without cracking a few skulls!' Percy Bysshe Shelley's Dreambook. 'It's getting a little better all the time.' (*Laughs.*)

MARY: And should Shelley not indulge in Dreams and Aspirations? Cannot a poet be also . . . a teacher of the intellect and moral nature as well as merely of the senses and the imagination?

BYRON: *Merely* the senses and the imagination. There is nothing else *but* the senses and the imagination. All else is Humbug and Bubbles, Mrs Shelley! You know in the cool clarity of your heart-of-hearts you are *not* the over-optimistic sort. You are not the child who ran away with Percy Shelley! Mary, you are getting good and sick, I know it, of Ariel's head-in-the-clouds hopefulness. Come on, come down to earth, where you belong, come and curl up with old Clubfooted Caliban! (MARY *and* BYRON *hold for a long moment. Break as* MARY *turns away. He flicks her mother's pendant.*) Write that story! And, let me tell you it won't be made of nebulous ideas, pretty philosophies, or pointless, pointless politics! Everything I write is a creature who can only live by what he sees, hears, smells, tastes, touches and grabs, Mrs Shelley! And rather than starved and skinny living on air I'd have him rich and fat with facts, facts, facts. (*Pause.*)

And any plain fact looked at without flinching is funny! At any rate One Has to Laugh! Or doesn't this one? Don't you, Mary, I look at you, Mary, and I see someone who is holding it all within. A lovely lady, who yet suppresses every gust, every gale, every giggle. Don't sit on your wit just to please Shelley.

MARY: 'Like a sword without a scabbard it wounds the wearer . . .' What good does wit do a woman? Wit in a woman is always sour.

BYRON (*full of open sexual threat*): So then is my sour wit womanish? I think *Not*, Mary. (*Whispers.*) I'll prove it to you . . . (*Suddenly brisk as* CLAIRE *enters.*) We'll have Claire here sign me an affidavit!

MARY *spins around shocked to gawp at* CLAIRE.

Claire, come here! (*She does.* BYRON *kisses her full and lewdly on the lips.*) Lord, Lord I think I have found me Polidori's Vampyre! (*Confidentially.*) You know, Claire, Mary's virtue is much affronted that there is so much . . . to-ing and fro-ing between your villa and mine. She does not like to be too near the foul stye or the hot breath of the Two-Backed Beast!

CLAIRE: Albé, Albé, do not tease Mary so! Now you know I told you she is the best and the sweetest of sisters, but so, so serious! You know you are *diabolique* to say such betises! (*Giggles.*) Mary does not realise you are joking. Mary, Shelley is calm now, he's sleeping, sleeping like a baby. Polidori gave him a draught — I went and fetched him, told him Shelley had had a fit, he said he is sure it is not serious. Something he will sleep off. Everything will be better in the morning. Go and sleep, Mary. It will all be right in the morning.

Black music. A wind gets up, then a thunderstorm. In its lurid light we see, near the original area of MARY's *old circle of candelight, her lying by* SHELLEY's *side asleep. He is flat out covered in the sheet. What we see of his head is turned away.* MARY *begins to struggle as in a nightmare.*

MARY: No! No! I can't . . . you're stifling me! Can't breathe, can't. No! (*Wakes up, sits up terrified.*) No! Shelley! (*Shakes at him gently. He does not stir. Gets out of bed, still panting.*) I saw him! The pale student of unhallowed arts kneeling beside the thing he had put together. I saw the hideous, hideous phantasm of a man stretched out, and then with a jolt from some powerful engine stir with an uneasy half movement then snap up rigid and live. Was it a dream? Why won't it fade? I cannot shrug it off. Oh, how such success would terrify the artist; he would rush away from his handiwork, horror-stricken. He would begin to hope that, left to itself, this slight . . . spark of life would fade . . . this thing would . . . He sleeps. But he is awakened. He opens his eyes. Behold, it stands by his bedside looking down at him with yellow, watery but hungry eyes.

Hallelujah! I have found it. What terrifies me will terrify others. I need simply describe what haunted my midnight pillow.

I have thought of a story! (*Sits down and begins to write.*) It was on a dreary night in November . . .

Black.

ACT TWO

Scene One

MARY *alone in the ghostly nursery. She is sadly toying with a doll, of a curiosity sort. It is a doll like MARY herself, clothed in her costume with hair in the colour and style of the actress who has the 'MARY' role. Under the skirt of the doll (although we do not know it yet) is actually not the lower half of a body but another top half, that of a doll with the head, hairstyle and costume of the actress who is to play ELISE. The skirt of this doll turns inside out and on the underside is doll-ELISE's skirt, which will cover doll-MARY's head.*

Just now, MARY has her own doll-image in her hand, right side up. She also has a copy of Frankenstein.

MARY: Frankenstein, by Mrs Shelley ... Once upon a time Mary Shelley had a dream and wrote a book. (*Pause. She puts the doll down, opens the book.*)

'Once upon a time there was a man called Walton. And this Captain Walton had a dream. That he should set off on a marvellous voyage of discovery, beyond the Pole, beyond the most extreme where he would discover not frost and desolation, but their banishment.

'A new and temperate region of wonder where men and women might live.

'So this Robert Walton, he furnished himself a fine ship and named it bravely, "The Endeavour".

MARY *sets the rocking-horse off and it bucks like a ship on high seas.*

'And he set sail in wild seas, northwards. "Read your own story", he said and now he is dead.

Pause until the rocking-horse stops. MARY *looks down at the book, reading:*

'And soon "The Endeavour" was icebound, clasped fat in the frigid grip of a hell of groans and groundseas. Stopped.'

Lights change.

Scene Two

CLAIRE, *unlaced, early morning, dishevelled.*

CLAIRE: Mary! Mary, there is a letter here from Byron, a package, he has written to me at last!

MARY: Claire ...

CLAIRE *rips open package, empty but for a single dark curl.*

CLAIRE: The lock of hair I begged from him, of little Allegra's, but there is not a single word of her, why doesn't he tell me she's well? Surely she — my baby, I should not have let her go to him!

MARY: Allegra is fine, Claire. Everything is well, he wrote Shelley this morning, I asked him not to wake you. You were sleeping, Claire, I crept in, and I knew what disturbed nights you've been having lately so I begged Shelley let you sleep, while you could.

CLAIRE: Let me see the letter!

MARY: Shelley has it with him, he'll be back soon, he'll ... read you the parts that refer to Allegra. She runs everywhere these days, apparently. And prattles in English and Italian equally never confusing one for the other, and has twelve teeth and —

CLAIRE: What does he say about me?

MARY: Nothing, Claire — I am sure he wishes you no harm ...

CLAIRE: He won't see me!

MARY: He ... I'm sure we can prevail on him to send Allegra back with a nursemaid to visit or perhaps some disinterested third party may look after her for a spell, and you could go there — the Hoppner's say —

CLAIRE: Surely he'll adore her. Mary,

won't he? Albé will be a good father to my little girl?

MARY (*gently*): I'm sure he will be a good father.

CLAIRE: A child needs her father, no? I am sure I did the right thing, Mary. Allegra is the image of me, didn't you say so yourself. She looks like me, yes, and like Albé too, I know he will adore her. If only he would agree to see me! If only I could be as merry, and as slender, as that first bright summer in Switzerland, I really think he may love me again, yes?

MARY: Claire . . . (*Pity, anguish, irritation, equal measure.*)

ELISE *comes in with something. CLAIRE is fidgeting with her dress.*

CLAIRE: Lace me nice and small, Elise. Of course it fits me!

Little flashback now and MARY is back in Switzerland at the mirror scene in Act One – (so there should be a definite sound cue or lighting cue which is like the sound or lighting cue for the flashback within the mirror scene in Act One) – CLAIRE's voice should be light and gay when she next speaks, as opposed to frantic in her last speech which has triggered MARY's mind back.

. . . Nice and small, Elise, make me beautiful! (*Tinkling.*) . . . Haven't we always shared everything? . . . Perhaps it has happened already. Peut-être. There is no stronger a bond between a man and a woman than the making of a child.

MARY *snapping back from then by sheer will. ELISE has already retreated to her menacing shadow presence again.*

MARY: No! That time is long over. It's past. (*Very much believing she's being cruel to be kind.*) Claire, it is already three summers ago we were all in Switzerland together. Allegra is two years old. When she was born, when

you were back in England, alone, with us, he did not so much as write to you; just, by attorney, he let it be known he's made some financial arrangements. And now we are back in Italy he allows that Allegra can come to him and he and *his mistress* shall care for her. 'The Countess is very fond of children,' he writes to Shelley. (*With pity.*) Claire, how can you possibly hope after all this time – how could you wish it!

CLAIRE: You cannot begin to understand how I feel. A mother separated from her child! You have not suffered a moment's separation from *your* children.

MARY: My little baby died . . . my first little –

CLAIRE: Before the year was out you had William, and now little Clara and she flourishes fat and bonny! (*Genuinely upset.*) You cannot know how I miss my Allegra!

MARY: Oh Claire, there was so much talk! Allegra needs –

CLAIRE: Shelley understands how I feel. He knows what it is to lose his children.

MARY: Had you not been adding to our scandal with your little bastard brat, then that Judge should never have found in favour of Harriet's father!

CLAIRE: You were glad when Harriet drowned herself . . .

MARY: How can you say that?

CLAIRE: Glad, glad, glad! 'Mrs Harriet Shelley, a respectable woman far advanced in pregnancy has been taken from the Serpentine River having been missed at her lodgings for nearly six weeks . . . She had a valuable ring on her finger . . .'

MARY: Claire, if Shelley should hear you now – he suffered such – to read it like that, cold in The Times, poor Shelley . . .

CLAIRE: And *you* could be married! Mary could be Mrs Shelley. A respectable woman! And dine at her Daddy's again — Godwin — who cares so very very little for the way the vulgar world judges such things — is pleased as *punch* at 'My daughter the Baronet's son's wife'. Oh not, *not* because Mr Shelley can borrow against his inheritance and balance the books for a publisher whose pamphlets are ever too true to be popular!

MARY: The only reason I wanted to be married was so we could gain custody of the children. Harriet's father was determined Shelley should be deprived of his own children.

CLAIRE: And he won.

MARY: Only because of you. There you were, swollen and scandalous, spoiling everything.

CLAIRE: And if the Judge had granted you the children wouldn't *that* have spoiled everything? If I remember aright, Mary dried up her milk working, working, working at her famous story. She had no time for her own William, far less she'd let dead Harriet plant two more little cuckoos in the nest . . . Doesn't she haunt you, Mary?

Involuntarily MARY *looks round and catches her breath at the dim shape of* ELISE.

You'd have been as jealous of Charles and Ianthe as you are of my Allegra. (*She bursts into tears.*)

MARY: Why should I be jealous of Allegra? (*Pause.*) Claire, Claire, of course you miss her. Claire . . . you let her go so she should have all the advantages her father can give her. Of course he will love her, who could but love such a creature . . . Claire, you have no money, no fortune, you did a good and a brave thing, Claire —

CLAIRE: Shelley will come with me. He understands so he will come with me.

He promised me. He said if Byron refused to let me come and be with my own child he would travel with me and prevail upon his finer feelings and take me to see the child I gave birth to.

Shelley promised me we will go.

Black

Scene Three

MARY *alone again continuing telling herself her own story in the ghostly nursery. At first she's muttering some* 'Ancient Mariner'.

MARY:
'The ice was here, the ice was there
The ice was all around
It cracked and growled, and roared and howled
Like noises in a swound.' (*She picks up the book, the* 'Frankenstein' *and quotes from it.*) 'About two o'clock the mist cleared away and we beheld stretched out in every direction vast and irregular plains of ice which seemed to have no end.'

Then suddenly 'Look!' — a low carriage . . . fixed on a sledge, and drawn by dogs, half a mile away, going North. On it a being which had the shape of a man but of gigantic stature, a colossus!

Coming after this creature was another of more normal aspect but . . . strange still. And he whipped his ailing dogs in a frenzy till the leader burst his heart and great gobbets of blood spattered the snow. Weeping, the man slumped beside the exhausted yelping creatures.

So Captain Walton's mariners fetched him to the ship, they dried him, rubbed his limbs, gave him brandy, revived him and soon Captain Walton was alone with a stranger who sat up and began this tale:
He said, 'My name is Victor Frankenstein and I had a dream.' (*Pause.*)

And Frankenstein told Walton of his secret art, his passion, out of which he made a new kind of creature in a new way. And he gave him life. And he lived. And Frankenstein saw that it was not good. And in horror he recoiled from his own creation. When he saw what a maimed and twisted thing was this life he had made, he ran away.

But the creature went out into the world. A child called William was killed. And a maid was unjustly accused.

Scene Four

MARY *begins sadly to put toys away in a trunk, with the heaviness and calmness of grief; we see something awful has happened.* ELISE *enters, is moved by pity.*

ELISE: Madame, let me help you.

MARY (*icy*): No, thank you, Elise. I shall manage. (*Completes task. Pause.*) I meant exactly what I said.

ELISE: Yes, Madame.

MARY: You have till tomorrow morning to pack up your belongings.

ELISE: Won't take me that long, Madame! (*Changing again as she sees* MARY *with an agonisingly familiar little toy of William's — perhaps a little wooden puppet that when you pull the string its arms and legs fly up.*) Mrs Shelley, Madame, it is not good for you to do such a sad task alone. Let me —

MARY: I don't need your help, Elise.

ELISE: I'm grieving, too, for him. I have been with you since he was six months old, I loved your little Willmouse . . . Mr Shelley, he weeps in one room and you here all alone in another, it is not good to be alone with such dark thoughts, you should go to him.

MARY: That is quite enough! How dare you be so familiar. You!

ELISE: I think he did not suffer. At the end it was easier for him, Madame, the fever eased and he seemed to be released. —

MARY: I want you to be gone by tomorrow morning. I cannot bear to look at your face. When I look at your face I see the face of my little daughter with the spasms and convulsions racking her as if death had picked her up and shook her like a dog with a rat. I see the face of that physician you fetched bending over that huddled little bundle on the Fusina ferry. I see the great red ham face of that customs man making his endless endless delays with the passports, I see the white faces of Shelley and Claire when I got there and told them 'my baby is dead'. My baby is dead . . .

ELISE: She had only the slightest temperature when we set out, we thought she was only teething, there did not seem to be any reason not to travel, the doctor said we should not blame —

MARY: I look at your face and I see my little William! I see you bending over him and smoothing him with death's hands. I see you the other side of the bed from me helping me hold the blankets on while he twists and twists a hangman's rope of the sheets and his golden curls are glued to his forehead with sweat and I see in your face that he is going to die. And that moment killed him as surely as your fingers were round his throat. Because when I, his own mother, gave up hope, then my child was dead already.

ELISE: I told you . . .

MARY: Be quiet.

ELISE: I told you, I have done all the packing, but —

MARY: Go away, Elise, be quiet!

The sound/lighting cue which has become our convention for timechange/flashback.

ELISE: Madame, I have done all the packing as you asked and Paolo will bring the coach round first thing in the morning . . . but I really think the baby is not well enough to travel.

MARY: Nonsense, she is teething, that's all . . . a little fretful. I must go and join my husband, Elise. And my sister, they say the villa Byron has lent so Miss Clairmont can spend time with her daughter is a very pretty pleasant place.

ELISE: But, Madame!

MARY: They need me! I'll be the one to decide.

ELISE: Yes, Madame. Only . . . I think she has quite a fever. Both she and William are running a temperature. I think you ought to come and look at the children.

Flashback over, we go back to present time.

MARY: You are a wicked girl.

ELISE: Why, what have I done?

MARY: You must marry at once, we cannot afford any more gossip, I cannot bear it. You are dismissed from service in this family.

ELISE: I think you are a cruel and a heartless woman, Madame.

MARY: How dare you speak to me —

ELISE: Easily! Now that to tell the truth costs me nothing.

MARY: Elise!

ELISE: Yes, Madame. And irresponsible. And a hypocrite too.

MARY: That is enough. Go. Both of you. Paolo is waiting. You will thank me some day.

ELISE: Thank you? For what?

MARY: A child needs a father, Elise, how can you, a servant girl of no fortune, manage to support a —

ELISE: Oh, so free love is not to be afforded to the working classes!

MARY: Love is never free to any woman, Elise.

ELISE: How can you be her daughter and say that?

MARY: Because I am her daughter I must say that! (*Fingering miniature.*) Oh, what do you understand of —

ELISE: Well, I read the book too! You were always encouraging me to improve my mind, were you not? Even although I was only a maid-servant. Indeed I understood it very well. The Rights of Woman. The marvellous Mary Wollstonecraft was very keen on freedom for Woman. At least freedom for the Woman with six hundred a year and a mill-owning husband to support her — and a bevy of maid-servants sweeping and starching and giving suck to her squalling infants — not to speak of her rutting husband.

MARY *slaps her hard.* ELISE *and* MARY *looking at each other. Echoing the* CLAIRE/MARY *mirror scene in Act One.*

Don't you think we are sisters? Are we not somewhat alike?

MARY: Go with Paolo! He is your husband now, he will marry you. Shelley talked to him, he says he is responsible. (*Goes. Her glower never flinching.*)

ELISE: Oh yes, *he* is responsible!

Scene Five

MARY *alone again talking to herself.*

MARY: And Frankenstein knew, oh, he knew who was responsible. (*Looking down at the book and reading quotes.*) So Frankenstein set off after his creature —

Voice, faint, distorted, of CLAIRE *as from Act One —*

CLAIRE: Getting warmer, getting colder — getting warmer . . . getting colder . . . col . . . der.

MARY: — over vast rivers of ice winding among the icy and glittering peaks of mountain summits. And he found him, waiting for him on a high alp.

Black and instantly up again on.

Scene Six

BYRON *with* MARY.

MARY: Why, when we never showed you anything but kindness and affection, how can you return this by —

BYRON: Telling the truth? Allowing the truth to be told? Mary Shelley, such hypocrisy from you, I should never have expected it.

MARY: Truly, you are a —

BYRON: Monster? (*Laughs.*) Mrs Shelley, I can guess why you've sent for me. You want to beg my daughter back. Well, the answer is no. The nuns will bring her up good and God-fearing.

MARY: Byron, listen to me, I must — (*Is overruled.*)

BYRON: I asked myself, reasonably enough I should have thought, whether Mademoiselle Claire Clairmont was the right person to bring up Allegra. Does a mother knew best? Not, I suggest, if that Mama is Claire.

You see, Fair Claire is most keen that Allegra be at once Our Little Secret and at the same time bruited abroad as the Dazzling Daughter (albeit Wrong Side of Blanket) of a Peer of the Realm (although my realm is darkness and exile as the world well knows). An impossible desire you might think, but then Claire Clairmont never was one to let impossibility stand in the way of her desires.

MARY: Are any of us? Byron, I must tell —

BYRON: I suppose not, although Claire does take *mangeing* her gateau and having it to some ridiculous extremes.

In fact that particular confection by now must be a mere icing shell, so long has Claire nibbled away from the inside like a secret mouse in a wedding cake.

MARY: Oh Byron, we are treated like monsters, Shelley and I, cut off from all the world. I was sixteen years old, my mother wrote it, my father wrote it, my lover wrote it! 'Marriage was a sad charade: it ought not to be prolonged for one moment longer than the natural affections did spontaneously dictate.'

I did not know when I ran away with him we would be exiles from all society, the subject of vile and vicious rumour, hounded —

BYRON: — From spa to spa to splendid ruin by smell-a-rat expatriates! *and* silly — bitch Claire making three, not to speak of her whelp . . .

MARY: . . . You should have let us raise the child . . .

BYRON (*not hearing her*): Oh, don't whine, Mary! You were never a sniveller. That I always thought was your saving grace. So: you ran away with your amazing flaming boy and if he blazed about a bit then that was part of the bargain, was it not? Did you think you could quench him of his wenching?

MARY: Shelley does not —

BYRON: Sorry, I mean his little . . . spiritual attachments. I'm *sure* he's quite above the attachment of the dog and the bitch, except occasionally, in the marriage bed, Mrs Shelley. What did you expect?

MARY: A new way to live.

BYRON: Ah yes, I think I've heard that somewhere before . . .

MARY: I was sixteen.

BYRON: Old enough, obviously. Only sixteen! Well, a girl of sixteen had better be a woman with all her wiles about her, she's twice as much in need of her wits at Sweet Sixteen than she is at vinegar thirty. How old was Harriet? (*Silence.*) Not sure, eh? No more am I, but I'll warrant she wasn't one-and-twenty when they dragged her from the river, so by a process of simple arithmetic —

MARY: — Oh cruel . . .

BYRON: Let me see, one year for child number one, a year . . . child two, a year to woo *you* . . . you'd been together, what? another two, makes five . . . from twenty-one makes . . . sixteen! Harriet ran away at sixteen. There's coincidence. (*Pause.*) Did her little dripping wet sixteen year old ghost visit you on your wedding night? Were you jealous? Are you? Come on, Mary, take it like a man.

MARY: Like a man! Oh yes, and write poems about it! If she wounds you between the sheets, then cut her down to size upon the page. If she is unfaithful to you, then that is nothing to the cuckoldry of books! You can publish volumes, and every ode dedicated to someone else. That'll freeze her and make her burn.

BYRON: Aha! So your green-eyed monster is even more jealous than I thought. Want to be his only muse, do you — the mother of all his poems!

MARY: I'd trade every poem ever written to be once again the mother of his sweet children.

BYRON (*reaching out to her, stricken, sorry*): Ah Mary, Mary —

MARY: You should have let us raise her. You should have let us keep Allegra, we would have loved her like our own. (*Pause.*) I know what you said. About us. I know. All about your treachery. The Hoppners told me! 'Have the Shelleys raised one? I do not want Allegra to die of starvation and green fruit and to be brought up to believe there is no Deity!' How can you be so malign?

BYRON: Oh, so the gossipy Hoppners carried tittle-tattle! Well, I cannot eat my words, would that I could swallow them unsaid — and I should never have said them to your face, Mary, I would not have looked in your eyes and wanted to wound you. I think you know how I grieved for you. Little William too. And the baby. But, think on it, Mary. When our . . . mutual friends the Hoppners parrotted out my gaudy scrap of cruel wit who or what exactly did they wish to wound? My reputation in your eyes? — which has never been a fulsome or healthy animal anyway — or did they wish to wound you, Mary Shelley? Ask yourself.

MARY: And did you defend us? When the Hoppners wrote you that . . . unspeakable rumour did you tell them it was all a lie?

BYRON: Unspeakable? Unspeakable? Don't be mim-mouthed, Mary, speak it out. If it is a lie then look it in the face. If you must know, Mrs Shelley, I told the Hoppners: Don't believe everything you hear from a dismissed servant — and if Elise says Claire Clairmont bore Shelley's bastard in the Spring, then I am sure it is just a venomous lie even although it *would* have been just a gestation time away from the time Shelley and Claire spent alone at my villa in Este. Why, Mrs Hoppner, I said, Shelley only accompanied Claire to prevail with me on her behalf, I won't stay half an hour in any town that minx sets foot in. I said: Mrs Hoppner, can you believe that a man of Shelley's burning idealism could enter into a love affair with his wife's own sister — oh, I mean *half* sister, whatever — while his wife struggled alone across Europe with an ailing infant? I said: there is not a word of truth in it, I swear on the head of my own Allegra.

MARY: Well, she is dead! (BYRON *slumps.*) Claire wanted me to tell you.

She cannot look at you. I tried, you would not listen. There has been an epidemic swept through that cold Capuccin Convent and your little love child is among the first to be borne away. (MARY *looks at the broken BYRON eventually beginning to stir with pity, goes to reach out to touch him, pulls away again. He sobs, not knowing even that she has tried to make herself reach out.*) Byron, oh Byron, there is something wrong in how we all live.

BYRON: Oh yes, look in the mirror of my grief and see yourself.

Pause, they look at each other, might reach out, but don't.

'All men hate the wretched.' Isn't that one of yours, Mary? And the wretched hate each other. Oh, don't trust me, not one inch. I am utterly, utterly malicious. And so are you. We are malicious because we are miserable.

Pause, MARY now inadvertently admitting a core of her misery.

MARY: Shelley does not love Claire!

BYRON (*laughing horribly*): Of course he does not love Claire! Who could love Claire? Even Claire has a hard job loving Claire. I never pretended to love her, but if a girl of eighteen will come prancing to a man at all hours then there is but one way! Pleasure, freedom, wine, women, song, apes, peacocks, vinegar purges, boys, opium, ocean-going, orgies — and I won't give up any of it, I'll double any gluttony and double it again. All just to kill time, eh, Mary? It will be the death of us, eh?

MARY: We do not live as you do.

BYRON: Oh, I forgot, the Shelleys are political! The Shelleys are principled! The Shelleys do not eat dead animals. How about dead children?

MARY: My Firstborn, then Clara . . . then William. My own little Willmouse. The worst pain a mother ever bore, to have her child die before her. An unnatural, monstrous thing . . .

BYRON: And yet you can encompass it. As I will. I will live with my guilt. Can you live with yours?

MARY: But I am not guilty! I loved my children and I will not cease from grieving even when my new child is born!

BYRON: A new baby, eh? Congratulations. And to Shiloh too. Is there to be no end to this Creation? Well, better luck this time. If *luck* is all you will acknowledge is in control of our lives . . . as is evidently the case if you will not admit your own responsibility. Culpability.

MARY: You are accusing me of never questioning myself! Since . . . I became a mother no more . . . I have been constantly tormenting myself by examining my past conduct. Nor do I find it blameable!

BYRON: You don't. (*Sniggers.*)

MARY: I lived for my children.

BYRON: Well, I have never pretended to live for anyone but myself. And there's where we differ. Infants do benefit from travel, don't they? Florence, Venice, Padua, a bit of culture and cholera does broaden the mind.

MARY: You are a twisted person.

BYRON: Oh yes, Mary, there is something in us which is very ugly. Do you not think we are somewhat alike? We are put together all wrong.

MARY: Loathsome.

BYRON: Well if I am the monster, who or what are you? Mary Shelley. (MARY *turns away, afraid.*) Oh yes, I have read your book. Very powerful it is too. Remarkable for a young girl of . . . what were you? Nineteen? I'm sure I cannot imagine where you got your ideas, can you?

MARY: Damn that book! A silly work of

fantasy is my albatross. It's only a book . . . an idea.

BYRON: Only a book, eh? A very popular one, though. Why, Mrs Shelley's scribblings outsell Shiloh's — and even mine — several times over. Everyone knows the story . . .

MARY: Popular! People confuse things so — they scramble together Frankenstein and the creature he brought to life, mix one with the other —

BYRON: Oh, everyone thinks they know the story.

MARY: It's nothing to do with anything in real life.

BYRON: Have you read your book? Oh, I know you *wrote* it, have you read it though, recently?

I'm sure it is silly of me to read between the lines though. Oh, if only the naughty reader would keep his gladeyes on the text. No profit in noticing an author name a character after her beloved baba, blonde curls and all, and then strangle him to death on page sixty-nine — oh, not many mamas, especially not busy fingered distracted mamas, who have not occasionally, en passant, wished to silence the little darling.

MARY: I am afraid of you.

BYRON: Don't be afraid, Mary. Courage! (*Flicks her Mama's pendant as in Act One.*) Read that story. Read your story.

Black.

Scene Seven

MARY *alone, reading* Frankenstein.

MARY: And the creature told Frankenstein, 'You made me ugly, you put me together all wrong. You made me unfit for the sweet society of men, I was a foul abortion, they recoiled from me.' He said, 'You hate me! All men hate the wretched.'

The creature said, 'Frankenstein make me a mate! Make me one who will share the desert places. Shall every beast of the field cleave to its mate and I have none to lay my sweet head beside? Make me a mate!'

So Frankenstein robbed the grave again and stitched his long secret sutures — belly, breast, oh, he could fancy the putrefaction already starting in her softness, the corruption, the yeasts beginning to bubble . . .

And he saw the creature at the casement, waiting, gloating, exultant.

But Frankenstein said 'No! What is repellent in the male will be ten times more disgusting in the female, I cannot grant it life.' And he withheld his spark, he smashed his machine and trampled its intricacies underfoot and ripped and burned his last marvellous formula. And he flung the ragdoll-sack of organs at his creature who cradled her, keening. And Frankenstein said, 'She is dead meat, the worms can get drunk on her. I will never make another like you.'

And the creature said to Frankenstein, 'I shall be with you on your wedding night.'

Enter SHELLEY.

SHELLEY: Mary! Mary, what are you doing here. In the dark. All alone. Muttering . . .

MARY: Shall I be alone?

SHELLEY: The moon is out. Come and see her. She is arrived.

MARY: Your new love.

SHELLEY: My new boat! The bonniest boat that ever sailed the seas.

MARY: 'The Endeavour'!

SHELLEY: What 'Endeavour'? Stop this, Mary! You know it is 'The Ariel', I wish you'd sail . . .

MARY: I cannot.

SHELLEY: Oh yes she is 'The Ariel' all right! I told Roberts, I told him long before the building was done, I said 'We have changed our mind.' It is *not* to be called in Byron's honour, and yet it sails in, monstrous letters blazed across the mainsail — 'The Don Juan'. Bright and clear!

MARY (*shivering*): The devil's brand!

SHELLEY: What devil? Oh, that name won't stick, depend on it. We have already set to with turpentine, buckets of hot water, soap and brushes, we'll shift that stain, don't fret about that!

MARY: We'll never shift that stain.

SHELLEY: Oh, we'll shift it, and if it won't come off we'll cut it out the mainsail and insert a clean patch.

MARY: The Don Juan!

SHELLEY: The Ariel! I told you! Mary, listen . . .

MARY (*fey*): 'If you will set sail in a philanderer's barque, then beware of the fickle seas . . .'

SHELLEY: Now that's riddles! Morbid talk! I won't hear it! (*Shaking her gently.*) Mary, enough of this melancholy.

MARY: He has come home to us. He lives with us at last.

SHELLEY: Melancholy? I'll not give him house-room. I'll take my Best Mary and I'll wrap her up warm and I'll rush her out of doors, out of this damp and dreary summer-house and I'll sit her at the prow of my bonny boat like a proud figurehead, and the winds will undo her hair and whip roses to her cheeks and blow the last black wisps of melancholy away from her, just as I promised her when she was a pretty child in a graveyard.

MARY: You can take your Best Mary, and you can sail away with her, but I'll still be sitting here with my own thoughts in an empty nursery.

SHELLEY: We can have another baby, Mary.

MARY: I nearly died, Shelley.

SHELLEY: I saved you.

MARY: I, Am, In, Pain. I thought this is what it means . . . to be In Pain. It was a dark river drowning me, I wanted to drown in it. I hoped to die.

SHELLEY: I saved you. It was pure instinct, the ice!

MARY: . . . I thought, it is my element. I swim in it and I do not die.

SHELLEY: You lost so much blood, I had never seen such . . . I ran, ran all the way to the Ice House, I woke Umberto, I made him pack the last shard of ice, we packed a bath of it. Claire would not help me; she said the shock would kill you, but I lifted you up in my arms and I plunged you in that bath of ice and that stopped the flow. I saved you.

MARY: No baby.

SHELLEY: It's my loss. too. Why is it every woman thinks she has the patent out on pain?

MARY: You bleed on paper. I bled through every bit of bedlinen in this house. I lost it. I wonder, was it a boy or a girl? Or a monster. What are little girls made of? Slime and snails and . . .

What are monsters made of?

'I met murder on the way. He had a mask like Castlereagh.'

(*Laughs.*) I like that one. You should have written more like that. I used to like your poetry when you were being romantic. Now I prefer the political. You put more passion into it, ultimately.

SHELLEY: Mary. Mary, listen —

MARY: What?

SHELLEY: Remember, I'll never turn from you. To turn sometimes to others is not to turn from you.

MARY: Oh, Shelley, Shelley — to live in the spirit as much as you do puts a great deal of strain on the body. I don't know if I can bear it. Can I change myself? I must take myself to bits, put myself together again, leave out the bit that makes me . . . jealous. Can I do it?

SHELLEY: But Mary, you agreed —

MARY: I did not know what I was agreeing to! (*Pause.*)

SHELLEY: Back in that graveyard — you were just a girl — but I knew I had found everything I ever dreamed of — beauty without taint of vanity, intellect without longwindedness, love without —

MARY: Responsibility?

SHELLEY: Love *With* Full and Mutual Freedom. And you said yes!

MARY: In a graveyard.

SHELLEY: Yes!

MARY: By the cold slab of my mother's grave.

SHELLEY: Oh yes. She died. Yes, it *is* a terrible terrible thing that childbed was her deathbed.

MARY: Oh, Shelley, as it is for so many.

SHELLEY: Yes. You bled, Mary, but you didn't die.

MARY (*fey again*): '. . . So Many . . . and so beautiful and they all dead do lie . . . and (*Shivering self disgust.*) . . . a thousand thousand slimy things live on and so do I.'

SHELLEY: Stop it! (*Shakes her.*) Stop this, Mary. Yes, that women die making babies is terrible. Yes it is unfair. But it's getting better. Things must improve.

MARY: — How can —

SHELLEY: Daily. Daily doctors and scientists make themselves explorers and chart unknown regions of disease and infection.

MARY: Doctors! Scientists!

SHELLEY: Men. Yes. But they need not be. They *must* not be. Oh yes, I am a man. You're right, I won't die of childbirth, I know . . . But listen, Mary, I can never know the joy of creating new life.

MARY: Just poems.

SHELLEY: Just cold words on a cold page.

MARY: You do not mean that for one minute! Your pride in your creation is that of the Lord Almighty.

SHELLEY: Mary, Woman is the door to all life. I sink to my knees and worship at her —

MARY: God save all women from men who worship 'Woman'. (*Pause.*)

(*Fey.*) A pretty doll in a purple silk dress . . . A pretty doll!

SHELLEY: What are you saying. I don't know what you are talking about.

MARY: Harriet. That's how Claire described her. When I asked her. I said 'What is Mr Shelley's wife like? Is she pretty?' She said — I was sixteen — she said, 'Oh yes, but she is no wife for Shelley.'

SHELLEY: Mary, listen, are we to be ripped apart by what so powerfully dragged us together?

MARY (*shivering*): I don't want to be alone. I am standing here, and the cracks appear, and I find myself on a smaller and smaller island of ice. And you floating away like an impossible dream.

SHELLEY: Mary, you're shivering.

MARY: A good job my mother isn't alive to see me now! She tried to find Freedom, enter that region where Reason and Love would flourish and the Lion should lie down with the Lamb. And she died, giving birth to me. Drowned in that river of blood.

SHELLEY: Lions and lambs? — Mary

this is not like you. Man is not a lion and Woman not a helpless lamb . . .

MARY: I did not say she was! When man and woman lie down together they are at once each other's strange wild savage beasts and each other's sacrificial victims. And Death sits at the bedhead. Oh, not the Little Death the poets talk of, the moment's love-swoon after which each animal feels a little sweetly sad. But the Death they talk about below stairs, down there, down among the women where cook, shelling peas and slicing carrots, has parlour maid all agog and saucer-eyed over the tale of how the Mistress had a hard time of it when she was brought to bed this time. 'Midwife says the babe will live, but though doctor has set puppies to suck at her breasts to see if they can make the afterbirth come down, she has little hopes for the mother! And it looks as though reading or writing or love or money isn't going to stop her dying exactly the way Cook's own sister the laundress did! The blood will not stop.'

SHELLEY: Mary, I cannot reach you.

MARY: To be born poor is to be born a slave. To be born a woman is to be born a slave. Poor Elise, you were a slave's slave – and that's a jumbled up collection of wood and wires! I should not have sent you away. (*She flips the Mary-doll inside out. Showing the Elise-doll and frightening* SHELLEY.)

SHELLEY: Macabre toy! What a hideous –

MARY: Elise made it. She had quite the talent for needlework, she fashioned many a puppet, this was for Clara but how it did make little Willmouse screech and laugh – to see his mama, and how under her skirt she was but a maid!

SHELLEY: Throw it away. Mary, tomorrow I'm going to get Umberto and we'll clear this room. We'll –

MARY: Or maybe it was to see a maid who had a thinking head in her loins for a change. A certain sort of Jack-in-the-Box effect for the naughty child who would, as all children will do, flip a doll over to see what it has under its dress.

SHELLEY: Mary, I am afraid for you.

MARY: Save your fear for yourself! I had a dream, Shelley, it made me shudder.

SHELLEY: Mary, we should leave this place. Take the boat and –

MARY: I dreamed Elise was back and she was making something, something here in the nursery and it was a secret, she would not let me in, so I spied on her. And she was making a doll, a life-size puppet – it was spread out here on the couch, long pale limbs, cadaver-loins gleaming whitely. Its dress was over its head, Claire-flounces turned inside out covering the whole top half of its body. And Elise was stitching. 'Long secret sutures,' she said, she spoke it out loud. 'A la victime is à la mode for all time, is it?' And she smiled to herself. 'How shall I make her perfect. How shall I make her whole.' And she took my mother's book. 'Mary Wollstonecraft's Pattern Book' she said, 'Hints on the stitching up and finishing of ladies.' 'Satin stitch, French hemming, blanket stitch, and I'll finish with a strong knot where I join between the thighs lest it shall unravel,' and she bent down and bit off the end of the cotton with a snap. And then you came in . . . You were naked and had seaweed tangled in your hair and you said, 'No.' And Elise said, 'Will you deny your spark of life to your female fellow creature?' You went and you lay down on top of her and you said, 'Claire', and you began to pull at the flounces peel them back from where they were flipped over her head and you fought with them to reveal – above the waist of your hellish creature was my belly, my loins, my thighs my screaming vulva and my limbs tangled with your head and pulled you down, down, down. (MARY *grabs* SHELLEY *and kisses him. They kiss. He breaks, flees from her. Leaves her alone.*)

(*A cry:*) Elise, I should not have sent you away. Claire, I should have sent you away long ago! Shelley!

Music swells, goes.

Scene Eight

MARY *alone as at the beginning of the play.*

MARY: They only knew him by — they found in his pocket that volume of Keats, bent open at the place he was reading . . . His face, his hands, all parts of him not . . . protected by his clothing had been eaten away by fishes.

I wonder what it is like to drown? Did he expect to breathe easy in a brand new element, plunge straight in, embracing it, I would not put it past him. What bobbed up at him from the lone and level sands of the sea bottom?

Nymphs? Nereids? Mermaids? All the flimsy impossible women, glittering hermaphrodites, did they tangle with him, did he clasp his sweet ideal at last? Or was he beating useless limbs, dragged down by sodden duds among the bladderwrack and nosing dogfish, fighting his way back, gulping and struggling with bursting lungs back to his flesh and blood Mary?

Lord Byron is dead. I wonder if Claire knows? Is she sobbing in her Moscow schoolroom to see the last tatter of her scarlet past is blown away. The news came yesterday. Gone to fight for the Brave Cause of Greek Indpendence. Oh he died of a cold, some say, or the pox . . . or for love of a beautiful boy who did not love him back, oh, who

knows the truth of the matter. But he went to fight for freedom.

And I read my story. 'Read it,' he said. 'Understand your freedom. Understand what keeps your freedom from you. Or you will never own it.'

I thought: I am Frankenstein, the creator who loves creation and hates its results. Then I thought: no, I am the monster, poor misunderstood creature feared and hated by all mankind. And then I thought: it is worse, worse than that, I am the female monster, gross, gashed, ten times more hideous than my male counterpart, denied life, tied to the monster bed for ever.

I wonder what it is like to die? The dead have entered a new element, they are beyond us utterly, utterly . . . unchanged. Un-sea-changed, the dead we have always with us. The dead come back. Back they come, large as life, and twice as . . .

The dead are constantly reassembling themselves. We are continuously putting them together again. Everybody ends up on the monster bed sometime. The news came. Lord Byron is dead.

'Read that story.'

But now I see who I am, in my book. I am Captain Walton, explorer. Survivor. My own cool narrator. The one who once dreamed of that land of wonder, where, way beyond the pole, sailing over a calm sea, further than the flickering Northern Lights — Men and Woman Might Live In Freedom.

The one who turned back.

The one who, when the ice came, stuck fast, unable to go back or forward. The one who saw what it might cost and promised if they would be released would turn south, head for more moderate regions.

The one who could not go on without the concensus of all fellow travellers.

I gave up all I once most dearly hoped for.

I am Captain Walton, survivor.

I dreamed I found my baby, she wasn't dead but . . . cold merely.

I dreamed I saw my dead mother. I wanted to join her, for death to join us and we should part no more. I reached to kiss her and I found that in my arms I clasped my own Shelley, hot and living with all his senses and his five straight limbs. And my heart sickened at the workings of my loins. (*Pause.*) Claire dreamed she saw Shelley walk with his own ghost in the garden a week before he drowned. I dreamed Shelley walked naked into the room, blood-stained, skin in tatters, seaweed tangled in his hair, crying out, 'The Sea is Invading The House!'

The ice is invading the house.

This house? A blood bath. A bath of ice.

Will the ice save me?

It saved me once. Will it save me twice?

And I hear Frankenstein, calling from my own book. He says 'Walton! Walton, you'd have your sons and daughters say you had not strength enough to endure the cold, but you scuttled back to the warm firesides of the withdrawing rooms of England?

'Persuade your mariners. Lead them, Walton. Tell them be men or more-than-men. The ice cannot stop you if your hot hearts say it shall not!' (*Pause.* MARY *sits down at her writing table. Quietly, but resignedly going on.*) Oh, Shelley. (*Begins to write.*)

Blood and Ice

Blood and Ice was my first attempt at a stage play and my relationship with it has been as intense and almost as troubled as Mary Shelley's with her great novel — or the fictional Frankenstein's with his maimed and misunderstood creature. And as much of an ongoing passion too.

In the summer of 1980 I was in New York, staying with a friend who worked all the time, day and night almost. I wanted a big fat piece of work to do. I was at that time a poet waiting for my second full-sized collection to come out. I was used to travelling all over the UK to do poetry readings, which had been getting gradually more theatrical until I'd collaborated with playwright Marcella Evaristi on a revue called *Sugar and Spite*, which people seemed to have enjoyed a lot. We'd been asked to repeat it in some places anyway, and done a radio version. And suddenly I was hooked. I wanted to write something for the stage. There, in New York that summer, I began to read up a lot about Mary Wollstonecraft, who'd written *A Vindication of the Rights of Woman* — and yet who'd lived an interestingly contradictory life before dying, like so many women of all social classes, in childbirth. She died giving birth to the girl child who was to become Mary Shelley, the myth-maker, Frankenstein the creator's creator. And it niggled at me, that the daughter of a great rationalist would grow up to write Gothic Horror. Why? (Because in my utter ignorance — I hadn't even read *Frankenstein* because I didn't think it'd be very good and who needed to? One Knew The Story — I thought *Frankenstein* was a Gothic Novel!)

So I read *Frankenstein*, an obsession was born, and any fantasies of writing a play about Wollstonecraft evaporated. I wrote like a being possessed.

The first fumbling version — *Mary and the Monster* (ugh — see what I mean?) was produced at the studio of the Belgrade Theatre, Coventry, in March 1981, and is not a production either my very good friend, the director, Michael Boyd, or I are proud of. When I tell you that the *Birmingham Evening Post* said they'd *rather be at the dentist* (and that I, Michael and every member of the valiant and talented cast agreed with them) you will maybe see what I mean. And after reading the *Guardian* review I thought I'd rather be at the mortuary.

A few months later I recovered, wrote another revue, *True Confessions*, which was great fun, and a short, one-act play for the Scottish Youth Theatre called *Disgusting Objects*, which they seemed really pleased with, and, fortified, started the Mary Shelley and Frankenstein play All Over Again. Peter Lichtenfels at the Traverse Theatre in Edinburgh read this one, loved it and a production of a slightly more complex and difficult version than the one you can read here went on at the Traverse at the Edinburgh Festival of 1982. This one was certainly a lot more like the Thing — and some, especially *posh*, papers, reviewed it very well — and some members of the audience came to find me sometimes and tell me they had found it very moving. But it still didn't work. Not properly. Not all of it. And despite the passion and intelligence of Gerda Stevenson, the terrific actress who played Mary, what she had to do disintegrated in its imagery at the level of my writing before the long difficult monologue ending of the play. A play about a woman and loneliness and isolation made both me and Gerda actually feel lonely and isolated. The casting of that production had not gelled — as far as good working chemistry between the actors, and the director Kenny Ireland and I fought bitterly about this. Thank goodness we made it up, and he was helpful about *this* version. But not a happy time . . .

The next nightmare about this play began when RADA contacted me in the summer of 1983 to say that some students loved the play and wanted to put it on, and I went to London to see Helena Kant-Howson who had been hired, freelance, to direct it. During this meeting, disturbing talk about 'workshopping' the material and 'improvising' other scenes to add alerted me to the fact that Ms Kant-Howson seemed to think I had handed her a rag-bag of research material and not a play. Don't get me wrong — a writing 'workshop' with actors at an early stage can be absolutely fantastic — and I'd just written something like this for Borderline, the Scottish Touring Theatre Company, and loved the whole experience. But *Blood and Ice* was a *play*. A play I'd rewritten, totally, three times, living with and making for three years. Certainly *and* production requires rewrites and *always* cuts — to suit the particular cast and the particular production, but I had a very uneasy feeling about Ms Kant-Howson. Which turned out to be right. I put all these doubts and fears on paper to her, said that if she didn't want to do my play but to completely take it to bits and reconstruct it, then she *couldn't*. I outlined my rewrites. Did them. Submitted it. She said all was well and ten days into their rehearsal period I visited, making a special trip South again. To find that the script they were doing went up to my page four, then they did a little *piece* of the doll-speech on my page eighty-four, then a bit of my page sixteen before a new scene they'd invented — with Byron and Shelley on a boat (and *no* Mary Shelley, in whose consciousness my *entire play* takes place) discussing what year they had been at Eton (like a jokey clumsy bit of information-imparting in *The Real Inspector Hound*).

I was naturally furious and said, not for the first time, that unless they returned substantially to my script, permission would be refused by my agent. So we cancelled. Later RADA put on, at what ought to have been *our* date, a play called 'Grave Thoughts' a semi-improved piece about Mary, Claire, Shelley and Byron. I made no accusations of plagiarism despite the fact they'd had my work all summer and for the first two weeks of rehearsal . . .

Just over a month after this upsetting business a small, young, enthusiastic London-based fringe theatre group called, then, Pepper's Ghost, asked if they could do *Blood and Ice*. I sent them the script that's here. They liked it. They did it. Very well. With no budget to speak of in a grim North London pub. It worked. My relations with the entire company were entirely cordial — as indeed they have been with every cast and every director of every other play or production I have ever been involved with. Except *Blood and Ice*.

But, despite the Bogey Men, I still love this play. More than anything else I have ever done. Until . . . well, I am *now* working on an adaptation, which is turning out to be a free adaptation, of *Dracula*, Bram Stoker's sick masterpiece. So the monster's on the move again . . .

Liz Lochhead. 1984

Liz Lochhead

Stage Plays

Sugar and Spite, 1978; review, written with Marcella Evaristi.

True Confessions, 1981; review, Tron Theatre, Glasgow.

Disgusting Objects, 1982; Scottish Youth Theatre.

Shanghaied, 1983; Borderline Theatre Company.

Red Hot Shoes, 1983; Tron Theatre, Glasgow.

Blood and Ice, 1984; Pepper's Ghost Theatre Co. (Earlier versions of this play were: *Mary and the Monster*, 1981; Belgrade Theatre, Coventry, and *Blood and Ice*, 1982; Traverse Theatre, Edinburgh.)

Same Difference, 1984; Wildcat Theatre Company.

Rosaleen's Baby, 1984; Scottish Youth Theatre.

PINBALL

Pinball was first produced at the Nimrod Theatre Downstairs, Sydney, Australia, on 9 September 1981 with the following cast:

THEENIE	Jenny Ludlam
AXIS	Natalie Bate
VANDELOPE/MIRIAM	Kerry Walker
LOUISE/VIOLET	Cecily Polson
SYLVESTER/ARCHIBALD	Roger Leach
SOLOMON (KURT, WAITER, SERGEANT)	Paul Bertram

Directed by Chris Johnson
Designed by Kate JasonSmith
Lighting by Kevin McKie
Sound Effects by Michael Carlos
Stage Managed by Stephanie Walkem

Thanks to: Robin Boord, Nick Enright, Ron Hoenig, Chris Johnson, Fay Mokotow and the cast at Nimrod and at Troupe for their invaluable work on the script. Special thanks to my writing group: Robyn Clark, Carole Deagan, Jeannie Edgar, Janne Ellen, Kerryn Higgs, Mariana Jones, Jan McKemmish, Drusilla Modjeska, Jill Sutton. And to Tim Hughes for his sense of humour. And to Roma and Ian Cooper and friends at The Craggs for great encouragement. And to Chris Westwood and Sue Hill for inspiring courage and giving much support at Nimrod and in the Women and Theatre Project. And to many other friends: thank you.

Thanks to Refractory Girl, Issue No 20/21, 1980, and to the Lesbian Mothers for their research.

The song, 'Don't be too Polite, Girls', was written by Glen Tomasetti.

PROLOGUE

Pinball machines lit.
    Electronic firing.
    *Organ music to suit Old Testament
drowns pinball machine.*
    Pinball machines go out.
    Stained glass window lit.

    SOLOMON *enters wearing biblical
robes.*

SOLOMON (*reads from 1 Kings 3, v
    9–28*): '. . . and God said to
    Solomon . . . Behold I give you a wise
    and discerning mind, so that none like
    you has been before you and none
    like you shall arise after you. I give
    you also what you have not asked,
    both riches and honour . . .'

And Solomon awoke and behold, it
was a dream . . .

Then two harlots came to the king . . .
The one woman said, 'Oh, my lord,
this woman and I dwell in the same
house: and I gave birth to a child . . .
Then on the third day after I was
delivered, this woman also gave birth;
and we were alone; there was no one
else with us in the house; only we two
were in the house. And this woman's
son died in the night, because she lay
on it. And she arose at midnight and
took my son from beside me . . . and
laid it in her bosom, and laid her dead
son in my bosom. When I rose in the
morning to nurse my child, behold it
was dead, but when I looked at it
closely in the morning, behold, it was
not the child that I had borne.' But
the other woman said, 'No, the living
child is mine and the dead child is
yours.'

Then the king said, 'Bring me a sword.'
So a sword was brought before the
king, and the king said, 'Divide the
living child in two, and give half to the
one, and half to the other.'

Organ music.
ALABASTAR's *voice making a sound
of firing, builds up to a sound battle
with the organ music.*
The organ music, defeated, fades.
Stained glass window fades.
Blackout.

ACT ONE

Scene One

Pinball parlour. VANDELOPE *enters.*
Pinball machines.

SOLOMON: The child, Alabastar, here in a pinball parlour? (*He introduces himself to the audience.*) Solomon's the name. (*He looks with disdain at a machine.*) Caveman's the game? Sometimes one needs an audience while collecting evidence. Thirteen boys, three girls and you have to look in the dictionary before you know what that one is.

VANDELOPE: Piss off! (*She plays a video game.*) Jeep! Blllll! Loooppppp! (*She makes electronic firing noises.*) Score 200!

SOLOMON: I prefer the old fashioned kind with flippers. One can see where the balls go.

VANDELOPE (*firing noises*): Bluumm! Tank! You beauty, Score 500! Brrip! United Nations truck. (*Swears.*) Soyabeans. Lose three seconds.

SOLOMON: 'And the voice of the turtle dove
is heard in our land.'

VANDELOPE: Ooops, Vandelope, there goes El Salvador.

SOLOMON: This is the space age. Why aren't they home playing cowboys and indians like we did?

VANDELOPE: They send kids here to school. Teaches them how to talk to coloured lights bipping, face to face.

SOLOMON; Where is the boy? He must be somebody's son. Madam! I'm looking for the owner of a son.

VANDELOPE: I'm not into that. I'm an anarcho-lesbian bicyclist.

SOLOMON: He was last seen with a pile of coins, asking for a cigarette, and he must be all of ten.

VANDELOPE: See if he'll lend me twenty cents.

SOLOMON: This little boy has potential.

VANDELOPE: If men had to give birth to children, they'd pop out of their skulls just like that — fully clothed and brainwashed, drooling, 'Come to where the flavour is'.

SOLOMON: You women have gone out to work, and a whole generation suffers from neglect.

VANDELOPE: You know why I wear overalls? So when a jerk like you pops out at me, I can put my arms in here and give myself a cuddle.

SOLOMON: 'I compare you, my love to a mare of Pharaoh's chariots.'

VANDELOPE: Get knackered. Give him an inch and he thinks he's Ben Hur.

SOLOMON: I'll remember that.

VANDELOPE: I come here to get away from it and the patriarchy follows me. It thinks I'm an addict. (*She checks her pockets.*) Destitute! You know they're making a fortune out of you, so you have another game to take your mind off it. Pigs. I was going to hang onto enough for a thickshake. (*She pulls down a sign with graffiti on it: 'THE RICH COME HERE TO FORGET, THE POOR TO DREAM'. She goes out.*)

SOLOMON: Bring in the harlots,
I'll judge who's his mother.
Sharpen my sword,
I've already won . . .
Only a harlot would cut up a son.

He sees what VANDELOPE *has done.*

Concubine! Vandal!

VANDELOPE (*off*): Yep!

SOLOMON: I'll catch her later. Now there are more important visitors.

Scene Two

SOLOMON *conjures the pinball machine into a table. Uses his biblical robe to make a formal table cloth, revealing him dressed as an elegant* WAITER. *He discovers that the cloth has graffiti on it: 'EAT THE RICH'. He hastily turns the cloth over. Adds two chairs. An expensive menu.*

   Lights out on pinball machines.

WAITER: 'He brought me to the
   banqueting house,
and his banner over me was love.'

   LOUISE *enters with a thick folder of notes.*

WAITER: Madam, table for one?

LOUISE: Two. Three. (*She sits.*) *Merci.* A perfectly easy restaurant. They can't possibly be late. I wonder if ten-year-olds like steak without chips. It's going to be a big responsibility. Someone's life to organise. I want to give the boy the choice that leads men up.

WAITER: She is the perfect flower who married the father yesterday.

   SYLVESTER *arrives and gives* LOUISE *a kiss.*

SYLVESTER: Louise, darling.

LOUISE: Darling.

SYLVESTER: Sorry I'm late, Professor Sinclair wanted to see me.

LOUISE: I've put your notes together for you. (*She hands him the notes.*) I've added a piece on Althusser, picking up the themes of collaboration and resistance.

SYLVESTER: Darling, that's wonderful. The Prof was delighted with the first draft. He's given me a pat on the back.

LOUISE: Darling.

SYLVESTER: You've been such a support. I should put your name on it, as co-author.

LOUISE: No, darling, I couldn't do that.

SYLVESTER: Yes, we could, darling.

LOUISE: No, really, darling, I couldn't. It's yours.

SYLVESTER: We're so happy together. Shall we start with the terrine?

WAITER: 'Eat, O friends, and drink: Drink deeply, O lovers!'

LOUISE: Mmm. Darling, weren't we going to do this with Alabastar?

SYLVESTER: Darling, could you persuade him to have quail in orange brandy when he's walking past Big Mac in neon lights?

LOUISE: You left him there? For lunch? To do what he wants? Darling, you don't know who might be there.

SYLVESTER: Louise, darling, relax. They do the garlic prawns beautifully here.

WAITER: Garlic prawn.

SYLVESTER: Alabastar would be bumping the table leg every time you and I looked at one another.

WAITER: Take your time, sir.

LOUISE: I love it when we're perfect together.

WAITER: Rack of lamb, Madam?
   'Your cheecks are like halves of a
      pomegranate
behind your veil.'

LOUISE: I do so want to get on well with Alabaster.

SYLVESTER: I want you to think of him as ours.

LOUISE: After lunch should we take him to the museum? The art gallery? Sylvester darling? You have organised the afternoon free?

SYLVESTER: Mnn. Yes, darling. The art gallery, no. Perhaps the fish soup?

WAITER: *Bouillabaise.*

LOUISE: Mmnmn. Do you think he could do with some shopping, now we've got him in town? New jeans? A cricket bat?

SYLVESTER: He wants a space invaders machine — to take home.

LOUISE: That's ridiculous. I mean, that can't be good for him.

SYLVESTER: I had to promise it to him, darling. It's been difficult for him, for both of us. Please understand.

LOUISE: Darling, if he's going to spend puberty with a pinball machine, you ought to book him into a decent school.

The WAITER *covers the graffiti sign with chalkboard menu: 'SPECIALS OF THE DAY'.*

SYLVESTER: We can't move fast, my darling. Theenie won't let us. I know she won't. Louise, I love you. Louise, Theenie wouldn't just make an issue out of it, she'd make a revolution.

LOUISE: Let her keep her ugly old sandshoes and struggles, but if she goes on dragging Alabastar into them, he'll never learn how to sit down to dinner in the right company. She's not his mother any more. She is his ex.

SYLVESTER: My ex, darling. Would you prefer the Balmain bugs *au beurre*? He's happy and learning at Edgebank Public. Plenty of his friends will be going on to the local high school. It's not as though we live in an unsavoury area.

LOUISE: I'm rather taken by the rainbow trout. Be reasonable, darling. I've seen how it hurts you when people ask what school you went to and you have to answer Cardigan Boys High.

SYLVESTER: That was while I was fighting for a lectureship. Now that next semester I've been offered the Marxist Studies Course, it's good that I've had exposure to the mixed lens of humanity. You know what those students are into. Anything that flies in the face of convention. Consciousness raising. Food co-ops. I can't send Alabastar to a private school. Student assessment of lecturer: nil.

LOUISE: But remember how you suffered. How you lost that tooth for reading *Pride and Prejudice* in the playground. Do you know what my favourite is, dearest? Avocado vinaigrette.

WAITER: Avocado vinaigrette. (*He goes.*)

SYLVESTER: Superb. Louise, don't you see, I can bite on that capped tooth and remember. When you were at school, didn't you feel that life had breadth?

LOUISE: Darling, it was enriching at Lamington Ladies College: Hockey, front row, Byron, Chapel at eight, Michelangelo, the annual GPS Regatta, and *Oedipus Rex*. We must get Alabastar off to a good start.

SYLVESTER: We have.

LOUISE: If we can get the tomato sauce off his tee shirt.

WAITER (*re-enters with table napkins*): 'As an apple tree among the trees of the wood, so is my beloved among young men.'

SYLVESTER: You're growing to love him, aren't you? The shoulders on him!

WAITER: 'His neck is like the tower of David Built for an arsenal.'

He goes.

SYLVESTER: He's more Theenie's build than mine.

LOUISE: Sylvester, let's not think of her any more, darling. The point is, we can afford the fees, he's probably scholarship material anyway, and he needs a private school as an antidote to that woman.

SYLVESTER: Theenie is not *that* woman. And don't worry about Alabastar. Theenie's done the groundwork — Vitamin B, books from

Dr Seuss, and a set of Scrabble on his seventh birthday. He'll make it whatever school we send him to.

LOUISE: She's a better mother by the minute. I don't know why you bothered to get a divorce.

SYLVESTER: Darling, I did it for you. I knew I loved you when I found myself looking forward to my lectures, because you'd be in the front row, sitting there with your folder open. You made me feel I had somewhere to belong.

LOUISE: It's all right for you. Wherever you go someone's going to make you belong there. Fifty per cent of the time, you said. Alabastar's got to be with us fifty per cent of the time. But how am I going to belong with you if Alabastar's hers?

SYLVESTER: Darling. Stop it! I can't bear that I've hurt you. I had no idea. Darling? I'll canvass my colleagues for the best of all possible schools.

The WAITER re-enters.

LOUISE: Sylvester. I can't bear us to quarrel. Darling, look, if his future's out of danger, and he's set his heart on that video game, we could buy it, now, a present from both of us.

SYLVESTER: No, no darling. From you! As your welcome to Alabastar.

LOUISE: Darling, I knew you could be tender and perceptive. *Garcon*! where could we find the Space Invaders?

WAITER: 'How much better is your love than wine,
And the fragrance of your oils than any spice!'

LOUISE: Where's the pinball department?

WAITER: On the mezzanine, Madam. Santa Claus is in Aladdin's cave, on the right as you come off the escalator.

LOUISE *and* SYLVESTER *go out,*

SYLVESTER *giving the* WAITER *a small tip on the way.*

WAITER: Merde! So well dressed and so rude.

'And when the Queen of Sheba
had seen all the wisdom of Solomon,
the house that he had built,
the food of his table,
and his burnt offerings
which he offered at the house of the Lord,
there was no more spirit in her.'

A good old lesson. Harlots! Take note. Now, does anybody else want a piece of this child?

THEENIE *enters*

Scene Three

WAITER *removes coat. Takes off table cloth, puts on dirty apron. Covers chalkboard menu with Coca-Cola advertisement: 'SMILE, COKE ADDS LIFE'. Turns menu inside out. Now a cheap Lebanese restaurant.*

WAITER (*during the above activities*):
'King Solomon made himself a palanquin
from the wood of Lebanon.
He made its posts of silver,
its back of gold, its seat of purple:
it was lovingly wrought within
by the daughters of Jerusalem.'

You come up in the world, you come down in the world.'

Lebanese music.

'What is that coming up from the wilderness,
like a column of smoke,
perfumed with myrrh and frankincense?'

AXIS *enters with a bicycle helmet, a luminous jacket, and a smog mask.*

AXIS: As I rose out of the evening peak
head down head choking
bicycle past news of sieges . . .

THEENIE: Sounds like where we live. (*She embraces* AXIS.)

WAITER: Two of them! In all my born days. (*He goes.*)

THEENIE: Hi!

AXIS: Did you get anything done?

THEENIE: I've been standing in front of the canvas for hours, not painting, stabbing.

AXIS: Don't give up Theenie. Anybody who tries to paint humanity with confidence is going to have days when nothing happens.

THEENIE: I'm sick of 'almost'. I want it magnificent. Have you seen the way Alabastar's hands move? Zap, zap, sideways, dodging, and it's on the screen that very instant, as if any second his life is going to blow up.

AXIS: If he's got twenty cents he gets another one.

THEENIE: I hate those machines. Why couldn't I work today? I get an idea, I try to do it . . . (*Pause.*)

AXIS: Stop worrying about what other people are going to think.

THEENIE: I'm not good enough.

AXIS: You are. It's your palette and your brush. Go on, say it, 'I'm a painter, and I'm good.'

THEENIE: I'm . . . I'm . . . Oh Axis. (*She hugs her.*) Thanks. How was your day?

AXIS: Don't ask. I'll get onto the latest government cuts at the clinic.

THEENIE: Is that going to send you all into another collective depression?

AXIS: We're not going to let it. I've been doing pregnancy tests all day. When the last one came out positive I didn't know how to break the news to the woman, she looked like she'd fall apart. But she was thrilled. Been trying to have a kid for years.

THEENIE: Hooray!

WAITER (*re-enters*): 'Your two breasts are like two fawns . . .'

AXIS: Two large mixed plates please.

WAITER: 'twins of a gazelle that feed among the lilies.'

AXIS: Hang on — one vegetarian.

WAITER: Vegetarian.

THEENIE: And if we could please, a carafe of white wine.

WAITER: White wine.

THEENIE: Almond cakes, coffee.

WAITER: Almond cakes, coffee.

THEENIE: Oh, and Turkish delight.

WAITER: Turkish delight. (*He goes.*)

AXIS: Theenie, are we having a party?

THEENIE: A funeral for Western society. Sylvester's bought a Space Invaders console.

AXIS: For himself, or his students?

THEENIE: For Alabastar!

AXIS: How are we going to afford to switch him on?

THEENIE: He's back with us tomorrow. It's our month.

AXIS: Hope you fixed it so we always get the short months.

THEENIE: I want to see him. (*Pause.*) When he's home with me I can't ever go into the studio and shut the door.

AXIS: Guilt.

THEENIE: Crap. When he's gone, it hurts, there's something missing.

AXIS: Yeah, dirty socks. I'll find something to turn him on. Do-it-yourself bread? Bicycle maintenance? Creative graffiti?

THEENIE: We spent hours with him making that billycart. He rode it down the hill *once,* and he was back inside demanding more money for the robot in the laundromat.

AXIS: Maybe we can save up, to buy him a hang-glider. Sorry, Theenie.

Every time we try to eat, try to get to know each other, in come the update on Alabastar, and you plonk him in the middle of the bed . . . I mean the table.

THEENIE: He has learnt to knock.

AXIS: He's nearly ten.

THEENIE: When he was born they gave me bowls of peaches. They covered the end of the bed with blue forget-me-nots, pansies and shawls. Now they're teaching him to open fire.

AXIS: Well, you could have had a girl child.

THEENIE: Is that the only way you can think of making paradise?

AXIS: All I mean is, if you'd had a girl, it would be easier. She wouldn't be anybody's hero, she wouldn't have anything to inherit. You could take a girl with you to self-defence classes.

THEENIE: What the hell do you want? Keep a knife by the bedside in case one pops out, and then cut it off and tuck it in? Expose them on the hillside like they did with unwanted girls? It craps me off when people give up hope for Alabastar because he was born a boy. That's as senseless as blaming everything on Eve or Pandora.

AXIS: Calm down.

THEENIE: I won't have people telling me that evil comes because of that male piece of punctuation. If I have to believe that, I'm running out of here like Jocasta, to hang myself.

AXIS: Shut up. I want to get drunk. And I love you.

THEENIE: And Alabastar?

AXIS: Sometimes I don't think you see me.

THEENIE: Axis, let's get off this tightrope.

AXIS: I don't think we own the ground down there. Or the wire we're balancing on.

WAITER (*enters with a basket of bread*): 'How graceful are your feet in sandals, O queenly maiden.' (*Exits.*)

THEENIE: There's nothing we can do about it. My brother gave Alabastar a gun for Christmas. When we got home Vandelope was there.

Light change.

AXIS: Our friend the pacifist.

THEENIE: In her jungle greens. (*She plays a mock firing game with* AXIS *and the invisible* ALABASTAR.)

VANDELOPE *enters.*

VANDELOPE: So this is Alabastar. I've met him. On the pinnies.

Firing video game noises.

He thinks he can bring a gun in here, does he? Good one. Boom. Got 'im.

Firing noises.

THEENIE: Alabastar dear. Put it away.

VANDELOPE: Away? Smash it. You know what little macho shits grow into? Big macho shits. As if having a gun cocked with bullets isn't enough, they grow their own, the fuckers. Put it down, Alabastar. I said, put it down. Only pigs and warmongers have guns — Stalin, Reagan, Pinochet and Alabastar. Aw Shulamith, now I've made him cry.

THEENIE: Don't cry, Albie. It's all right. She didn't mean to jump on you.

AXIS: Go on, Vandelope. Explain to him that right now we have to fight our way out from under, but when the anger's all come out and changed the world we're gonna live in peace.

VANDELOPE: If you put your commitment to male children above your commitment to women . . .

AXIS: Heavy.

THEENIE: Albie, we'll get you a soccer ball.

VANDELOPE: If you put your commitment to male children above your commitment to women . . . Holy Germaine! Anybody coming? I've got a few billboards to bugger up. (*She goes.*)

THEENIE: Go if you want to, Axis, follow her. She's so lucky, so pure, she's never even had a tampon inside her.

AXIS: You don't have to send me away, Theenie. (*They embrace.*)

Light change.

THEENIE: The sun's come out.

AXIS: Okay, Alabastar, let's go down the canal and play. (*She plays a game with* THEENIE *and the invisible* ALABASTAR. *Invisible ball!*)

VANDELOPE *enters. Writes graffiti on Coca-cola billboard: 'SMILE: WHILE U STILL GOT TEETH.' Then joins the ball game.*

Improvised shouts of ball game between AXIS, THEENIE, VANDELOPE *and* ALABASTAR.

WAITER (*re-enters, tries to join the game*): 'Catch us the foxes, the little foxes,
that spoil the vineyards,
for our vineyards are in blossom.'

AXIS *and* THEENIE *collide and embrace at the moment when the* WAITER *gets the ball unexpectedly.* VANDELOPE *goes.*

WAITER (*hit in the middle with the ball*): Oof! (*He kicks it away.*) Howzat. (*He notices* THEENIE *and* AXIS *kissing.*) Harlots! Break it up. You'll put the customers off their food.

THEENIE: Appeal to his rationality, Axis. His inbred sense of justice.

AXIS: I'll phone Vandelope. She'll know a lawyer. Arrest this restaurant. (*She kisses* THEENIE.)

WAITER: 'The juice of my pomegranates.' What a waste! (*He separates* AXIS *and* THEENIE.)

AXIS: How come you're not molesting that couple of heterosexists up the back?

WAITER: They have a right to enjoy their evening in peace.

AXIS: Enjoy their evening? They're canoodling, paddling up to their necks, and because they're a man and a woman it'll turn up on children's TV.

THEENIE: Axis, don't. Let's go.

AXIS: I haven't eaten my dinner.

THEENIE: We can't fight the whole world.

AXIS: He's discriminating against women on the grounds of sex. Call the cops.

WAITER: Get out of here. You sluts are ruining my business.

AXIS: Stuff your business!

THEENIE: Come home, Axis, come home,
The kettle calls on the stove;
The curtains keep out the cold.
The walls, the walls make us free.

AXIS: I want justice! Do I have to turn the tables over before I can have a quiet dinner? Lay my head on a woman's breast, and you insult me. Vandelope! Help! Slander! Ho! Police!

WAITER (*enters wearing* SERGEANT's *coat and hat*): Behold, the paddy wagon!
'About it are sixty mighty men . . .
All girt with swords
and expert in war . . .
each with his sword at his thigh.'

THEENIE: Axis, we can reason our way out of this.

AXIS: Good evening, officer, sir, would you be so helpful as to register formal charges against this place of business and its manager for violating the Anti-Discrimination Act.

SERGEANT: You'll have to come down to the station.

AXIS: You don't understand. You have to book the restaurant.

SERGEANT: I've had dinner, love.

THEENIE: Axis, he's bigger than us.

AXIS: I'm not going to have him call me love.

SERGEANT (*seizes* AXIS): Come on, love.

THEENIE: You're hurting her. Police don't hurt people.

AXIS: You're breaking my arm, you dickwit.

THEENIE: Please stop.

SERGEANT: Are you coming quietly, lady, or head first and noisy?

AXIS: Let me go.

SERGEANT: Bloody communist drug-fiends!

AXIS: Radioactive mine owner from Queensland!

VANDELOPE *strolls through with a sandwich-board the front of which reads: 'SISTERS, KEEP A SMILE ON YOUR LIPS AND A SONG IN YOUR HEART', and on the back: 'WHILE YOU'RE SMASHING THE STATE'. She rearranges chairs for the next scene.*

VANDELOPE (*sings*):
Don't be too polite, girls
Don't be too polite.
Show a little fight, girls,
Show a little fight.
Don't be fearful of offending in case
    you get the sack,
Just recognise your value, and you
    won't look back.

All among the bull, girls
All among the bull . . .

She goes.
SOLOMON *enters.*

SOLOMON: Manhater! Hijacking harlot!

VANDELOPE, *off, blows a raspberry.*

(SOLOMON *covers* VANDELOPE'*s coca-cola ad. graffiti.*) Give them their heads and they'd change the scenery. I'm the one with the overall view. (*He*

hangs up a banner: 'HAPPY BIRTHDAY ALABASTAR'.) The child is turning ten. Now's the time to infiltrate the party. (*Changes coat to become* KURT.) Disguise myself as a plant in the heart of the nuclear family. The boy needs his uncle, Kurt, a capital man, of my own calibre. He'll know what the boy wants in a mother.

'I would lead you and bring you
into the house of my mother,
and into the chamber of her that
    conceived me.'

He goes.

Scene Four

VIOLET *enters during* KURT'*s last speech, followed by* ARCHIBALD, *both wearing party hats, and carrying punch bowl and tray of punch cups.*
    Light opera music, eg. Gilbert and Sullivan medley.

VIOLET: The children can eat in the rumpus room, they'll be less of a mess and bother.

ARCHIBALD: Theenie rang to say she's bringing that woman.

VIOLET: We'll need another chair for the adults then, dear.

ARCHIBALD: My dear Violet! Must you encourage my daughter in that unspeakable house full of bandwagons? Last year a pro-communist war, this year women's lib, next month the Aborigines and any moment now they'll discover something useful, like rainforests.

VIOLET: Dearest, she believes in good causes. There but for the grace of God go you or I.

ARCHIBALD: I would not want her to be insensitive to injustice, but she embarrasses. Any excuse to demonstrate the disruption of our peace, from government bashing to graffiti, and our daughter is in attendance. Doesn't she realise our country is being handed over on a platter to the very bus-stop collection of union-mongers and liberationists who are plunging it into bankruptcy?

VIOLET: On your grandson's tenth birthday.

THEENIE *and* AXIS *enter.*

THEENIE: Hello, mum.

VIOLET: Hullo, Theenie.

THEENIE: Hullo, dad. This is Axis. My parents. Violet and Archibald.

ARCHIBALD. How do you do, Axis? Axis. First names already. I'll save my protests. (*Pause.*)

VIOLET: Arch.

ARCHIBALD: Would you ladies like a party punch?

AXIS: Thanks.

THEENIE: Cheers!

VIOLET: Where's our Alabastar?

THEENIE: Hiding in the willows. He's a tree pirate.

ARCHIBALD: Pirate eh? (*He calls.*) Alabastar? Here comes the big cwocodile. (*To* THEENIE.) Remember? Coming to get you. Tick tock, tick, tock. (*He goes.*)

VIOLET: Be good to your father, won't you? He's feeling the strain of work. There's so little decency left in the world.

THEENIE: I'll be good. I care for you both, you know that. (*Hugs* VIOLET.)

VIOLET: That's my girl. (*To* AXIS.) And you dear, it's nice of you to come, it's nice of you to have each other, and be friends. (*To* THEENIE.) Theen, anytime you want to invite her over for a meal, dear, just let me know, and it's nice for you and Alabastar, having an auntie in the house. Now I wonder where the others are, come and we'll get out the good teaset, not much use saving it till I'm dead and gone. (*She goes off.*) Arch! Alabastar!

THEENIE: Thanks for coming.

AXIS: Your old man wants to put me in the zoo.

VIOLET (*off*): Come on, Theen.

THEENIE *goes.*

AXIS: Write me a message that I don't exist.

VIOLET *enters carrying a jug with more punch.*

VIOLET: Oh dear, Alabastar does need a haircut, he can't possible see out, dear, you have to find the wisdom to choose, the good Lord gave Theenie the brains to use, heaven knows.

AXIS: We were going to do it for him this morning. Only we had a bit of trouble finding the scissors in the chaos. Theenie's working on a new painting.

VIOLET: When she was little she loved bright colours. I'd get her those pots of fingerpaint and we were always running out of red.

AXIS: She still loves to rub her fingers in the paint.

VIOLET: One day she painted a whole story on the lounge-room wall. It's still there, under the wallpaper. And what do you do, dear?

AXIS: I see people. In a clinic. I get fed up with it sometimes.

VIOLET: Oh, you're a nurse, aren't you?

AXIS: Not exactly. We have . . .

ARCHIBALD *enters with a chair. There are now three chairs.*

VIOLET: Over there, dear. We'll need the cake tray down from the top shelf and a ribbon to tie on the knife. (*She goes.*)

AXIS: It's a beautiful old jug. Is it crystal?

ARCHIBALD: Young lady. You do appreciate . . . You have a responsibility to consider Alabastar.

AXIS: I do.

ARCHIBALD: It is important that you tell me what you think . . . of our landscape. An original.

AXIS: It's very nice.

ARCHIBALD: Ah! Do you dabble with the brush too? Like our Theenie?

AXIS: Dabble! It's Theenie's work.

SOLOMON *enters as* KURT *with a bottle of brandy.*

KURT: Behold! A wise and kingly spirit.

ARCHIBALD: Son, how do you do?

KURT: How do you do, father?

ARCHIBALD: Napoleon, ah.

KURT: 'Who is this that looks forth like the dawn,
fair as the moon, bright as the sun . . .'

AXIS *gives* KURT *a dirty look.*

'terrible as an army with banners?'

ARCHIBALD: Allow me to introduce a relative newcomer to the family, currently establishing her reputation as an art critic. Kurt Havistock, may I present Miss Axis . . . Axis mm.

KURT: We've met. An art lover, eh? Did you have time to study the collection of Old Masters when you were at Central Court?

AXIS: I am outnumbered. (*She goes.*)

ARCHIBALD: What was she doing in court?

KURT: It would not be very loyal of me to tell you.

ARCHIBALD: Loyal?

KURT: To Theenie. She is entitled to her secrets.

ARCHIBALD: Kurt, we are a family. We have our name.

VIOLET (*off*): Arch dear, the ham. Are you ready with the carving knife?

ARCHIBALD: Now is neither the time nor the place, but this is no light matter, son. (*He goes.*)

MIRIAM (*off*): Darling! (*Enters, pregnant, bearing a pavlova pudding.*)

KURT: Christ!

MIRIAM: Darling, is there anything else to bring in out of the car? I do hope Sarah and Matthew behave themselves, it's boring when they don't.

AXIS *enters with things for the table.*

Hullo! Who's this?

AXIS: Well, I'm . . .

KURT: Theenie's latest.

MIRIAM: Beautiful hair. It does set off your head short like that, but how long did you leave the henna in? (*To* KURT.) She's actually beautiful, darling, what a waste!

AXIS: Don't turn away. Teach me how you wrap the sugar round the put-down.

THEENIE *enters bearing a dish.*

THEENIE: Oh, my God. Don't take them on, Axis.

AXIS: I'm taking them off.

VIOLET *enters.*

VIOLET: Don't upset your father, Theenie, Kurt. There's the worry of his kidneys.

AXIS: Truce.

VIOLET (*calls*): Alabastar! (*She takes the dish from* THEENIE.) Come on, darling, call the others. Children! Your frankfurters are ready in the rumpus room. Grandad's waiting. (*She goes.*)

KURT: Give Miriam the comfortable chair.

'The fig tree puts forth its figs,
And the vines are in blossom.'

Would you like a cushion for your back?

MIRIAM: Please. Thank you, darling. Happy mummy, happy baby.

VIOLET *enters.*

VIOLET: I didn't buy enough yo-yos.

Isn't it funny how everybody wants one? Children, children. It takes two to make a quarrel.

THEENIE: Do sit down, Violet.

AXIS *stands to give* VIOLET *her chair.* VIOLET *glares at* KURT *who has remained seated.*

VIOLET: Theenie, what have you been up to, dear?

THEENIE: I've started a . . .

ARCHIBALD (*enters from the rumpus room*): Little children should be seen and not heard.

THEENIE: Actually, I've . . .

ARCHIBALD: May I help anyone to a glass of liquid refreshment? Would you do the honours, son!

KURT: I think Theenie was about to tell us what she's been up to. Theenie? (*He offers her a drink. Calls.*) I don't care who started it. Matthew, you hit your sister again and you can forget about the football.

ARCHIBALD: I would venture to suggest without fear of contradiction that the behaviour of the children is the fault of our schools, where rampant left-wing influences exult in the subversion of discipline, diligence and decorum.

VIOLET: A growing boy needs his vitamins. I hope you're taking them every day now, Miriam.

KURT: Yes, mother, she is. Sarah! Let your mother have her rest.

MIRIAM: There's no need to take it out on the children. Sarah and Matthew are at very good schools. They have their altercations, naturally, but they adore one another. (*She exits to the rumpus room.*)

VIOLET (*to* ARCHIBALD): I'll have a drop more, thank you, dear. I wouldn't entirely blame the schools. There's more nonsense on television . . .

KURT: It's the Teachers' Federation, mother. I've told you that.

MIRIAM (*re-enters with a child's stained white dress*): Sarah! Kurt, she wanted to wear her new white dress and now look! If you knew how it makes me tired. (*She goes out with the dress.*)

KURT (*to* ARCHIBALD): Don't fill Miriam's glass. She becomes uncontrollable. (*He shouts.*) No more crisis-mongering in there, Sarah. I've told you not to cry. Don't cry. Thank you. Okay. Just don't cry. (*To* VIOLET.) I wouldn't put it past her to pull his hair.

AXIS: Theenie, you've got to say something.

THEENIE: Where would I start?

MIRIAM (*returns*): My charming Mr Havistock senior, now that the children have promised to be good, may I? (*She holds up her glass.*)

VIOLET: Miriam, you have your baby to think of.

KURT: She's drinking for two.

ARCHIBALD: For the blossoming Mrs Havistock junior, a pleasure.

VIOLET: Arch, dear, you haven't answered me. You always change the subject when what I say about television is right.

KURT: Mother, television is a powerful vehicle for freedom of choice, an indispensable part of the market, and of your financial destiny as an Australian shareholder.

VIOLET: We can have a destiny, and a sense of responsibility.

MIRIAM: I consider television a godsend for the mother with a commitment to her husband's career.

VIOLET: Are the children ready for their chocolate crackles?

KURT: Just a minute, mother. No sweets for Matthew and Sarah until they've got every sandwich off their plate.

THEENIE: Aren't you being a bit savage, Kurt? You're piling so many rules in front of them they'll never see over the top.

MIRIAM: Waste not, want not. Think of the starving millions.

KURT: You might be my sister, but you mind your own bloody business.

VIOLET: Don't use language here, Kurt.

KURT: Yes mother, I'll swear in my father's house if I bloody well want to. (*To* THEENIE:) How dare you criticise the upbringing of my children, when I suffer in silence the aberrations of you and your illtrained offspring.

VIOLET: Theenie, a soft answer turneth away wrath.

THEENIE: It's okay, Violet, I don't want to quarrel. (*She gives her a kiss.*)

ARCHIBALD: The disgrace is not the food, but the language. A generation is growing to adulthood with the grammar of the gutter. It comes this very afternoon from my grandson's mouth, 'I done whatcha said.' The greatest work of genius in the history of mankind is the English language. It catches at an old man's heart when the treasure house of centuries is ransacked.

THEENIE: No, Dad. It's changing, growing. If we did a Rip Van Winkle backwards for a hundred years, we'd find the language very different.

ARCHIBALD: That argument does not hold. I knew a time when it was the great men of letters who moved the language forward.

AXIS: And the women.

ARCHIBALD: I'll start again. I knew a time when it was the great men of letters and history – includes Jane Austen and George Eliot – who created our language and its beauty. Now it has become fashionable to adopt the speech and manners of the proletariat. The children of the least educated are dictating to us how we shall talk. 'I done whatcha said.'

VIOLET (*perfectly modulated*): I did what you said.

ARCHIBALD: Thank you, Violet.

MIRIAM: I did enjoy the claret cup.

THEENIE: Are you sure it's a choice between *I done* and *I did?* I mean once we used to say, 'I have done', then someone invented 'I've done', and now the adults are saying it so quickly, all the children hear is 'I done'. We're moving to a faster language, away from the restrictions of the apostrophe.

ARCHIBALD: My dear daughter! What we have lost in clarity and precision . . .

AXIS: Our Alabastar's helping. The other day he told me, 'I already undone them there knots meself, but.'

ARCHIBALD: Theenie, you must move.

VIOLET: Arch dear, couldn't we manage somehow to send Alabastar to a private school?

AXIS: I don't think they'd like my sandshoes on parent-teacher nights.

THEENIE: Don't tease them, Axis, I can't bear it.

MIRIAM: Have you ever had the opportunity to have children, Axis dear?

KURT: Are you being optimistic, or ridiculous? How can women's libbers have a sensible conversation about motherhood? Look in the media. They tirade against it. But notice how she says, 'Our Alabastar.' Mark my words, as soon as these women realise their control over the next generation is slipping out from under them, you'll see an immediate revival of the maternal instinct they've been so busy thwarting.

AXIS: Bullshit.

ARCHIBALD: I will not have the language of the tavern in my house.

AXIS: I'm sorry. But do give me a moment to defend myself.

KURT: Moment! Have an hour. Take the chair.

MIRIAM: Kurt.

AXIS: I can choose to give birth if I want to, and right now I've got other things to do. How come, when you can't have a baby yourself, you think you have a god-given right to tell me how to run my maternal instinct? You're not going to put me down.

KURT: Nobody put you up in the first place.

THEENIE: Axis.

MIRIAM: Go on, Axis, spit at him, like you did at the policeman in court. Oh! Sorry! Is it a secret?

VIOLET: Kurt, get your father his tablets.

AXIS: This is so fucking real, I'm getting out of here.

THEENIE: Wait. Please, Axis.

AXIS: I've got to apologise again, have I?

THEENIE: No. No. This time he has. Listen, Kurt, you may be my brother, and I used to love playing marbles with you, but I didn't come here for your judgement. I came because I love my warm-hearted mother and I love my dear old conservative dad, and we enjoy our odd conversations on language and the death of the King's English. And you can't turn Alabastar into a dog that you train how to bark, and you can't turn me into you. I'm going out to the kitchen to stuff myself on the biggest piece of Pavlova since the Sydney Opera House. (*To* AXIS:) Are you proud of me?

AXIS: Yep. For sanity's sake, let's go.

THEENIE: Yes. No. Everybody's ideology's at stake, but I can't leave before the birthday cake.

AXIS: I can smell the passionfruit and cream. (*She takes the pavlova.*)

THEENIE *and* AXIS *go out.* AXIS *carries the pavlova.*

MIRIAM: I need to do my yoga breathing to plan my reduced serving of Pavlova. (*She goes.*)

KURT: Father, why have you allowed Theenie and that woman such a disgraceful exhibition?

VIOLET: Now Kurt, Theenie's got an opportunity my generation didn't have to work it out for herself.

ARCHIBALD: Work it out? You expect me to welcome the female involvement society? The multi-cultural society? Do you know what lies behind that balderdash? Every troublesome, unqualified, ungrammatical, pill popping dishmop of a housewife to be found in this country, and every guttural, lisping tinpot god of a migrant desperate to settle here, thinks he . . . or she, is entitled to the freedom to dictate to everybody else. Already at Havistock Credit we do our market research in sixteen languages and three sexes. And an upstart Turk comes into the office, the sort that hangs gold rings in the nose of half a dozen wives, devoid of any understanding of democracy, and dammit, he's an indispensable multi-national contact!

VIOLET: Arch dear, your daughter's just like you, she cares.

ARCHIBALD: Yes, Violet, you are right. Our daughter is only a symptom, but she has a heart. She hasn't been left an easy life since that business of the divorce. Sylvester was a lovely boy. I'm worried about the polarisation, son. I'm worried that the decent people, the intelligent people, are going to be forced to build a high wall around their heritage, and patrol the boundaries with machine guns against the pillage of this vile generation. And that is not the freedom I have worked for in my life.

KURT: It will be Theenie's friends we'll
have to shoot.

ARCHIBALD: That is harsh, my son.

VIOLET: It's no wonder there are wars.

MIRIAM *enters.*

ARCHIBALD: My dear, sit down. Let
your old father-in-law have a kind
womanly smile.

MIRIAM *smiles and takes* ARCH's *cup
of punch.*

KURT: 'You have ravished my heart
with a glance of your eyes.'

Look at her. Ready for another baby,
and still Bo Derek.

MIRIAM: And look at him. My brilliant
lawyer and judge-to-be. As wise as
Solomon. She just dropped a willow
pattern jug, your sister's wife.

VIOLET: I don't know why you all can't
live and let live.

MIRIAM: Kurt, they're unnatural.
Theenie kissed her. On the lips. (*She
puts her arms around* KURT *for
reassurance.*)

KURT: Well? You could have said
something.

MIRIAM: I walked out.

KURT: It's time you learned to present
an intelligent argument. (*He calls.*)
Theenie! Axis!

MIRIAM: Don't bring them in here. I'm
relaxing.

KURT: Don't give me instructions. Stand
up for what you believe in.

MIRIAM: Darling, you're embarrassing
me.

KURT: You're letting the side down.
Challenge them or they'll have you in
a factory like the women in Russia.

VIOLET: Arch, you marshall the children
while we bring in the birthday
surprise. Come along, Miriam, get your
punch-bowl. And after that you must
put your feet up.

VIOLET *and* MIRIAM *go out.*

ARCHIBALD: Now's the time, son.

KURT: Theenie and that woman are both
in court like a couple of witches. On
charges of indecent language, immoral
acts in public, offensive behaviour,
assaulting a police officer in the
execution of his duty, malicious
damage to the interior of a paddy
wagon, and resisting arrest.

ARCHIBALD: Don't tell your mother.

KURT: And Alabastar? How are you
going to protect Alabastar?

ARCHIBALD: Oh, my Theenie.

KURT: Are you going to let her behave
like that and keep custody? Do we sit
by and lose a Havistock to the other
side?

ARCHIBALD: Get me Sylvester's phone
number. We'll save my grandchild if
we have to take it to the highest court
in the land.

ARCHIBALD *goes out.*
VIOLET, MIRIAM, AXIS *and*
THEENIE *enter,* THEENIE *carrying a
birthday cake, made like a pinball
machine with ten candles lit.*

THEENIE: It's lovely, Violet.

Lights out.

ARCHIBALD (*off*): Line up behind the
birthday boy. Get your guns ready.
Straight line. Wait for it. Quick march.
(*He enters with invisible children.*)
Left, right, left, right. Halt!

ALL (*sing*): Happy birthday to you
Happy birthday to you
Happy birthday, dear Alabastar
Happy birthday to you.

ARCHIBALD: Hip hip . . .

ALL: Hooray.

VIOLET: Make a wish, Alabastar, make a
wish. (*Candles blown out.*)

ALL (*go out in the dark, clearing props
from the party scene, while singing*):
For he's a jolly good fellow . . . etc.

Scene Five

Plush old country hotel. Green light on the table. Imaginary billiard balls. AXIS *and* THEENIE *enter with billiard cues. Billiard balls, pinball machines.*

AXIS: Lovely cut! I've got my eye in now. (*She plays.*) Blew it! Theen. Theenie!

THEENIE: What? What are you doing?

AXIS: I sunk four in a row. (*She kisses* THEENIE.)

SOLOMON *enters, disguised as a hotel guest. With billiard cue.*

AXIS (*to* THEENIE): It's your turn.

GUEST: Ladies. Excuse me.

AXIS: I'd be on the red, you've got a nice shot there.

GUEST: 'Your shoots are an orchard of pomegranates
with all choicest fruits.'

When I was at school a man stood up for a lady, and women did not play billiards.

THEENIE: I can't concentrate.

AXIS: Ignore him. (THEENIE *plays.*) Good shot.

THEENIE: It is lovely here. Cedar architraves, tinkling glass, moths in the velvet walls. I can't breathe.

AXIS: Stop worrying.

THEENIE: I want to rip up everything felt.

GUEST: She will ruin the cloth.

'You are stately as a palm tree
And your breasts are like its clusters.'

(*Attempting to show* THEENIE *how to use the cue.*) Madam, this is how you hold it.

AXIS: We got here first, thank you, sir. Get out.

GUEST: 'I say I will climb the palm tree
And lay hold of its branches.'

AXIS: Fuck off!

The GUEST *goes out.*

Wow! Did you see that?

THEENIE: Kiss me again. Come up to our room . . . Axis.

AXIS: Alabastar's with us and it's fine.

THEENIE: Why do they want to take him away from me?

AXIS: They're scared of me and you together.

THEENIE: They don't understand it.

AXIS: They can't control it. Alabastar has to turn out perfect or their empire falls in ruins. You have to work out whose life you're living. They'd force that child on you if they could split us up.

THEENIE: Don't say that. If I'm not holding onto you, nothing's real, nothing's safe.

AXIS: I can't be you. I want to finish the game.

THEENIE: I'll go.
Out. Up and down
This cold haunted town.
Run out and play baddies
Rape girls and old ladies,
Make havoc; why can't I?
I'm unnatural, aren't I?

If men can't have me, or my lover
They'll build a court and damn me,
Morally unfit to be a mother.

AXIS: Don't let politics leave you without a corner for yourself, or for me.

THEENIE: They're going to sue me.

AXIS: Oh shit, Theenie. This was supposed to be our decadent weekend away. If it didn't rain all the time in these painful mountains we could go out.

THEENIE: Alabastar doesn't want to go bushwalking.

AXIS: Alabastar? Alabastar! He's the only one enjoying this. Ice creams at Echo Point, rides on the Scenic Railway.

'Knock knock . . .
Who's there?
Walter.
Walter who?
Wall to wall carpet . . .'

Chocolates at the Paragon Café, and here, beside the log fire, in this stunning old camp hotel, Space Invaders.

Pinball machines.

You gotta smile. He's winning enough free games to flog them off to the other kids. With a bit of luck he'll get up to paying the hotel bill.

THEENIE: You don't like him, do you?

AXIS: I don't want to be torn to pieces. I'll support you if you have to fight for him, but right now I've got to have some space for myself.

THEENIE: You want me to lose him. Go on, admit it, you want his father to get him.

AXIS: Don't be crazy.

THEENIE: You wish he didn't exist.

AXIS *moves to go.*

THEENIE: Axis, where are you going? Where are you going?

AXIS: Out. (*She goes.*)

THEENIE: Let me come with you. (*She calls.*) Alabastar! (*Pause.*) Axis! Wait! It's raining. Please. (*No answer.*) Alabastar, get your raincoat. We're going out to hug a gumtree. (*She goes.*)

Blackout.

Scene Six

KURT *and* MIRIAM's *house.* MIRIAM *enters with a new baby wrapped in a shawl of purple, white and green, the suffragette colours.*

MIRIAM (*sings*): I have a dolly
With eyes of blue
And hair that's curly brown.

She wakes whenever I pick her up,
And she sleeps
When I lay her down.

KURT *enters with a towel. Doing his morning exercises.*

KURT: 'My head is wet with dew,
my locks with the drops of the night.'

Why am I the one to have a dream about Axis? I'm too busy. But someone has to lie her down and do it. That way she would learn. Someone has to make the world safe. She'll have my sister – do you know how close I was to my sister? – parade around the court, demanding rights. Rights! The filthy, sanctimonious, demonstrating lesos.

MIRIAM (*refers to the baby*): She looks like you darling. Don't you think?

KURT: Of course, sweetheart. But she's got your chin, God help her. (*Pause.*) My colleagues trust me. Damn it! I won't have my reputation diminished by deviants dragging my sister into their clitoral insurgency.

MIRIAM: Don't swear, Kurt, she'll hear you.

KURT: Daddy's ittie girl. Sleeping.

'Your eyes are doves
Behind your veil.'

I'm not going to let Alabastar down.

MIRIAM: Little fingers curled like warm shells.

KURT: 'Round and round the garden
Chased the teddy bear . . .'

When he gets in his bookcase Sylvester might look like a Marxist, but he and Louise are thoroughly decent people.

MIRIAM: I know, I know, Louise is perfect. But can't you worry about them some other time? A baby is for ever, yet when you have one, it only lasts a little while.

'Rock a bye baby
In the tree top . . .'

KURT: Will you ring Theenie up? See if

she can be reasonable. Tell her it's in the boy's best interests if she hands him over quietly without the messy business of a court case.

MIRIAM: 'When the wind blows . . .'

KURT: I've got it! Invite her to the christening.

MIRIAM: She has to be there, silly, she's the star performer.

'The cradle will rock . . .'

Look, she's smiling.

KURT: Darling, at that age it's wind. (*He sighs.*) I'm discussing Theenie, Auntie perilous Theenie.

MIRIAM: Theen and Axis sent his hand crocheted shawl. And don't you swear. Feel how soft it is. (*The shawl drops open to reveal a women's symbol worked into the cloth.*)

KURT: Good God, look at it. I warned you. The moment you have anything to do with them, they start hostilities.

MIRIAM: You forget, they grow so fast, this milk-warm baby smell.

KURT: Nothing matters to you, does it? Can you take time out to listen to me, Miriam? Freedom has to be fought for, it's very fragile. A red flag . . .

MIRIAM: 'It's very fragile. A red flag waver can come and break it, like that.' (*She waves a squeaky toy in front of the baby.*) Look, there's Daddy. Daddy!

KURT: Don't mock me, dear. Give me that. (*He grabs the toy.*) Do you think I'm working day and night simply for what you and I can get out of it?

MIRIAM: Don't you raise your voice at me, Kurt, I'm a nursing mother.

KURT: If I didn't care about Australia, I'd have sold out years ago. We could have bought an island in the South Pacific for a song, and let this country go to the bitches.

MIRIAM: You're frightening her.

KURT (*takes the baby*): There!

MIRIAM: Careful, Kurt.

KURT: I'll be careful.

MIRIAM: Careful. Don't you have to go in to work?

KURT: Miriam. There are moments when I almost wish I was you. I could forget about everything. Oh Gawd. (*To the baby:*) Are you puking? All right. I'm sorry. I'll fix it. Where do you keep the cloth?

MIRIAM: Baby! (*She takes the baby.*) If you knew how it makes me tired.

KURT: How it makes you tired!

MIRIAM (*she goes out, singing*): 'When the bough breaks
the cradle will fall,
and down will come baby
cradle and all.'

KURT *changes lights with a karate gesture and goes.*

Scene Seven

Back at the hotel.

AXIS (*enters*): Where is she? It's nearly dark. She wanted me to hold her, and I had to run away.

VANDELOPE *enters with a billiard cue.*

AXIS: Where is she?

VANDELOPE: I bet she's at the Paragon, knocking herself off with scones, jam and cream. (*She plays billiards.*)

AXIS: Vandelope, we just come from there. What if they wandered off the track?

VANDELOPE: She's probably stopped somewhere to do a rock carving. So much for your decadent weekend.

AXIS: She was driving me round the twist. We need to get away, I say, of course Alabastar can come — there's no escaping kids — and she accuses me of hating him.

VANDELOPE: She's gotta put that Alabastar in a big basket and dump it on his dad's doorstep.

AXIS: He's not a bloody cross-eyed kitten.

VANDELOPE: Sylvester can cope. Their house is air-conditioned.

AXIS: Vandelope, it's taken me a while, but when you live in a house with a kid, their friends come and visit, they talk to you, and you get fond of them.

VANDELOPE: It's your go. Axis love, you're holding it like a toothpick.

AXIS (*plays*): The table won't keep still! She knows the bush, I know she knows the bush.

VANDELOPE: This isn't a game, it's a nervous breakdown.

AXIS: Last week she ripped the knife through her big canvas, that's why we came up here.

VANDELOPE: I can see it's bad, it's in your eyes.

AXIS: Why can't she see that?

VANDELOPE: Have you given her the chance?

AXIS: We hardly see each other anymore. I'm either at the clinic or barmaiding. If we have to go through the courts to keep the kid, there'll be all those illegal fees, thousands. Theenie doesn't realise. I feel like I'll get punished whatever I do.

VANDELOPE (*holds* AXIS): There's the world out there to get angry with and we keep turning the knives on ourselves.

THEENIE (*off*): You'd better run upstairs, Alabastar, and get some dry clothes.

VANDELOPE: Wouldn't you know it? Right on dinner-time.

THEENIE *enters.*

THEENIE: I thought you'd caught the train.

AXIS: I haven't, have I?

AXIS *and* THEENIE *embrace.*

VANDELOPE: Well, you didn't think I'd let you two bust up, did you?

AXIS: Hours. Hours and hours.

THEENIE: The wattle was in flower.

VANDELOPE: Well, I come up to the mountains for fresh air and a capuccino, and there's Axis, staring into her cup of froth at the Paragon — Well, that was a fortuitous conjunction of the charts, wasn't it? Half the ghetto turns up, into the waffles, polishing off with a little bushwalk round the cliffs.

THEENIE: We saw the lyrebird.

AXIS: Did you?

THEENIE: She came out of the bush in front of us . . .

VANDELOPE: Some people have all the fun.

THEENIE: She fluffed her wings like an old woman gathering her skirts and ran, ran on her skinny legs down the track and disappeared.

AXIS: I wish I'd been there.

THEENIE: So do I. I was okay in the bush. I walk out of the tree ferns and the world's still everywhere.

VANDELOPE: I'm going to put my butt in, even if it gives you the shits. It doesn't matter where he lives from now on.

THEENIE: Don't you start driving me mad. (*She turns to go.*)

AXIS: Come back. Theenie. We've got to work it out.

VANDELOPE: Let me finish. Theenie, they'll stick the kid in an old school tie, keep his vowels open, and try to teach him to despise us. But he won't turn out like them. He's been with you, he's got your sensitive world with him in here — (*She indicates her head.*) — and in here — (*Heart.*) — and he's missed out on one or two of the cockfights that usually come with the balls.

THEENIE: You mean he's not a macho pig after all, and I still have to give him up?

VANDELOPE: But it's safe to let go of him, he doesn't throw beer cans at lyrebirds. Sure, he'll love life with the upwardly mobile, until he realises he has to swap honesty for knives and forks.

AXIS: He'll tell them where to stick it. And when he's older he'll rebel and marry a feminist.

VANDELOPE: With a bit of luck he'll just live with him.

THEENIE: I don't care what fancy reasons you think up, and I don't care if he grows cloven hoofs as well as a tail, he's my kid.

VANDELOPE: I know it's hard, but are you and Axis going to ruin your lives and alienate your friends just to save Alabastar from the nuclear family?

THEENIE: I love him, and I'll be as emotional and irrational as I like, and I won't let anyone take him away, whether they attack from the right, or they attack from the left. And everyone screaming at me, 'It's for your own good, you understand, and we're sure it's in the best interests of the child.' (*She goes.*)

AXIS: How come a touch of honest feminism goes down like poison?

VANDELOPE: I meant it as an antidote. Run after her, tell her I didn't understand she was struck on him. Tell her I'll help. We'll raise the money and fight.

AXIS: Thanks. Wish me luck. (*She goes.*)

VANDELOPE: We could do with a good campaign. We're down on morale.

ACT TWO

Scene One

Lights dim. A street very late at night outside SYLVESTER's *house. 'LESBIAN M' has been painted on the wall.*
　　Car passing close. Headlights sweep by. VANDELOPE *and* AXIS *hide. They have a torch, and* AXIS *has a pot of paint and a brush.*

VANDELOPE: They've gone.

AXIS: A taxi, fuck it. He'll have a radio.

VANDELOPE: Did he see us?

AXIS: Dunno. Got three more letters. (AXIS *paints on wall by torchlight: 'UMS.'*)

Police siren, car.

VANDELOPE: Pigs! We can get through those bushes and over the fence.

AXIS: They've got a sausage dog called Yappy.

VANDELOPE: They would have. (VANDELOPE *and* AXIS *hide.*)

SERGEANT (*off*): Mongrels!

Dog barks. Car drives away. Siren fades.

　　Street lights on AXIS *and* VANDELOPE. *They give one another a victory sign and a hug.*

VANDELOPE (*shines her torch on the graffiti*): You little ripper.

　　VANDELOPE *and* AXIS *exit.*

Scene Two

Daylight outside SYLVESTER *and* LOUISE's *house. The graffiti on the wall is now visible. 'LESBIAN MUMS.'* SYLVESTER *and* KURT *enter.*

SYLVESTER (*indicates the graffiti*): There!

KURT: Barbarians! On your own property. I've rung the papers. If she's forcing this case to court, you'll need evidence of this infantile smearing.

SYLVESTER: Will you give me a moment to think? There has to be a rational way to give Alabastar the stability he needs. How did Theenie get mixed up in this idiotic extremism? We used to sit up for hours talking philosophy. Well she's not going to make me guilty because I earn enough to buy this house. Alabastar likes it here. He's my son and I want him here, he's a great little person.

KURT: Inform her officially you're not sending Alabastar back, and if she doesn't call off this . . . war, you'll inform her employer she's a lesbian.

SYLVESTER: She's freelance. Your publicity will double the price of her paintings.

KURT: Freelance! You can establish in court that she doesn't have a steady income.

SYLVESTER: Will you lay off.

KURT: I've got it. Does Axis work? Get onto her boss. The top man.

SYLVESTER: She works at the Women's Clinic.

KURT: How promiscuous are they? You can prove it isn't a stable relationship. (*Pause.*) Family! That's it. Say you'll spill the beans. The impenetrable Axis must have a mother and a father.

SYLVESTER: My God. Can't you base your arguments on a modicum of good taste?

KURT: Don't shrug your self-righteous shoulders at me, Syl old boy, I didn't scribble on your wall.

LOUISE *enters with tray of coffee things.*

KURT: Ah, Louise.
'Let me hear your voice,
For your voice is sweet
And your face is comely.'

LOUISE: Why Kurt! You're such a funny, gallant man.

KURT: The age of chivalry is not dead, and is that the flower of pregnancy blooming on your cheeks?

LOUISE: Oh you! Lucky you and Miriam.

KURT (*offers* LOUISE *a chair*): I am at your service any time. (*Kisses her hand.*)

'O that you would kiss me
with the kisses of your mouth!
For you love is better than wine.'

LOUISE (*pours coffee*): Milk?

KURT: I'll have my women white, and my coffee black.

SYLVESTER: Let's have some semblance of respect for humanity.

KURT: Haven't you married delectable milk white skin? Humanity will lose you Alabastar.

SYLVESTER: God knows why I ever let you interfere in what was a very convenient arrangement between Theenie and myself.

LOUISE: Dearest love, that wasn't working, you said that yourself — a month here with us, a month in that commune, the poor boy didn't know whether he was Arthur or Martha. He's nearly a teenager, he needs a routine. And look at our house. Just when the sauna arrives, she attacks us.

SYLVESTER: You don't think, darling, we provoked her, by keeping him here. It is her month.

LOUISE: Suppose I walk over here and stand in her shoes and there's her precious Alabastar on the other side of the wall. It looks like we kidnapped him. So she turns us into capitalist monsters whose house should be ruined. He wants to stay here. I thought we were doing the best we could for him sending him to Bedlingham Grammar, but if she thinks he's going to be happy mucking around way below his ability in an ordinary state school for the sake of her revolutionary principles, then I give up. I'm sorry. He needs the guidance. Violin and homework, and then he can play pinball.

KURT: Play! He should be making them.

SYLVESTER: You have overdrawn my patience.

KURT: That's where we're steering Matthew – computers.

LOUISE: Alabastar's artistic. Can't you see him in the Senate?

SYLVESTER: I wish I could give Alabastar life on a Mozart record. He was asking this morning when he was going to see his other mother – both of them. I want him to be happy, but so in her own strange way does Theenie.

LOUISE: Well, you'll be pleased to know we had a phone call from the Undone Graffiti Company. Don't look so worried. They specialise in sandstock bricks.

SYLVESTER: Cross your fingers they get here ahead of the press. (*He goes, taking the coffee tray.*)

KURT: 'O-fairest among women . . .'

You're the only woman I can talk to. Miriam won't listen. You can feel free to talk to me. I know you're worried and I want to help. He's your boy now. What's on your mind?

LOUISE: I'm doing anything I can for Sylvester.

KURT: Do you think he's descended into apathy, or downright complicity?

LOUISE: He's carrying an enormous burden.

VANDELOPE *and* AXIS *enter disguised as workers from the Undone Graffiti Company. AXIS has a cleaning machine, and a concealed pot of paint and brush. VANDELOPE has a cassette player, with Greek music –*

loud. If desired, AXIS *could be the cleaning machine itself, operated by* VANDELOPE *by remote control.*

Hooray. There's the wall, we want it all off, do you hear, all off, completely off, it's got to be totally off, clean.

VANDELOPE: Buenos noces, madame et m'sieur. Santa Lucia.

Tinafto portoleni agapi, sa gapo,
    volpone
Ik ike ok
Waynee weedy winky
Amo amas amat
Hoki mai, wahine,

LOUISE: What?

VANDELOPE: Qu'ils mangent de la brioche.

LOUISE: Turn it off.

VANDELOPE: What you say, lady?

LOUISE: Turn it off. (*Turning towards* AXIS.)

VANDELOPE: Hey! Honi soit qui mal y pense.
Sul mar a luciar lustro dargento.

LOUISE: I don't speak Greek.

AXIS *has painted during the above another word on the wall: 'OK!'* AXIS *and* VANDELOPE *exchange a look.*

VANDELOPE (*miming needing a hose*): Psshhh.

LOUISE: Oh, round the back.

VANDELOPE: No, no, lady, you don't understand. Psshh.

LOUISE: Round the back.

VANDELOPE: Danke schön lady. (*To* KURT.) Guten Tag, Mettwurst.

VANDELOPE *and* AXIS *go.*

LOUISE: I don't think anybody understands.

KURT: You can trust me.

'O my love, in the clefts of the rock . . .'

LOUISE: I'm not in the mood. It's the

past. I haven't got a past. Not like
Sylvester has. No child of my own. No
great love to look back on. Apart from
the curtains in the loungeroom I can't
point to something and say 'That's
what I did.' As long as that boy is
here, or there, or anywhere, Sylvester
is tied to *her*.

SYLVESTER *enters. Unseen by*
KURT *and* LOUISE.

KURT: You just need to be reminded
how beautiful you are.

LOUISE: No!

KURT: Sylvester needs you, and my
nephew needs both of you. You can
hold this family together. Otherwise
Sylvester will dither away on his
well-cleaned academic bum, until
Theenie has manipulated Alabastar
into a suitable case for a lobotomy.

SYLVESTER: Get out of here. Now.

LOUISE: Darling!

KURT (*sees what has been added to the
wall graffiti*): More! See.

LOUISE: What? Oh, no, Sylvester!

KURT: The ratbags. Fraternise with them
and you turn this country into a
cesspit for subversives. Hey you!
Where are you taking the kid? They're
kidnapping Alabastar. Harlots! (*He
runs off.*)

LOUISE: Sylvester, do something.

SYLVESTER: It's their month.

LOUISE: I could shake you at a time like
this.

SYLVESTER: Don't darling. Don't make
it harder than it already is.

LOUISE: I'm not. It's just the strain of
not knowing where we are.

SYLVESTER: Bear with me. I need you,
sweet one.

LOUISE: All right, darling. I'm sorry.
What would you like for dinner,
darling?

LOUISE *and* SYLVESTER *go.*

Scene Three

KURT *arrives. Cues in organ music, and
lights for stained glass window. Moves
table.*
　　MIRIAM *arrives with the baby in a
christening robe.*
　　MIRIAM *poses for flash photo.*
　　KURT *takes the baby.*

MIRIAM: Careful!

KURT: 'My dove, my perfect one, is only
　　one,
　　the darling of her mother,
　　flawless to her that bore her.'

　　KURT *and* MIRIAM *pose together for
four photos.*

　　VIOLET *and* ARCHIBALD *enter.*

ARCHIBALD: I trust Theenie is not
bringing her life's companion, the
misfit?

VIOLET: Ssh, Arch. We're in church.
Hullo, Miriam.

　　KURT *gives* VIOLET *the baby.*
　　Photo flash of VIOLET *and the baby.*
　　VIOLET *hands the baby to*
ARCHIBALD.

Careful!

Flash of ARCHIBALD *and the baby.
The baby gets passed along the line to*
MIRIAM.

*Photo flash of each change of holding
the baby. Change of lights.*

What a lovely service! But a bit rushed,
don't you think?

ARCHIBALD: Come and sit down,
Miriam.

The baby cries. MIRIAM *finds a
dummy.*

VIOLET: Miriam, not a dummy, that is
naughty. You'll make her a smoker in
later life!

KURT: 'We have a little daughter,
　　and she has no breasts.
　　What shall we do for our daughter
　　on the day when she is spoken for?'

KURT *goes.*

ARCHIBALD: Miriam, my dear, the best thing I could do for her was to sign a pink slip of paper.

VIOLET: Now dear, it ought to be banked, for when she wants to go to university.

MIRIAM: Oh Archibald, you darling generous fairy godfather. Thank you! She's too little to tell you herself. (*She shows the baby the cheque.*) Look!

ARCHIBALD: May she grow to have the delicate charm and modest demeanour of her mother. And her grandmother.

VIOLET: And this, Miriam, belonged to her great great grandmother. It's her diary, her poetry, and pressed flowers.

MIRIAM: Oh. A treasure. For my wittle Sleeping Beauty.

KURT *enters with a huge package.*

KURT: Roll up, ladies and gents. Here in this tent we have the world's most proud, most lavish daddy. Guilty, ladies and gentlemen, of bringing you from the seven corners of the globe, the world's biggest, quadrophonic, walk-in, battery-operated — young Matthew can show her the wiring — *dolls' house.* (*He opens the box away from the audience.*)

The baby cries.

VIOLET: Careful, Kurt, careful.

KURT (*takes the baby*): For Daddy's noo girl? Can Sarah play too? If you can learn to stack the dishwasher half as quickly as your big sister Sarah, Daddy will be proud of you.

The baby cries.

VIOLET *takes the baby.*

The crying stops.

VIOLET: He earns at the bar more money than sense. And she ought to be feeding her baby now.

KURT: Well, darling, what does my favourite wife think of it?

MIRIAM: It's very very . . . everything. How will she manage? It makes me want to crawl in there and hide.

KURT: Have you lost your contact lenses, woman? Don't thank me, will you?

MIRIAM: I was going to thank you, Kurt, of course I was.

KURT: No, just don't thank me.

MIRIAM: Baby. (*She takes the baby.*) This little piggy went to market, this little piggy stayed home . . .

THEENIE *and* AXIS *enter.*

ARCHIBALD: Good afternoon, ladies.

THEENIE: Hullo.

VIOLET: Hullo, darling, hullo, Axis.

KURT: That settles it. Theenie, there is no basis for negotiation if you bring into my house, that that . . . black witch.

ARCHIBALD: Son, will you have the intelligence to meet a crisis with the dignity of a gentleman.

AXIS: Oh double bubble, I forgot the cauldron. Can I have a hold of her?

KURT: No!

MIRIAM: I don't think I should let you.

VIOLET (*to* AXIS): Keep your hand under her head. (*She takes the baby from* MIRIAM *and gives her to* AXIS.)

AXIS (*sings*): A caterpillar on a tree
Found a leaf to eat for tea.
Humpity humpity hump.

One day she felt the strangest things
Her body was growing legs and wings.
Humpity humpity hump.

She stretched herself, and climbed up high,
Bumpity bumpity bump
Left the branch and learnt to fly.
Humpity humpity hump.

KURT: Father, they're already turning Alabastar into a fairy. And we allow ourselves to be intimidated while she casts spells on my daughter. Look.

ARCHIBALD: Enough. I will speak to Theenie.

VIOLET: Come along, Miriam dear. I'll get you your cuppa, and you can feed her.

ARCHIBALD: Subtlety is more valuable than kingdoms.

AXIS: Alabastar can come too. He wants to see the baby.

THEENIE: Thanks, Axis.

AXIS: Courage! There's a full moon. Look at her funny baby nose.

VIOLET *and* AXIS, *with the baby, go out.*

KURT: Run after them, go on, save your baby.

MIRIAM: Oooh! (*She goes.*)

THEENIE: I want to ask you to stop insulting Axis. And me.

ARCHIBALD: You're very precious to me, Theenie. What's in the parcel?

THEENIE: It's a book.

KURT: The complete works of Ima Crank.

THEENIE: The pages are blank.

ARCHIBALD: For photographs.

THEENIE: Or drawings, paintings. One day she might write in it herself. (*She gives the parcel to* KURT.)

KURT: I can see returning the helpful sister I remember.

ARCHIBALD: We all know and love a very attractive and intelligent Theenie.

KURT: We used to share our toys, remember, you loved marbles. I don't like to see you seduced into something that isn't you.

ARCHIBALD: I appreciate, my dear, the enormity of the sacrifice that has to be made, but I feel certain that the young lady, out of decency and loyalty towards you, will understand that you care too deeply for Alabastar to let him be taken away.

KURT: Think what it would mean to me personally, and to the whole family, if you left the proselytising to the frustrated fanatics and returned to being yourself.

ARCHIBALD: Of course, come over to us for as long as you need. Your mother will be delighted.

KURT: Miriam'll love to take you shopping, we'll arrange introductions, gallery openings . . .

ARCHIBALD: Kurt, we could convert your old room to a studio for her. And as for Alabastar's school fees, he shall have his share now while we're still alive.

THEENIE: No, thank you.

Pause.

KURT: Did I hear you?

Pause.

ARCHIBALD: It would behove you to explain, my dear daughter.

THEENIE: There's nothing I can say. Nothing.

ARCHIBALD: Nothing will come of nothing. Speak again.

THEENIE: I could paint the willow trees, the pretty willows hanging in the garden, I could eat steak and jacket potatoes with sour cream and chives. I could lie still at night with my curtains open and watch the moon make my bed cold. I could paint a branch hanging in the garden. I could wash and iron and put away my thoughts and my dreams until strength became my wardrobe door and all my joy its mothballs.

KURT: You're mad.

THEENIE: We'll sit at Sunday lunch and talk of veins in leaves and lineages, make kind, safe touches of the brush, and when I've learnt to sit there, silent, soft, false and vulnerable, like the tub of table margarine, you will nod your satisfaction, 'She is good enough for Alabastar.'

KURT: Every word she plunges deeper.

ARCHIBALD: My sometime daughter. I wipe my hands.

KURT *and* ARCHIBALD *go out.* MIRIAM *enters.*

MIRIAM: Oh, there you are. Thank you for the empty book.

THEENIE: Help me. Please. What Axis and I do isn't going to hurt Alabastar. Please tell Kurt.

MIRIAM: You make everything so difficult! You have to come into lunch.

THEENIE: Wait. Who's going to tell Alabastar I can't see him any more?

MIRIAM: There's too much danger that he'll grow up a . . .

THEENIE: Yes, he will grow up. And as for the other unmentionable, he might. Or he might not. I don't know why Kurt's so scared of it — tell him it's free enterprise.

MIRIAM: Actually, I quite like Alabastar. He offered to babysit if I ever wanted to go to a meeting, but I do most of our entertaining here.

THEENIE: Tell him Alabastar can't be cut in half.

MIRIAM: What makes you think Kurt would listen to me? If I agreed with you . . . which I can't.

THEENIE: Ask him to drop the case or he can't screw you.

MIRIAM: I've just had a baby.

THEENIE: Suppose he was trying to take your baby away from you?

MIRIAM: He might, if I behaved like you. (*She goes.*)

THEENIE: Miriam! (*Pause.*) Axis, come and find me. I don't want to go on being an idealist. I keep getting disappointed.

I paint split-second canvasses. In my head the walls come down. I hang a picture here,

violet, purple, lavender, different, and not punished.

This arms race ends, power and its weapons rot — and boldly from the compost grow celery and walnuts.

VIOLET *enters with a photo album.*

VIOLET: The way you adults behave, you're worse than the children. You're shouting this whole house and family to pieces. Kurt, don't you raise your hand to her. Stop him, Arch! Where's your father, he needs his cup of tea. (*She sees* THEENIE.) Theenie, it's not good for you to be sitting in the draught, dear. There aren't enough hours in the day to be miserable, dear. If only you'd given Alabastar a little brother or sister while there was still time. I go inside my head and make up stories. You've got a minute, haven't you? (*She opens the album.*)

THEENIE: It's nice, mum. Do you know where Alabastar is? Violet, have you seen Alabastar and Axis?

VIOLET: What, darling? In this one you were — you would have been six, that's your big brother, he'll be seven and a half, we like our picnic by the paperbarks. Now what have I done with it? Always losing things, your silly mother. Theenie? Have you got it? the bag of bread to feed the ducks?

THEENIE: Mum. This is now. I'm grown up. Don't go mad. You're cold.

VIOLET: It doesn't matter what the weather's like, dear, as long as you wear your warm singlet and don't sit on the concrete.

THEENIE: Will I get you a rug?

VIOLET: My helpful little Gappy.

THEENIE: This is not happening.

VIOLET: Don't you go worrying about me. Look at you. You'll get your two front teeth for Christmas, but you must put your paints away now and have your bath, your father's coming home, I've only got one pair of hands.

THEENIE: What have we done? Where are you? That's more than twenty years ago.

VIOLET: You mustn't cry, my darling daughter, you know I'm never unhappy. Brush your hair and it will shine like gold. Your father knows. He's bringing you home another box of paper. I've got all your paintings, safe and sound. Oh no, he has to load the rubbish on the trailer for the tip. 'If you can keep your head when all about are losing theirs . . .'

AXIS *enters.*

AXIS: They've taken Alabastar. The fucking shits have taken Alabastar.

VIOLET: There she is. Stop shouting. Everybody's shouting.

AXIS: You've got to tell them all to get stuffed.

THEENIE: I can't.

VIOLET: I've got too much to do to sit here all day. There's only one thing that worries me, and that's when you children fight, it's the bane of my existence. (*She cries.*)

THEENIE: Mother, we won't fight any more.

AXIS: I'm sorry she's upset, but so am I.

THEENIE: Sssh!

AXIS: Will you listen to me. You've got to stand up to them, or they'll suck you in until you've gone as mad as the rest of them.

THEENIE: I told them what I wanted. I told Kurt. I told Dad. Whatever I do, I —

VIOLET: You can't go on shouting at your party.

AXIS: You're never going to satisfy them.

THEENIE: Where's Alabastar? He didn't come and say goodbye.

AXIS: He ran out to their car. With all the kids. Louise came and said they'd go disco-skating.

THEENIE: Why didn't you call me?

AXIS: I was screaming for you, this house is huge and fucking soundproof, I tried to run after Albie, Kurt grabbed my arms, I kicked him, we've got to get out of here.

THEENIE, *crying, wipes her nose on her sleeve.*

VIOLET: Go and get a handkerchief, a sleeve is a sleeve.

THEENIE: Mum.

VIOLET: No, you don't have to hold onto me, it's a beautiful moon for a new baby. Where's your father, he needs his cup of tea. My strength is as the strength of ten, because my heart is pure. (*She goes.*)

THEENIE: I'll get her to lie down and sleep.

AXIS (*stops her going*): Your father's there.

THEENIE: When she wakes up tomorrow, the world might have gotten better.

AXIS: Come back. You can't live her life.

THEENIE: When I look at the back of my hand I see my mother's, how it looked when I was small, and when I look in her face, it's too late. I love her. The only mirrors here are pinball screens. Help me. I want to find a picture of myself. (AXIS *hugs her.*) I shouldn't have brought you here, it's so sad.

AXIS: What about you?

THEENIE: You know how the raindrops hang in the morning on a blade of grass? She used to look for beauty, very early, before we kids woke up, and Dad wanted marmalade. I'd find her in the garden with her hands folded, breathing the sunrise, and the sparrows. She was patient for years and years, and now Kurt and I are fighting and they've taken Alabastar.

AXIS: You live in this dreamworld. It drives me crazy. You've got to act, Theenie. In the court.

THEENIE: How can I fight them? I could if prejudice was a dragon and I didn't know its name. But it's not. It's my family.

AXIS: That doesn't mean you've got to give up yourself. They might learn something if they hear you being honest, out loud.

THEENIE: Not in public, I can't. (*Pause.*) Mum used to like what I painted.

AXIS: *You*'ve got to like it. You. I'm sick of our silence, Theenie. There's a lot of people supporting you, you know. If it has to go to court, they'll be ready, really fast. We'll have a paste-up, leaflets, money coming in, a big demo, a bail fund, a dance at Balmain Town Hall.

THEENIE: You're scaring me shitless.

AXIS: Smile. Come on. Vandelope's out there raffling a few deals.

THEENIE (*laughs*): I'll have an exhibition. 'For Axis, who wouldn't let me give up.' We'll get Albie back. You're wonderful.

AXIS: That's the good news. (*She takes out a letter.*) Louise brought an agreement for you to sign. (*She reads.*) 'To obviate the stress of a court case with its concomitant emotional and financial embarrassment, agreement must be reached for Alabastar to continue at Bedlingham Grammar School . . .'

THEENIE: Axis, we'll accept. It's only a stuck up school, we can go back to month and month about, we can have our turn.

AXIS: I thought you were ready to fight. (*She gives THEENIE the letter.*) There's more.

THEENIE (*reads*): He grants me access, one weekend in five, the Easter Break from the morning of Good Friday until Children's Day is over at the Show. And three weeks at Christmas, with alternating Christmas Days. All, Sylvester, is that all? Do we have to go down on our knees and beg for scraps of candles?

AXIS: That's not all God wants. Read the rest.

THEENIE (*reads*): 'I undertake during any period of access to refrain from any word or act which may reasonably be calculated to suggest to Alabastar that I am, or any friend of mine is, a lesbian, such acts to include remaining overnight with any lover, or engaging in any public display of affection.' (*She screams.*) You kiss me back to life and then they kill me for it.

Scene Four

The court. AXIS *and* THEENIE *watch as* SOLOMON *enters in the robes of a judge, with books, gavel, concealed flask of brandy.* VANDELOPE *enters with leaflets, collection bucket, books and papers ready to demonstrate against him.* SOLOMON *and* VANDELOPE *fight for control of the stage as they move the chairs and table into position.* SOLOMON *pushes* VANDELOPE's *books onto the floor.*

VANDELOPE (*giving the books and papers to* AXIS *and* THEENIE): Okay, sisters, hang in there.

SOLOMON: Out, vandal!

VANDELOPE: I'll be back. When you need me, yell.

SOLOMON (*calls*): Constable!

VANDELOPE (*moves to leave, shouts, joined by crowd of demonstrators offstage*):
You're in there for us
We're out here for you.

She goes.
Demonstrators offstage, singing, chanting, shouting.

SOLOMON: 'King Solomon excelled all
the kings of the earth
in riches and in wisdom.'

VANDELOPE & CROWD (*off, sings*):
We own our own bodies
We shall not be moved

SOLOMON: 'And the whole earth sought
the presence of Solomon
to hear the wisdom which God had
put into his mind.'

LOUISE *enters and takes up position
in court.* AXIS *and* THEENIE *move to
their positions opposite her.*

SOLOMON: Bring before me evil
perverted and unnatural
let it open and cavort —
we will sniff it out and kill it
in our Family Law Court.

VANDELOPE (*off*): Not the church, not
the state
Women must decide their fate.

SOLOMON: As I apprehend we have here
an application for custody, and the
issue for me to try is whether or not in
the pertaining circumstances, account
should be taken of the moral odium
which attaches itself to homosexuals.

VANDELOPE (*off*): Get your laws off
our bodies.

SOLOMON: I am given to understand
that a report has been entered by a
Dr Gareth Porteus, Fellow of the
Royal College of Psychiatry. (*Reads.*)
Homosexuality, in the literature,
would seem to be something of an
affliction, and while it may no longer
be recognised as a criminal offence, or
a disease, it is best avoided, especially
in the young. Bring in the boy.

LOUISE: It's not the boy.

SOLOMON: Not the boy?

LOUISE: It's the mother, Your Honour.

SOLOMON: Impossible! Dear lady,

'. . . you are going to tell the whole
world that there is such an offence, to
bring it to the notice of women who

have never heard of it, never thought
of it, never even dreamed of it. I think
that this is a very great mischief . . .'

And there you have the very words of
the Honourable Speaker of the House
of Lords, London 1921.

VANDELOPE (*off*): Get your Lords off
our bodies.

SOLOMON: The community in general is
still sufficiently old-fashioned to view
with disfavour and even abhorrence,
unnatural acts, whether between male
and female, or male and male, or
female and female, whether they be
illegal or not.

THEENIE (*offering reports and papers*):
Your Honour, we have a report which
counteracts . . .

SOLOMON: The grave problem about all
this is that I am already part heard on
other matters, and it is almost
impossible for me to take up any
extensive time with this matter;
however, it is clear that some
conclusion has to be reached on this
matter if it is at all possible before
lunch. (*He consults his papers.*)
Summon the grandfather. Mr
Archibald Havistock!

ARCHIBALD *enters.*

ARCHIBALD: Ask Alabastar what nine
sevens are and he does not know. Ask
him the capital of Tanganyika and he
says, 'Can you lend me twenty cents?'

THEENIE: Look at him. His hair pressed
onto his head; his tie, his neck held
tight.

ARCHIBALD: From the Department of
Education to the Gulag Archipelago
we have spawned a generation who
deny the distinction between good and
evil.

THEENIE: His shoulders caught inside
his suit, tight, tighter, his belly up
against his belt, his shoes too narrow
at the toes.

ARCHIBALD: To be modern is to stare at the destruction that flickers on the screen and have no way of knowing what it is.

THEENIE: He's frightened! He must hate it, when the world around him seems to be coming undone.

ARCHIBALD: Bereft of a standard to tell him right from wrong, like a boy who has come to the end of his pile of coins, twentieth century man stands before posterity, disconnected and disappointed.

THEENIE: I can't bear it. Can't we find a paradise where your truth and mine can meet? You, whose love once held me on your knee.

SOLOMON: Order, order.

AXIS: After what we've been through, are you asking me to have sympathy for him?

THEENIE: Yes. (*She cries.*)

ARCHIBALD: If the mother of my children were well and could be with us, she would agree with me. Her voice was ever soft, gentle and low. I shall go from here, an old, tired man. (*He goes.*)

AXIS (*concerned for* THEENIE): Adjournment, please, Your Honour!

SOLOMON: Five minutes! (*He pulls out a small transistor radio and listens.*)

The last few moments of a horse race. Meanwhile VANDELOPE *enters disguised as a doctor of laws, pours* AXIS *and* THEENIE *a cup of tea, dodges* SOLOMON's *view and adds a sign or graffiti: 'THE KOALA TEA OF MERCY IS NOT STRAINED'. She goes.*

SOLOMON 'Every one of them brought his present,
   articles of silver and gold,
   garments, myrrh, spices, horses and
      mules.'

That was the wrong bloody race! Time's up. Call the new wife.

LOUISE *moves forward.*

CROWD (*off*): No god, no master . . . No, No, Nanette,
   No god, no master . . . No, No, Nanette.

SOLOMON: Truly lovely.

'Our couch is green;
   the beams of our house are cedar.'

LOUISE: Your Honour, we do not want Alabastar to despise his former mother. We would rather have protected him from the shock of learning she is . . . is . . .

SOLOMON: A lesbian?

AXIS: The bitch! How long are we going to sit here and put up with this?

LOUISE: It's not the way most people live. We love Alabastar very much. He's very happy with us. We've found him an excellent school, when time and weather permit we take him sailing, and his friends. We like children. But we're worried that if he goes on living in that commune, he'll be a teenager soon, he'll want to take a girlfriend home, she'll find out his mother's a . . . a . . .

SOLOMON: Thingamebob?

LOUISE: He'll be so . . . embarrassed.

THEENIE: Objection!

SOLOMON: Order!

'I adjure you, O daughters of
      Jerusalem,
   that you stir not up nor awaken love
   until it please.'

LOUISE: Alabastar has expressed a wish to attend university, and we both encourage him in his studies. I do work part-time as my husband's research assistant, but I am always available to welcome Alabastar home from school, and his friends.

SOLOMON: A fair and far-sighted woman. Do you intend to have any children yourself with your current husband, out of curiosity, you understand?

LOUISE: Your Honour, well, at the moment, we are hoping. I'm not . . . I'm not . . .

SOLOMON: A lesbian. Thank you. Call the husband.

SYLVESTER *enters.*

LOUISE (*to* SYLVESTER): Stand up straight, darling, everybody's watching.

SYLVESTER: Your Honour, I am here reluctantly, without a bandwagon to push, or axes to grind. I remember with affection my former wife, and it is uncomfortable to be placed in opposition to her for the sake of a child we both love. Alabastar in his adolescence deserves a stable and consistent home with the love and role model of a father as well as a mother.

AXIS (*to* THEENIE): Tell him we want a world without straitjackets.

THEENIE: Wait. I've got to understand what they want.

SYLVESTER: I respect his mother's right to her lifestyle *qua* lifestyle. That is her own choice. What causes me distress is her obsessive need to advertise what she is, to drag the drama past her bedroom door and seek public acclaim for a private idiosyncrasy.

AXIS: People get married on billboards!

SYLVESTER: In such a household, a household for the most part without men, I would feel afraid for Alabastar.

AXIS: If I had a wart on my nose, and a cat, they'd burn us.

SOLOMON: Order! Words, words, as repetitive as muesli, Mahler, and our Asian future.

Affidavits have been heard to the effect that in the first year of the boy Alabastar's life, the respondent wife had the eccentricity to hold an exhibition of paintings, which provided entertainment to a heated crowd and a hot press . . .

AXIS: She made then look at things, and they hated it.

SOLOMON: . . . while the young husband, embarking on his career, had the burden of the child, and nobly filled the vacuuming.

THEENIE: Objection! Sylvester, tell them we shared the housework.

During the following dialogue between THEENIE, LOUISE *and* SYLVESTER, SOLOMON *swigs surreptitiously from his brandy flask.*

SYLVESTER: Objection, Your Honour.

LOUISE: You can't object to that, darling.

SYLVESTER: Christ, she's never neglected Alabastar. I was through my Ph.D. by then, I could afford childcare, we helped one another. Christ, if I'd had her talent. If the press hadn't given her a ducking. Louise, I need your support and your love.

LOUISE: You're my life, Sylvester.

THEENIE: Louise! If you put yourself in a cage, how can any of us be free?

SYLVESTER: I've said from the beginning this case can't go through if it means assassinating Theenie. Darling, let's go home. Now. You and me. Us.

LOUISE: If we walk out of here without Alabastar you'll never forgive me.

SYLVESTER: You're right. When he's with me I remember growing up. I'm not cut off from kangaroos and crazy things. And he's got those precious independent eyes. Theenie, I haven't any choice, we can't control this. Your Honour . . .

THEENIE: Sylvester, don't give him power over us.

SYLVESTER: Your Honour, objection withdrawn.

SOLOMON: *Ipso dipso,* the origins of the former wife's fractured family stem from the excesses of her artistic period.

CROWD (*off*): What do we want?
— Clear thinking.
When do we want it?
— Now.

SOLOMON: Who's next?

AXIS *and* THEENIE *move forward.*

SOLOMON: 'Who is that coming up from the wilderness,
leaning upon her beloved?'

Two of them. Custody confers the responsibility of proper training and example. This factor of your alternative admitted lifestyle which is not the normally considered life of the majority, does not make you, *per se,* an unfit mother, but it cannot, in conscience, be ignored.

SOLOMON *motions* THEENIE *to move back, and* AXIS *to take a position ready for being questioned.*

SOLOMON: In your fragmented family, do you not think the boy Alabastar will be subjected to social discomfort? To the ridicule of his peers?

AXIS: Not unless you give them lessons.

SOLOMON: Young lady, be warned.

AXIS: 'Solomon had seven hundred wives, princesses,
and three hundred concubines.'

SOLOMON: What was that?

AXIS: Kings, chapter eleven, verse 3.

SOLOMON: The devil would quote the scriptures, eh? I could have you charged for contempt of court. Alabastar would be at a disadvantage, would he not, in that normal parents would not allow their sons to mix with known homosexuals.

AXIS: Especially if they had halitosis or were blacks.

SOLOMON: Ms Axis, are you not denying yourself your own instinct for motherhood, if we try to complete the picture of the odd situation you have there?

AXIS: Get your laws off my body.

SOLOMON: I could use this as a further opportunity to deplore the sort of exceedingly imprecise language which does nothing to assist the court. Do you attend clubs of the type where homosexuals congregate?

CROWD (*off*): We want to be nuclear free.

SOLOMON: Don't mumble. What goes on at these clubs? Do you see anything wrong in the boy seeing you, and you, unclothed, at a beach designated 'nude'? Have you no thoughts on an old fashioned virtue called modesty?

AXIS: None.

SOLOMON: If the boy were to entertain notions of homosexuality would you not seek to dissuade him from these notions?

AXIS: Alabastar knows himself.

SOLOMON: Mmm. Ms Axis, in what role may we see you in relation to the child? A duplicate mother figure? A father figure?

AXIS: I won't fit into your boxes. You haven't got one that's my size.

SOLOMON: You do not see anything wrong with yourself, do you?

AXIS: No!

SOLOMON: How many of these unnatural relationships have you had?

AXIS: I'm going to explode.

SOLOMON: Do you, how shall I put it, in whatever it is that the two of you do together, involve the child?

AXIS: We make billycarts together. You're the porn-pusher, not us.

SOLOMON: What is it exactly that you and you do together? Is there no danger of you leaving, in the bedroom or the bathroom where the child may come upon them, any sexual instruments that you may use?

THEENIE: Your Honour, our love is not a violent thing.

CROWD (*off*): Free our bodies, free ourselves.

SOLOMON: You are of a religious, an evangelical nature, are you not?

Police siren.

AXIS: The pigs.

THEENIE: What if they're hurting people out there?

AXIS: Think of something.

THEENIE (*grabs books and papers*): We can produce evidence to refute the idea that homosexuality is linked with mental illness. Statistically lesbians are as well adjusted as their heterosexual counterparts, and in some cases may consume less valium. There is no evidence that homosexual households create homosexual children, any more than the other way round. Openness and acceptance of sexual diversity could contribute to a child's well-being and growth. There is clear statistical evidence that most sexual offences are committed by heterosexual men upon women, and not by lesbian women upon children.

AXIS: Put your hand up. See if he'll listen.

THEENIE: Sir!

SOLOMON: Yes, Theenie. You can be excused.

THEENIE: Sir! Could this case be considered not as a debate about sexual preference, but one about a world which does not trust and value women?

SOLOMON: You don't know what you're talking about. Out of order.

THEENIE: We've lost. I try to use their language, and still they refuse to understand.

AXIS *and* THEENIE *hold one another.*

SOLOMON: Order! This perverse affection cannot be allowed. I have weighed most carefully what I have heard. The law is cognisant of current debate about the position of women. Women deserve the respect and freedom of an equal partnership with men, and no higher compliment can be paid her, than that she devote herself to the welfare of her family within that partnership, as an equal. Servile wombs cannot create free men. However, when radical forces attack the familiar way of joining people together, they attack the cement of our society. It is my melancholy duty to uphold the sanctity of womanhood against those who wish to profane it.

THEENIE: Mr Justice Solomon, this is not a criminal court. Why have I been on trial since I began?

One child instead of two, guilty;
Three legs on my studio easel, guilty;
Four legs in bed and all of them gentle.
Five dirty socks found in the cupboard, guilty.
Six o'clock and it's not my turn for cooking, guilty;
Seven days in the weakness —

(*Sings.*) Eight ladies dancing, guilty,
Nine o'clock and he's up playing pinball, guilty;

(*Sings.*) There were ten in the bed
And the little one said . . .

Write this in your books: She stood in the court and said, Let the women ask the questions. (*She includes with gesture herself,* AXIS *and the women demonstrating outside the court.*)

VANDELOPE & CROWD (*off, singing*):
Just like the trees that grow
until the forest sings
We shall not be moved.

SOLOMON: Young lady, do you think a mere anyone can be initiated into the mysteries and ritual when it has taken us centuries to wrap the cloak around us? And you are merely a woman. After thorough deliberation the court awards the boy Alabastar to that dedicated family, man and wife, whose love, propriety and property will enable him to follow his chosen career, and to grow to manhood exercising responsibility for all that is worthwhile in our society.

'His legs are alabaster columns,
set upon bases of gold.'

Court dismissed. (*He gathers his books to leave.*)

THEENIE: No, please no.

AXIS (*calls*): Vandelope, help, ho!

CROWD (*off, singing*):
We own our own bodies
We shall not be moved.

VANDELOPE enters as a doctor of laws, disguised as a man.

Change of lights, puff of smoke to indicate fantasy.

VANDELOPE (*shakes hands with SOLOMON*): Dr Vandel Hope, QC. Give me leave to emulate your peroration.

SOLOMON: At last, a man after my own heart.

VANDELOPE & SOLOMON (*song and dance*):
You put your right hand in
You put your right hand out
You put your right hand in
And you shake it all about

You do the hokey pokey
And you turn around
And that's what it's all about.

SOLOMON (*offers flask*): Brandy?

VANDELOPE: Your Honour! (*Drinks.*)

CROWD (*off, shouting*).

SOLOMON: Attention those nincompoops attempting illegal entry by climbing through the skylight. You are endangering your own lives and you are endangering the lives of policemen. (*He calls.*) Constable! (*To VANDELOPE:*) Lunch, as soon as the police clear through to the gate.

VANDELOPE: I have startling new evidence.

SOLOMON (*checks his fob watch*): This is most irregular.

VANDELOPE: I would speak so the scroungers and riff-raff out there listen and learn.

SOLOMON: Order. The court will come to order.

Noise of crowd lessens.

VANDELOPE: Your honour, it is the concern of this court that the boy grow up responsible, is it not?

SOLOMON: Let the rabble listen and be ashamed.

VANDELOPE: You would agree that every man is the maker of his own fortune?

SOLOMON: You put it neatly.

VANDELOPE: Then the boy must be able to make his own decisions.

SOLOMON: What? The boy?

VANDELOPE: All of us. Take control of our own lives. We could do it, in time, if there was no prejudice between us, and no power above us.

SOLOMON: Abandon the rule of the law!

VANDELOPE: You can retire, Your Honour.

SOLOMON: Puppy! People come to Solomon begging for wisdom.

VANDELOPE (*takes a Bible off SOLOMON's table and opens it*): You would uphold the judgement of King Solomon?

SOLOMON: You mock me. (*He pulls the Bible from VANDELOPE.*) How can you, a doctor of law, make a plaything of our finest precedent? You invite the jungle to take over, and blood to flow in the streets.

VANDELOPE: You would stand by Solomon's ruling, no matter what?

SOLOMON: I have sworn it.

VANDELOPE: Have it your own way.

SOLOMON: Bring me a sword.

SYLVESTER *hands him the sword.*

VANDELOPE: 'And they stood in awe of the king
because they perceived
that the wisdom of God was in him
to render justice.'

SOLOMON: Have the women stand before me.

LOUISE *and* THEENIE *come forward.*

SOLOMON: 'Divide the living child in two
and give half to the one
and half to the other.'

THEENIE: You can't cut Albie in half.

SOLOMON (*indicates* THEENIE):
'The woman whose son was alive said to the king:
Oh, my lord, give her the living child and by no means slay it.'

THEENIE: At least let me go and hug him goodbye. I'll tell him. He's going to live with his dad for a while.

LOUISE: Alabastar will be very happy with us.

SOLOMON (*indicates* LOUISE):
'the other said,
It shall be neither mine nor yours: Divide it.'

LOUISE: We've moved the Space Invaders into his room. Theenie can come and see him if he wants to. Sylvester?

SOLOMON: 'Then the king said,
Give the living child to the first woman
And by no means slay it:
she is its mother.'

The law allows it and the court awards it.

THEENIE: Did he say?

AXIS: Yes.

THEENIE: Hooray! (*She hugs* AXIS.)

SOLOMON: What? The law awards the child to the natural mother, but this natural mother is unnatural. The law allows the ruin of the law?

VANDELOPE (*removing disguise*): You swore it, Sol, old pal.

SOLOMON (*his authority severely shaken*): You! You have spent hours obfuscating me. It has to be the other way around. There is too much at stake.

VANDELOPE: There's been fifty-eight people arrested, are you dropping the charges?

SOLOMON: Harlots! The law has to be cherished or you wreck the civilisation of centuries. (*Pause. Aside.*) The words are coming out, why aren't they rousing . . .?

(*He looks at* VANDELOPE, AXIS *and* THEENIE.) Why aren't you frightened of the damage you will cause?

Don't turn away from me. For my children's sakes I had an empire to hold onto, and I cannot have you telling me it's gone. And yet, you remind me of my wife, of Miriam, when she used to get up in the morning and sing. (*He goes, defeated.*)

VANDELOPE: In real life it could be a bit more difficult.

LOUISE: Well, do we talk about it, or what?

THEENIE: I've never talked to you. I'm going to need some coffee.

SYLVESTER: He says he doesn't want to play pinball any more. He won thirteen free games in a row and after that there's nothing else to do. I love him, don't you see. I love him too.

AXIS: I could do with some champagne.

THEENIE: I want to paint, a circus.

VANDELOPE: The law keeps itself
                strong
rewards those who make it,
invents endless reasons
why people should take it.

But you never know what
we could change
if we risk it.
Join hands friends
and we can go home
optimistic.

Pinball

What happens when women put into the mainstream, plays that seek to question very deeply the power lines of our society, including those in the theatre itself?

I've had the experience of a play of mine *Pinball* having an excellent professional production in a mainstream theatre, Nimrod, (Sydney) but I felt, and I can only find words for it at the distance of a couple of years, as though my play had been given a very attractive mask. The cast were lovely, I liked them very much, but I felt that on the whole their interest in the concerns of the play came from their desire to put on as good a performance as possible, rather than from an interest in a radical questioning of society and its effect on their own lives. It meant for me that my play was given a smile on the outside, that its heart was not quite understood.

My experience was quite different when that same play was performed by a theatre which has politics and political practice as the stated stuff of its life. I felt at home, I didn't have to explain to anyone why I was a feminist, or why I had a vision of us working to change the world. But when it came to performance, those earnest young revolutionaries who were working at Troupe Theatre (Adelaide) got so caught up in the serious message of the play that they tried to pretend that it wasn't a comedy. They couldn't see that they were spoiling it by damping down the belly laughs, or that the revolutionaries in the play do actually send themselves up. In several places they even altered my script or my stage directions to kill a laugh or a light-hearted or ironic moment. They forgot that the first requirement of the theatre is to entertain. We're not going to get an audience along to watch a theatre of sermons.

I've been quoting from a talk I gave at the 1983 Troupe Theatre Writers' Workshop, published later in *Australasian Drama Studies*, (Vol. 2, No. 2, April 1984, pp 35-36) under the title, 'Feminist Theatre: a monologue to start discussion'.

When I had to sit down and write this Afterword for *Pinball*'s publication, I was paralysed for days while the deadline got closer. It was the old problem of not trusting myself to write anything good enough. Back came the terrible fear that the critics would get me whatever I did. Hadn't Brian Hoad, when he was reviewing *Pinball*'s first production, dismissed the play as 'Yet another piece of crude and tedious female chauvinist piggery'? (*The Bulletin*, Sept. 29, 1981, p. 85.)

A friend found me hiding in the corner where my typewriter wouldn't get me, and coaxed me into making a little clearing in my head where I could go looking for ideas. That's when I remembered that I might be sane after all; I dug that earlier article out of the filing cabinet, and knew I had somewhere to begin.

Pinball had its beginning when I was at a demonstration in the centre of Sydney in January 1980. I can't remember what we were fighting for/against that day, but an urgently worried friend wanted me to buy five dollars'-worth of raffle tickets. She was trying to raise thousands of dollars because her lover, another woman, was having to fight a very expensive court case for custody of her children. 'I don't have five dollars,' I said, being an unemployed playwright. 'Perhaps I could write you a play?' Another lesbian friend who'd been through a similar custody battle lent me the transcript of her case; I heard of other cases through the Lesbian Mothers; some of their research was published in *Refractory Girl*, No 20/21, 1980.

In the court scene in *Pinball* a number of the questions the judge asks are taken directly from those real-life nightmare cases. They're so outrageously venomous I don't think I would have thought of making them up.

Pinball is about many things. I wanted to see what would happen if I wrote a play

where King Lear's daughter Cordelia (I called her Theenie) refused to let her father's
madness continue until it led her to her death. Theenie has to make a great effort
to separate herself from what her father insists she ought to be. Cordelia tries to do
that too, but her escape can only be temporary. In the end she has to come back to
her father and to her death because her world is limited and contained by his world,
and the forms and meanings of that world — nature and civilisation, sanity and
madness, truth and lies — can only be what her father has constructed them to be. To
agree with him, is to agree with right; to disagree with him, is to be wrong.

When King Lear finds, with increasing horror, that his definition of the world is
violently at odds with the evidence of his senses, he doesn't question his right to make
that definition. Rather, he calls on Cordelia to heal the breach in his mind by going
willingly with him to prison. Lear knows what he is doing to her, but it is in hallowed
tradition, and therefore it is All Right:

> Upon such sacrifices, my Cordelia,
> The gods themselves throw incense.
> (*King Lear,* Act V, Sc.3, 1.22-23.)

As dutifully as Agamemnon's daughter, Iphigenia, Cordelia allows herself to be taken
captive. And in prison she is hanged.

What I wanted to develop in Theenie in *Pinball* was the strength to refuse to make
that sacrifice. I wanted to show Theenie's sisters (in the Women's Movement sense of
women recognising each other's experience) giving her support, instead of fighting
with her and with one another, as Cordelia's sisters, Goneril and Regan, do in
Shakespeare's play.

For Theenie, Axis is the pivot, the support, the strength that has to be found inside
if she is going to keep on trying. Vandelope, whose name comes from a mixture of
Vandal and Hope, offers her an iconoclastic fighting spirit that teaches the taking of
risks until Theenie is forced to realise that her father/King Solomon/the judge is not
going to give up politely his control over the ground she is walking on.

Pinball wasn't easy to write. To make clear what the characters were saying I had to
confront their meaning in my life, in my connections with family, friends and
unhappy love. Whenever I got stuck, and it was often, the women in my writing group
would help me cry, pick me up off the floor and sit me back at my desk. Thank you to
them: Robyn Clark, Jeannie Edgar, Janne Ellen, Kerryn Higgs, Jan McKemmish,
Marianna Moonsun, Drusilla Modjeska, Jill Sutton and the late Carole Deagan.

Just as I was finishing *Pinball,* I was very lucky that the Women and Theatre Project
was starting in Sydney. It was the inspiration of two remarkable women, Chris
Westwood and Jude Kuring, and it brought together 140 women theatre workers to do
something creative about the lack of representation of women in professional theatre
in Sydney. Action was certainly needed, as Chris Westwood points out in an article,
'The Women and Theatre Project 1980–81', (*Australasian Drama Studies,* Vol. 1,
No. 1, Oct. 1982, p. 40):

> Women associated with the APG (Australian Performing Group) in Melbourne had
> tried to generate feminist theatre at the Pram Factory in the seventies, and in
> Adelaide in the late seventies there had been a strong semi-professional feminist
> theatre group. The Nimrod Theatre (in Sydney) had paid some attention to women
> in theatre in 1975, International Women's Year. But nothing had succeeded in
> making 'women' an ongoing and permanently integrated part of Australian theatre,
> and in 1980 the picture for women was pretty bleak all over the country. The
> landmark professional theatre, Nimrod, presents the extent of the problems
> through its first ten years. For a progressive professional theatre, it had produced

the work of only four women writers: Jennifer Compton, Alma de Groen, Eleanor Witcombe and Moya Henderson. It had used 214 actresses compared with 544 actors, thus reflecting the proportion of available female and male roles. There had been no female directors at all; 33 male composers/musical directors compared with 8 female; and only 26 female designers compared with 133 men. Nimrod's figures are readily available, hence it is being singled out, but throughout the fifties, sixties and seventies other theatres in Australia show a similar pattern.

With funding for twelve months from the Australia Council, the Women and Theatre Project was able to give many women a chance to workshop and stage their ideas. I didn't have a background working in theatre and was thrilled to be able to get to know other writers, directors and performers, and to get much valuable help with my script, especially from Fay Mokotow (sadly missed now) who directed a reading of *Pinball* for the Project, and Chris Johnson who directed the workshop and production provided by Nimrod later in that year (1981).

Sydney's reviewers were not impressed by what we women were doing. Chris Westwood sums it up in her article: 'Throughout the year of the Project's existence the majority of theatre critics reflected ambivalence and hostility . . . Few if any of the reviews in the major journals treated the plays seriously as deserving of a thorough critique.' (p. 47).

Now, as I'm writing this in 1984, it looks as though great progress has been made. In Nimrod's 1984 season six of the eleven plays were by women. But we can never sit back and think we've made it. Statistics of course can't tell us everything, but in their 1985 season Nimrod are doing only one play by a woman out of eleven, Dorothy Hewett's, *Bobbin Up*.

Now I've got to give myself some advice, so I can stay at my typewriter long enough to write another play. I've been noticing lately that male playwrights have been including in their plays their portraits of feminists. By doing that they take for themselves the power to say what feminists are, just as in the past the male writers have given us their images of wives and daughters. We've got to do it too. We have to tell our own story. We can't leave it to them.

Recently I met a woman who said she'd seen *Pinball* three times. She'd taken her parents to it, so she could explain to them that she was a lesbian. I was very moved.

Alison Lyssa
4 November 1984.

P.S. The Song, 'Don't be Too Polite, Girls', is a very popular one at feminist gatherings in Australia and was written by Glen Tomasetti.

Alison Lyssa

Stage Plays

The Year of the Migrant, 1980; reading at Nimrod Theatre, Sydney.

Pinball, 1981, reading as part of the Women and Theatre Project, followed by a full production, Nimrod Theatre, Sydney, 1981.

The Boiling Frog, 1982, reading at Nimrod Theatre; full production there in 1984.